PENGUIN BOOKS
# A LONG ROAD TO JUSTICE

Sylvia Yu Friedman is an award-winning filmmaker, investigative journalist, international speaker, serial entrepreneur, and advisor to philanthropists.

She is the author of two books: *Silenced No More: Voices of Comfort Women*, the only journalistic account of Japanese military sex slavery during the Second World War, and *Heart and Soul: The Life Story of Pastor Augustus Chao*. The first editions of both of these books sold out, and the former was #5 on the Amazon Kindle store's Asian History bestseller list in August 2018.

In 2017, Sylvia was listed in Assent Compliance's 'Top 100 Human Trafficking & Slavery Influence Leaders'. In 2013, she won the prestigious International Human Rights Press Award for her three-part documentary series on human trafficking in China, Hong Kong and Thailand.

After ten years of intensive research and interviews with elderly survivors, academics, lawyers and activists in different countries, Sylvia is considered a global expert on the victims of Japanese military sex slavery, known as 'comfort women'. She's been interviewed or featured by the BBC, CNN, CGTN, South China Morning Post, and The Globe and Mail, and covered widely in the media across China and the rest of Asia.

Sylvia is listed as a SheSource expert in the database of the Women's Media Center, which was founded by Jane Fonda and Gloria Steinem, and serves as a resource for journalists.

Sylvia believes her core calling is to use her business and communication skills to mobilise people and resources to help those suffering in the most marginalised places. Since 2005, Sylvia has managed and directed millions of dollars to major humanitarian portfolios, impacting the lives of more than a million people. This work has given her access to many influential networks in different countries.

Sylvia led a Hong Kong-based movement of 'passionate compassion' against human trafficking that involved more than 120 churches, NGOs and organisations, and later expanded to other countries, including Malaysia, China, Canada, South Africa and the US. Through more than 50 slavery awareness events over 18 months, her team has reached more than 25,000 people in universities, schools and major corporations like Goldman Sachs.

Sylvia is married to Matthew Friedman, a top-ranked inspirational keynote speaker and a leading global expert on slavery who is currently the CEO of The Mekong Club and was formerly a United Nations director and US diplomat. In the summer of 2016, they delivered 113 presentations in 27 US cities. She and Matthew are based in Hong Kong.

# A LONG ROAD TO JUSTICE

## STORIES FROM THE FRONTLINES IN ASIA

SYLVIA YU FRIEDMAN

PENGUIN BOOKS

An imprint of Penguin Random House

PENGUIN BOOKS

USA | Canada | UK | Ireland | Australia
New Zealand | India | South Africa | China | Southeast Asia

Penguin Books is part of the Penguin Random House group of companies
whose addresses can be found at global.penguinrandomhouse.com

Published by Penguin Random House SEA Pte Ltd
9, Changi South Street 3, Level 08-01,
Singapore 486361

Penguin
Random House
SEA

First published in Penguin Books by Penguin Random House SEA 2021

ISBN 9789814954341

Typeset in Adobe Garamond Pro by Manipal Technologies Limited, Manipal

www.penguin.sg

*I dedicate this book to all the children, women and men who have suffered unspeakable horrors for years in slavery and languished, even unto their graves, without a voice. Together, let's dream of a better world for the trafficked and poor.*

# Contents

# Introduction

Slavery is not just a historical issue; it exists even today. History is repeating itself. A constant stream of impoverished women and girls have been, and are being, enslaved and abused in the Asia Pacific region.

According to a report by the International Labour Organization (ILO), at any given time in 2016, there were an estimated 40.3 million people in modern slavery globally, including 15.4 million in forced marriage and 4.8 million in forced sexual exploitation. Women and girls accounted for ninety-nine per cent of the victims in the commercial sex industry, with seven in every ten of them being exploited in the Asia Pacific region. In other sectors of forced labour, women and girls accounted for 58 per cent of the victims.

Through my work in journalism, counter-trafficking, and philanthropy, I've had rare and incredible access to victims of sex trafficking and forced marriage in China, Hong Kong, Korea, Thailand, Cambodia, Myanmar, Singapore, Africa, and the Philippines.

Amid this terrible human suffering, frontline workers have been a source of light to help overcome the darkness in some of the most frightening places on Earth. With my husband Matthew Friedman, a leading international anti-slavery professional with thirty years of field experience, I've campaigned against slavery and informed and mobilized people, schools, faith-based groups such as churches, and organizations for this cause across China, the US, Canada, Malaysia, New Zealand, South Africa, Australia, and elsewhere.

This memoir describes my journey of fighting modern slavery; I have been supporting this cause through philanthropic initiatives and raising awareness through writing articles, producing films, and delivering presentations. In this book, I will share my personal setbacks, and how my awakening to social justice helped me come to terms with my identity issues and my Korean heritage. I write about the lessons—the good, the bad, and the ugly—and the unsung heroes and events that shaped me along the way.

By shining light on the women and children who are living in such desperate circumstances, I hope to bring them the attention and assistance they need from the global community. The overarching purpose of writing about my adventures on the frontlines in Asia—along with my personal coming-of-age story—is to inspire people to get involved in fighting modern slavery and to effect social change.

# Part I

# The Door of Hope

# 1

# Near-death Experience

The red-light district we were driving to was one of the most notorious in Yunnan province. While this region is best known for its diverse minority groups, delectable cuisine, breath-taking mountainous landscapes, Yunnan has a dark underbelly. Its proximity to the notorious Golden Triangle—an area in Southeast Asia that includes Myanmar, Laos, and Thailand—has meant that this province is rife with the trafficking of both drugs and humans.

This hidden enclave in the far outskirts of Yunnan's capital city Kunming was so remote that there wasn't a single street light to be seen. The utter darkness reminded me of a rural campsite. We could see the stars shining brightly against the black canvas above.

Why was I here? I had flown down to Yunnan in November 2012 for a week to film a news documentary on sex trafficking and exploitation in China. It was a familiar place as I had travelled to this diverse region—the Wild West of the Middle Kingdom—several times in the past. I had then met several survivors of sex trafficking and frontline workers in my role as a philanthropy advisor and manager of an HIV/AIDS fund in Yunnan and migrants fund in Beijing—a city I had lived in for more than six years. I had moved to Hong Kong from Beijing after writing the first draft of my book on Japanese military sex slavery before and during WWII. The move to Hong Kong was a fresh start and marked a new chapter in my journalism career of fourteen years as a reporter and producer of television and radio current affairs shows, executive editor of a magazine, columnist, and as a city council reporter for a newspaper.

This was my second trip in the first month as a producer of current affairs documentaries for a Hong Kong TV channel, and the pressure to perform was immense. As a perfectionist, I tended to expect a great deal of myself to the point of crushing self-flagellation. My executive producer and I had pitched a travel budget for a series on human trafficking in Thailand, Cambodia, and Mainland China, but the head of our department adamantly shot it down. I was too new and untested. We were ballsy and lobbied our big boss several times. My executive producer stormed out of the office of the head executive; she was visibly upset, and I was the following act. I went in there initially feeling intimidated by his stern face, but somehow was able to speak boldly from the heart, and I made a strong case to cover this under-reported story of the unspeakable sufferings of young women. It was our responsibility to share their stories with the world. I emphasized my prior experience in the region, and the remarkable and unprecedented access I had through my contacts.

I learnt later that my mother had been praying hard for a breakthrough in this meeting. I had told her of the roadblocks, and she appealed to a higher power than our department head. Her prayers had been answered!

Upon arriving at the hotel, I felt the dread of the looming deadline—I needed to get many interviews and footage in a short amount of time. This feeling of constant pressure was akin to low-grade anxiety, and I was with a cameraman who didn't speak English to boot! For several days, he had displayed a diva attitude, flinging around his tripod, with his eyebrows scrunched and nostrils flaring, in the small office of the non-profit organization that was hosting us so graciously. I felt at home immediately with a few of the local

Chinese staff whom I had met on previous trips. The expatriate staff, however, came across as nervous, because they were worried about the high risk from participating in an interview that could get them kicked out of the country.

This organization could not be named in the documentary, and even the names of its staff had to be changed. They feared being denied residence in the country if they went public, and this seemed to be a common sentiment among non-governmental organization (NGO) workers and missionaries. We agreed to refer to them by the name 'Door of Hope'.

Door of Hope is part of a grassroots movement initiated by Christians from the underground church, or now commonly referred to as house churches, fighting against human trafficking in the world's most populous nation, China. The organization also ran a safe home for trafficked women. It might take a while to change the mindset of house church Christians to view the works of social justice as part of their mission. However, when the Chinese church, made up of more than 100 million believers, embraces the fight against trafficking and prostitution, they could become the biggest global force in abolishing modern slavery.

One evening at around 10 pm, we drove down a busy road in a small white van resembling a loaf of bread. We were heading to an oppressive red-light area, closer to the city than the other brothels in the region. There were no street lights here, and the dark narrow road was lined with run-down stores closed for the night. I looked up at the ramshackle grey buildings and noticed that windows in the second floor were darkened. I felt a sense of dread and oppressive danger looking out at this pit of hell even as I was comfortably seated in the safety of the van.

I filmed girls in short skirts and tight dresses walking the streets. Some were riding pillion on motorcycles driven by men who served as pimps and delivered the girls to clients for a fee. A few men stood around smoking. They looked sinister and hunched over as if they were hiding from someone. I surreptitiously filmed many johns at different brothels through the windows of our van. Some of them were young Chinese men. I felt sick as I witnessed this flesh trade. The darkness of the exploitation of young women overwhelmed me.

The entire area had an ominous feel to it. I could feel gangsters staring at me as we filmed the exterior of one building where women were known to be exploited. These were the very streets that the Door of Hope team would visit to deliver their message of hope to the women as well as their pimps. But, I couldn't muster the courage to even stick my head out of the van window.

That night, I had a nightmare, and I woke up to my screams. I couldn't remember what I dreamt about. The entire building must have heard it. It was as if the oppressive force in that brothel area had clung to me, and it wasn't my scream but the piercing plea of an abused woman crying for help. As a highly sensitive person, I wondered if I had felt the pain of the women who were engulfed by the lust of men late at night in that dank and seedy part of town. That was a profound moment for me as a woman, that I was able to identify a little more with the women in the red-light district, despite knowing that I had nothing in common with their plight. I felt this would help me to tell their stories more authentically.

Amy, the head of Door of Hope, was a devoted Christian. She had dark blonde tresses and a strong jawline that accentuated a kind smile which appeared now and then. There was an intensity in her gaze that complemented her tough, no-nonsense speaking style. She came across as someone who had overcome a great deal of adversity as a trauma survivor herself. Though she never opened up about her childhood or family, I could sense that she had overcome something dark; it was the source of her immense inner strength.

I first met Amy in 2005 when she was just starting to set up her NGO. The philanthropy advisory company I worked for had a client—a foundation—that wanted to donate a van for their work, and I had helped in the process. On several occasions, when

I interviewed her, she humbly emphasized that she was just your average housewife and mother, and she depended on God daily for strength and love to carry out her often-harrowing work of reaching out to women in red-light districts.

Amy's fair complexion and blonde hair often drew people to openly stare at her on the streets. She used this curiosity in combination with her street-smart attitude, compassion, and openness to build relationships with traffickers, including mafia bosses and small-time profiteers. She had told me, 'These mafia [people] are curious and say, "I've never been out to dinner with a foreigner before." I tell them I'm a psychologist, which is a new area that's breaking ground in China. I also tell them, "This job of yours is very stressful. How do you manage that stress?"' Amy often felt that these men were in pain too and in need of a listening ear, and this question helped them open up to her easily. They would share more easily with her than with their own family members.

Amy also had an authoritative bearing that enabled her to pull off probing questions. It was a rare balance of toughness and compassion—a fearlessness that led her and her team of women into such dangerous red-light districts to talk with prostitutes and convince them that there was a safe place for them to turn to with free job training. If she was ever fearful when out in the red-light areas, she was able to overcome her fear by focusing on the suffering of the women and girls in forced prostitution. I don't know if there is another driving force in her life, other than her personal faith, to undertake this kind of justice mission.

The deep Christian faith of staff members and volunteers at Door of Hope motivated their rescue work. The all-women team was like a close-knit family, and the hardships of their mission bonded them. They were completely dedicated to their work but I could feel a sense of internal struggle as they grappled with the pain of the women who came out of exploitation. Somewhere they must have felt ill-equipped to handle the trauma. With the exception of Amy and another volunteer who was a professional counsellor, the rest of the women were ordinary housewives or young local Chinese women who were drawn to this meaningful work.

They all prayed regularly and brought their questions and frustrations to God. Every decision that Amy and the team took was bathed in prayer, a touching sign of their humility and child-like faith. Several of them made off-hand comments about how disgusting the johns were. It made me wonder though if these women were also united by a common hatred of men—a natural reaction to seeing exploited women.

Earlier in the day, before our traumatic near-death encounter with the thugs and mama-sans, Amy advised that I should walk through the dark alley and film it with my phone while pretending to be texting someone. I found her request rather odd but decided to place my trust in her. After all, here was a woman with several years' experience in rescuing women from the clutches of sexual exploitation at deadly red-light areas. I went to the brothel district with a junior missionary—an American woman named Mary from the Mid-West—in her mid-twenties and an older Chinese-American volunteer called Tina. Mary was talkative but awkward—almost child-like in her mannerisms and social interactions. We were like oil and water, but I admired her selflessness and passion to be involved in such rescue missions. The absence of street lights in the area was conspicuous.

Our car ride was mostly silent, and I was filled with a foreboding of what we would witness on arrival. We had to leave the cameraman behind because he refused to go to this red-light district. We giggled at his cowardice. But deep inside, I too was feeling antsy and terrified of the prospect of filming the trafficking victims myself. When we arrived at the brothel area, the stillness of the cool November night contrasted dramatically with the bright, garish lights of the wooden stalls selling fried egg dishes and candied hawthorn apples, along with other small vendors with electronic items and knick-knacks. I was too rattled to enjoy the sights, as I usually do at outdoor markets in smaller cities.

I wore sneakers and jogging pants and carried a backpack, partly in an effort to look like a tourist but also because I wanted to be able to run as fast as I could from the gangsters, should the need arise! I imagined different worst-case 'what if' scenarios as I tried to motivate myself to film the women there and look for signs of underage girls forced into sex slavery. I could feel my heart thumping erratically as if it would leap out of my chest like a rocket. I took a few deep breaths and sent out a silent prayer to protect me in a place where I could not count on help from the police. It felt like a suicide mission. In this part of the country, 'Romeo pimps', also known as 'loverboys' or 'boyfriend traffickers', were successfully plying their trade of manipulating young, vulnerable girls by pretending to be their boyfriends. These men would lie about owing money to a gang and claim that their lives were in danger unless their girlfriends voluntarily sold their bodies to pay off the debt. Door of Hope had met several girls who were victims of such deception. These girls were usually fatherless, children of divorced parents, or victims of abuse in their broken families.

In some of the side alleys in this night market area, there were small shopfronts with open windows designed for clients to come and pick the girl they wanted to pay for. The lighting was pink, the colour symbolizing a brothel establishment in Asia. Several young women in tight dresses sat on couches and chairs in every room. Each woman had an empty look on her wizened, heavily made-up face with bright red lips and pasty white skin. They looked like they were in their late twenties or younger. These young women were usually accompanied by their 'minders'—fierce-looking older women with garish make-up—or menacing young gangster-type men guarding their criminal activities. They were constantly on the lookout for anyone who could threaten their illegal ventures. These women were kept in a depressing prison, forced to entertain men all night long.

It was clear they could not leave of their own free will. Outside a few of the brothels, I noticed guard dogs growling and baring their ferocious teeth; they were undoubtedly used to intimidate women and prevent them from escaping this hell hole.

I felt an overwhelming sadness wash over me as I walked by. It was my first time in such a remote red-light district. I sensed the danger. I sensed the women were controlled and not free to happily walk away, and yet I was walking freely outside. This paradox was inconceivable and heart-breaking. I reflected on the unjust nature of life. It is just a matter of chance where one is born and into which family. This and a host of other circumstances beyond the control of these women had led them into a destiny of unimaginable trauma and enslavement.

I pretended to look at my phone but felt weighed down by the oppressive spirit of the place. What was I doing here? Amy had advised that I film in this particular alley, pretending to be a tourist who has lost her way. I depended on Amy for every step I took but now that I was here, it seemed too dangerous, too close for comfort; I couldn't shake off the feeling that I was possibly risking my own life.

I had to battle the impulse to run back to our waiting car. The darkness of this brothel alley made my skin crawl and the temptation to quit surged within me. But I told myself I need to expose this wicked racket. I quieted my panic by praying to God, asking for a sign. A wave of courage came over me. I felt my feet move ahead as my resolve to tell their story was strengthened.

I felt a rush of adrenaline as I held out my phone camera and walked by that surreal scene of window after window of young scantily-clad girls who looked like anguished mannequins with painted faces. I felt victorious once I had captured the undeniable images on both my phone and the small camera I had hidden in my backpack. No one had been able to get this on film before. It was a weighty coup that would expose evil. After feeling euphoric for a few seconds and thinking that I had outsmarted the gangsters, I walked back calmly to the jeep where Mary and Tina were waiting for me. If Amy were here with us, she would have asked how it went and helped us to process everything we had seen. But Amy was spending time with her family instead. She thought it was prudent not to be seen with me in the brothel area in case they found out I was filming because she has to be able to go there to build trust and relationships with the mama-sans and pimps.

All of a sudden, we were surrounded by three thugs in their twenties and menacing mama-sans in their forties. How could we have missed them! Instantly, I regretted putting my life in the hands of Amy and Mary. I felt I made a huge mistake and I was going to pay with my life. The men were dressed in black. Their eyes bulged out of their sockets. They had hard lines etched on their foreheads. I suspected the two mama-sans were former prostitutes who had clawed their way through the ranks to become brothel managers.

I wasn't sure who scared me more: the middle-aged women or the young male gangsters. They screamed at us in Chinese, saying, 'Give me your phone! Show me your phone! We saw you taking photos and posting them on Weibo!' They were screaming and pointing their fingers an inch away from our faces. I panicked and began sweating. I felt nauseated. I thought of my beloved mother and family and felt a deep anguish thinking I wouldn't be able to say my goodbyes.

Somehow, I had been able to take off the small camera from my backpack and throw it into the car-seat pocket. I hastily moved almost numb fingers across my phone and deleting the footage in a matter of seconds. This was a miracle in and of itself since I was not very familiar with my iPhone.

'What do we do? What do we do?' we asked in unison. The confusion and panic mingled together, choking us and, I'm convinced, cutting off the blood supply to our brains. Mary didn't have any answers either, and I felt like she was ready to throw me to the wolves.

Tina, the driver, froze and then suggested we get out of the car. She was terrified. In hindsight, that was a mistake. I was furious with her. But we had no idea whether or not these men had weapons or if they would have broken our windows and slashed our tyres.

Foolishly, I got out of the car after mixed signals from my accomplices. Mary crumbled and was barely coherent. Tina seemed like she was going to escape and leave Mary and me behind. I felt her sense of self-preservation kicking in. She didn't respond when Mary and I were asking for help. She had also kept quiet during the altercation.

I showed them my phone and said I had nothing. But they continued to scream obscenities and accused me of posting photos of their brothels on Weibo.

I imagined that our bodies would rot in a ditch nearby after they beat us up.

Then, unexpectedly, in the midst of the screaming, a man yelled, 'The police are coming! The police!' With these word, they scattered like cockroaches under a harsh spotlight. It was freakish. It was my first miracle. We bolted inside the jeep. Tina sat there like a rock. I was seething at her by now. Mary and I shouted, 'Drive! Let's go!'

Tina finally punched the gas and we drove away. My body was full of adrenaline and in shock. I was traumatized and could now better identify with the enslaved women in a way I had not been able to before. Then, I was just an outsider documenting their experiences. Now, I had a lived experience. I texted my family and friends right away to notify them briefly of what had happened. Ten minutes later as we left the brothel area far behind, my heart was still beating at a rapid pace.

Our ride back to the city centre was mostly silent, but I could feel an underlying anger in all of us. Tina probably blamed me for getting her into this mess. I blamed Tina and Mary for their lack of leadership, and Amy for giving me such foolish advice to openly film in front of mama-sans and gangsters. Mary was in a complete state of shock. It was her first brush with real danger since she began her work in the red-light district. Each of us was lost in thoughts, wondering if it was worth putting our lives at risk this way. I wondered if I would ever be able to cover this kind of frontline work again. Little did I know at this point that I would have signs of Post-Traumatic Stress (PTS) even months later, waking to the slightest creak and the lightest sound in the floor above me. Complete darkness was a welcome sight, and the terror of what I had experienced disappeared in the dead of night.

When I deleted the film footage of the brothel area, I also erased the film footage I had taken the other night of the most oppressive red-light areas in the city—the brothel street that caused me to scream in my sleep hours later. I knew it was an act of self preservation, yet I was inconsolable. I knew I did not want to return to that place ever again. But how would I produce my news documentary now? I needed footage of brothel areas, and I had none except what was recorded in the small hidden camera from my backpack. That thought helped quell some of the fear and anxiety.

Only after we reached Mary's home safely, was I able to let my guard down. Mary and I argued over how we could have better handled the confrontation with the gangsters and mama-sans. I couldn't share with her what was in my heart so I called a few friends and texted my prayer partners in Hong Kong, Beijing, the US, and Canada and told them what had happened. They had been praying all through my trip. It was inexplicable that we came out unscathed after being surrounded by the vicious mama-sans and gang members. There was no sign of police anywhere near that site. I believe a miracle happened and our lives were saved. It was a life-changing experience for me.

Most people in China accuse women of voluntarily selling their bodies out of greed. However, the viciousness and verbal violence of the mama-sans and thugs was terrifying, and I could understand how the girls would have been intimidated into compliance. It was profound to be able to stand in their shoes, to feel the danger and terror they face, and to have to face such menacing individuals myself.

This experience led me to have even more compassion for women and girls forced into sex slavery. I felt the ultimate purpose of my trip—to understand what the girls suffer in the brothels—had been accomplished. This understanding would better arm me to put a spotlight on the suffering of women and girls so that others could also empathize with them. To understand became a theme of my investigative work on human trafficking.

# 2

# Fearless Christian Women

Our near-death experience had caused a stir among the staff at Door of Hope. When Amy came in, she enquired what had happened. I was clearly traumatized, but I would not realize this until months later. I was in shock and could barely function, let alone speak about what had happened. I told Amy that it had not been wise to whip out my phone in the middle of that brothel alley. She responded with measured words and seemed to want to avoid taking responsibility. She was neither sympathetic nor callous but spoke in neutral, almost clinical, terms like a counsellor. I felt angry at her, and I was distressed on thinking about my experience, and the fact that there was nothing else I could do about it.

Our painful encounter brought to mind a memory from a few days earlier, when Amy had tried to convince me to film and expose a popular underground dance hall where the operators turned off the lights at random times. When the lights were off, the men had free rein to molest or do anything they wanted to their dancing partners. I had briefly considered filming the event and pondered on ways to protect myself but ultimately decided that it was too far out for me. It was not worth being collateral damage. Moreover, I was shocked into silence that Amy would even suggest I put myself in such a vulnerable situation. Perhaps to Amy, it was a tiny risk, considering what she had been through on the frontlines.

It is true that Amy had put herself in danger many times. On one occasion, a man near a brothel was punching a woman with full force. Amy leapt between them and held up the man's hand. She calmly spoke to him, and told him that it didn't reflect well on him to be seen hitting a woman. The man's hand went limp, and he stopped using her as a punching bag. The woman was able to get away.

I also learnt during my previous visits that the Door of Hope team consisting of Christian women, both Chinese and foreigners, had also walked into sleazy areas like the one where I had filmed. They had brought gifts to encourage the women and caused the mama-sans to look the other way. Socializing with any outsiders was discouraged. They had befriended a former trafficker named Guo and provided foster care to his three-year-old daughter, Chun. Their radical fearlessness inspired me, and I felt they were pioneering a truly meaningful work of rescue and reaching some of the most marginalized people in the country.

In 2003, Amy and several of her friends discovered that there were no social services being provided to prostitutes in red-light districts. Saddened by this knowledge, they began to investigate the area by walking in groups to learn more. They were thorough in their research, taking more than two years to get to know these unfortunate women and their needs. When they started, the team consisted of housewives and a few local women who had wished to help and pray for the women suffering in the brothels. Gradually, the team blossomed beyond everybody's expectations, even Amy's. At that time, Door of Hope was one of the few organizations to offer sustainable solutions to trafficking victims and prostituted women through their social enterprise, job training opportunities, creative outreaches, and rehabilitation centre. Their safe home was one of the first in Mainland China to be established. It has provided free medical support, mental health services, and ran a social enterprise selling jewellery made by rescued women and former prostitutes. I observed that they are not run like a professional organization, rather a family-run enterprise with both chaos among the staff and drama from the survivors in need of healing and stability. Despite all their setbacks, they are offering much-needed services to a group that had none previously.

In their journey to start an organization to help rescue women out of sex trafficking, they faced enormous obstacles like societal acceptance of prostitution and the women coming out of it, collusion and corruption in law enforcement agencies, and rampant use of prostitutes in the business arena, with foreigners being among the johns.

What they learnt was harrowing, and it made me shudder. On an average, the women are forced to have sex with four men daily and are paid $9 to $15 per john. The 'boss' takes a 30 to 40 per cent cut. Of those using prostitutes, about 60 per cent are married men and have children, while 30 per cent are students. The girls and young women face violence and the risk of contracting venereal disease and HIV/AIDS.

'One of the sick things many men like to do is burn these girls with cigarettes. They're leaving lasting scars all over their bodies, not just STDs, which is really sad,' said Alice, one of the volunteers during a conversation. I became quite close to this volunteer over several visits. Alice was an outgoing young woman, a recent university graduate, and about a year earlier, we enjoyed a fun all-day outing at the local zoo and ethnic minority park to let off some steam and release the stress of hearing terrifying stories of abuse.

In another conversation with Amy and one of the Chinese volunteers, one girl from a brothel was taken to the mountains and brutally raped, and then the man stole her money. When she made it back to the brothel, she had to face further violence from the 'owner' who was angry that the money was gone. This, instead of getting her

the urgent medical attention she desperately needed! Hopelessness
and unspeakable abuse permeate the atmosphere of these brothels.
Increasingly, these women are also at risk of being murdered.

According to Door of Hope, at least 80 per cent of prostitutes
in China have been trafficked. Official statistics (and they are
difficult to come by in China) state that there are four million
prostituted women. Amy believed the real number to be closer
to nine million because the official figures do not include women
working in karaoke bars (KTVs) and hotels—five-star to cheap
fleabag motels.

A code word for prostitution is 'massage', and in any given hotel
on the Mainland, if you are a single foreigner, there will invariably be
a knock on your door or a phone call at 11 p.m. asking if you want
a 'massage'.

It was an eye-opening experience to speak with the Chinese
Door of Hope volunteers who were going to brothel areas to reach
women who had been marginalized by society. These petite women
volunteers were from the local house churches. They told me that
they would not have been able to even shake hands with prostituted
women a few years earlier, but now they are able to embrace them
and show them love.

After I returned to Hong Kong from this filming trip, I received
a WhatsApp message from an unknown number in China. It was a
single photo of a young Asian woman in a sexual pose—a girl who
had eerily similar features and hairstyle as me. I thought of how
the Italian mafia sometimes send an intimidating life-threatening
message in the form of a symbolic image or object. This photo
seemed to suggest that someone in a position of authority knew about
my filming trip. I wondered if they were asking me to be careful. It
seemed too random to be from a clueless stranger as everything in
Mainland China is known to the authorities who have their eyes and
ears planted everywhere, even in personal devices. I felt unsafe as I
lived alone in an apartment. I immediately called my mentor, Lois,

to inform her of this WhatsApp message. I also showed it to my executive producer but she wasn't fazed by it.

I told myself to press forward to better understand the plight of women in the region, I spoke with one insightful researcher in Hong Kong, named Lo, who told me that Vietnamese and Hmong women were being bought and sold into prostitution through Romeo pimps using social media. She said that some parents even sold their daughters. These families had many children and ended up selling the girls. She said that some women wanted to go to China because 'it's wealthier'.

Lo likened it to 'mail order brides', with the demand coming from poor rural men who have a hard time finding suitable brides in the countryside. She had seen many abandoned girls who had been discriminated against because of their gender. Also, there have been multiple generations of opium addiction, with an ugly cycle of drug use and crime. I sensed an evil link between the historical opium-trafficking routes that paved the way for modern-day sex trafficking and the flourishing drug trade. Over the years, many women in the brothels I spoke with said they had parents and ancestors who smoked opium. I was dismayed on learning that there was a generational thread of pain that wove through families. As I've mentioned before, Yunnan is in the notorious Golden Triangle region where the roads of opium trading were well worn and wreaked evil and carnage on the communities in its path.

Lo observed that women view themselves as commodities that are less valuable than men. Their mindset reflects that of society. That's why it's easy for the pimps to target and sell these vulnerable women with low self-esteem. They are easy pickings.

It is in these dangerous neighbourhoods of China that Christian women like Amy and the staff and volunteers of Door of Hope are doing their work. They are working hard to change this mindset and helping the women overcome being frightened into submission and fear of pimps and traffickers in order to bring a radical transformative message of hope. They're reaching one of the most unreached people in China: prostitutes and young girls trapped in sex trafficking. What's astounding about this group's approach is that, unlike other non-profit organizations in the country, they extend their love of God and compassion to rehabilitation and alternative vocational options for traffickers, pimps, and others who make a living from selling girls. It is easy to despise these wicked people who inflict unending pain on the vulnerable for their own selfish monetary gain. I have little sympathy for them and would rather see them receive the harshest penalties for how they have destroyed lives.

Amy once told me, 'I used to walk down the street and hate them and pray against them. Then God broke my heart for mafia bosses and gave me opportunities to minister to them. This is the father heart of God.'

It's a profound concept to love your enemy. For Amy, anti-trafficking work also included praying for the perpetrators and pimps who sell children for sex. It was hard to take in at first. Their rehabilitation work with gangsters and pimps was not only gutsy, it was unprecedented.

Initially, Amy had felt unqualified to rescue women out of trafficking and brothels because of her lack of experience and inability to speak fluently in Mandarin. But she felt a nudge from God to just go and show love and compassion to prostitutes, pimps, and mafia bosses.

'Everything at a human level hates those perpetrators. That's my personal challenge. But God doesn't. It messes up your head totally, since in your mind you have your own justice system that separates the victim from the evil perpetrator,' Amy said. 'But I began to see that they're all victims. Even the traffickers and pimps are all trapped.'

She also described how emotionally taxing it was to see women exploited in such terrible ways. 'We do a lot of debriefing and crying together, building each other up.'

I felt drained from merely listening to Amy's stories and exploits. She had her fair share of ups and downs, but her commitment to help the voiceless was remarkable. My heart felt heavy, and I wondered if it was too stressful for me. I wondered if I had chosen the right path of kissing the comfortable, white-picket-fence lifestyle goodbye and taking on the fight against sex trafficking and modern-day slavery.

At this formative time of my life in my thirties that would determine the next decade, I felt so broken and lonely from a divorce. I was searching for identity and meaning. I didn't have a clear life purpose, and I often wrestled with the temptation to live a comfortable life back in North America that would not allow the suffering of others to pierce my perfect bubble. It was astounding to me to learn how Amy saw hope in the most depraved of humanity. I hope that is in God. She had an unshakable sense of purpose in her life that deeply moved me. I too wanted to have this hope and firm calling. She helped shape my thoughts on sex trafficking and this seedy underworld. She helped me to put my own personal pain in perspective, and understand how I could use my privilege as a professional woman with choices to help those who are voiceless and have had their decision-making power stolen from them. For that, I'm eternally grateful.

\* \* \*

On a previous trip in my role as a philanthropy advisor, I had met Sarah, a Christian attending a house church in 2009. We had a warm connection immediately, and she felt comfortable enough to hold my hand, a gesture common among Chinese women but I was not used to it. Sarah was an attractive, youthful thirty-year-old Chinese woman with long straight hair and delicate features. She had recently given birth to a baby girl. She had graduated from a college with an English major and helped serve as a translator for Door of Hope. I recorded her insights on the flesh trade in China and the stories of transformation. This is what she told me.

'It was difficult for me in the first several months when I was working as a translator at this ministry. I wasn't married, and when they talked about sex it was difficult for me to translate that. I was brought up to consider it shameful to talk about sex. One time, one of our sisters from Holland and I went to a brothel to teach them how to use a condom to protect them from sexually transmitted diseases (STDs). It was really embarrassing for me.

'I felt cynical and doubted these women would change. I helped translate for the counsellor earlier this year. They lied often. They talked about shameful things. When I listened to them pray, I felt God's power. We built relationships by bringing gifts or dropping by regularly to chat and asked questions about their lives. I told them about Door of Hope and that we can help them and they can come to our office at any time.

'If we have the chance, we'll share the gospel with them. If they give us their number, we'll stay in touch and call them. I did that for four months.

'We went to the make-up shops where prostitutes get their make-up and hair done for 30 kwai. Most of them do not have an education. Some have middle-school education only.

'First several months, I couldn't see their change. I knew their stories. One twenty-year-old woman with HIV was here for almost two years, but she still has sex with her Thai boyfriend—the man who gave the disease to her. She often says, 'I know God will heal me one hundred per cent.' She has a six-year-old daughter. Some of them had diseases from prostitution. Door of Hope helps them with medical care for free. Some of them were pregnant and they were helped.'

I asked Sarah why are women in prostitution? She said, 'I'd say ninety-nine per cent of these women are rejected by their parents. Some of them are rejected because they are girls. Some are from divorced families and poor families.'

She explained further as to why these women ended up in prostitution. It was heartrending.

'Most of the prostituted women choose to go into this work because they are uneducated and have few options—some of them have really poor families. Some are divorced and reluctantly go into this work. Many of their husbands abused them, or they broke up with their boyfriends. They are very depressed.'

She continued. 'Some women wanted a job in the city, but someone cheated them. Some of them wanted more money to lead a higher quality of life. Some of the women are uneducated and lazy. Working at a restaurant doesn't pay very well. Most of the girls I've met, two-thirds of the women, want to change their lives and really want to stop.'

Sarah said many of the women felt safe and secure for the first time in their lives at Door of Hope. They could stay at the shelter, receive counselling, and also take vocational training classes for learning English, computer, make-up artistry, and much more.

Most hear about the shelter through word of mouth, and when they first arrive they are distrustful and traumatized. But somehow through the kindness of the staff and volunteers, some of the women receive healing and are transformed. 'When I see their life change, even if it's a little, I am very happy,' said Sarah.

A woman named Feng Mian experienced profound change of heart. Sarah explained that her parents favoured her brother and showed him more love. So, she felt rejected. Several years ago, she had a boyfriend and a good relationship, but they broke up and she became inconsolable. She didn't have rent money, and was close to sleeping on the streets when someone suggested that she sell her body to survive.

'She felt worthless and decided to give it a try. But once she came to Door of Hope, she knew she would never go back to prostitution again. Feng Mian has a dream and wants to learn English in order to study jewellery design abroad,' said Sarah.

Another young woman named Yu Yan grew up without parents. She always felt alone and wanted to have a man in her life because she was insecure. But she was able to turn her life around after staying in the Door of Hope shelter and receiving care and counselling from the staff. Another young woman left prostitution and got married. She now has twins. Many others too are married now.

However, not all of the women have happy endings. Sarah looked visibly upset when she described the two or three girls who did not want to change and leave prostitution. Some of them refused to believe in God. To Sarah, this was like a personal failure as she is highly conscientious and takes her mission very seriously.

Many of the girls have difficulty getting pregnant when they want to start families of their own because they've had multiple abortions. 'Two of these women were told by the doctor that they cannot give birth. But here, because they pray and believe in Christ, we see miracles happen and they get pregnant. Overall, they feel happy, appreciated, and feel they are loved.'

Sarah believes that prostitution and trafficking are getting worse. One reason is that the cost of living is high, but salaries are abysmally low. Many university students cannot find good jobs. For many men, if they have several wives—like modern-day concubines—they have 'face' and feel they are more respected. There's no sense of morality.

Like myself, Sarah felt disbelief and shock when she first heard that many of the girls she met at the shelter were forced or deceived into prostitution. Some girls worked as dishwashers for little pay and were lured by the promise of a big salary and then deceived into prostitution. They felt too ashamed to leave.

The women working in KTV and in bars at big hotels who pour men alcoholic drinks are called 'princesses'. The bosses at these establishments try to lure these women into prostitution. Such an environment hardens these women to a level that they lose all sense of boundaries. Rich men and married men also seduce these women.

A profound sense of shame prevents some of the girls in the shelter from sharing their experiences and receiving help through counselling. Sarah explains that one girl was in prison for four months. When she was young, her father and grandfather loved her very much, like a little princess. They held her while she was sleeping. When she was eight, her father died and her grandfather became blind. She was raped by several family members. Her mother remarried and left her more vulnerable. She was abused by older teenagers and relatives.

When this young girl reached middle school, her mother stopped her schooling and wanted her to get married. So, she ran away from her family. Without a support system, she turned to prostitution in order to survive. Two months later, the police arrested her. After serving prison time, she learned about Door of Hope from the prison officials. She was only twenty years old at the time.

Another woman, Fei Hong, also feels safe in the shelter, knowing she can stay there for as long as she wants to, surrounded by an all-female staff that cares for her and shows her unconditional kindness.

Sarah also told me that often the women become vulnerable because they had been raped and abused by family members and family friends, the very people they were supposed to trust. They started to feel worthless and became vulnerable to exploitation. They turned to prostitution as a result of the rapes. All this also made the women suspicious of everyone around them, even those that tried to help.

I was touched by Sarah's noble compassion for these women and her willingness to meet with me even though she had a baby to care for. She overcame her own prejudices to extend kindness and support to these women who were debilitated by shame and betrayal. I asked her what do women recovering from forced prostitution need the most? I was moved by and surprised by her simple answer: 'Love, love. They need to find their worth. If they know they are so precious and valuable, they will act that way. They will live healthy lives.

Otherwise, it's difficult because they have broken families or were abused. They feel they have no value. I was moved by my foreign friends' love for the women in the red-light districts. I am Chinese, but I have not seen any Chinese people have this kind of love for the women.'

By reaching out to these vulnerable women, Sarah's life was also changed. She was able to process and heal similar personal issues in her own life, such as being rejected by her parents for her gender. She was the first to admit that she too had benefitted from her interactions with women in the sex trade. Sarah spoke to me at length.

'I was the third child. My parents thought they were having a son. My parents had to pay a fine to the government for having an extra child. I also felt I didn't have worth in this world. My mother left my family when I was seven. I thought it was because I was a bad daughter. When I was young, in my diary, I wrote unhappy things. I blamed myself. I believed that no one loved me or accepted me, and that everything I did was wrong.

'Jesus healed me of this lie. I know how important I am. Once you know God's love, you will know you are worthy. Only if you know God's love and forgiveness in a tangible, life-changing way [can you heal], otherwise, you cannot.

'The most challenging thing in this ministry is to understand their story. They need God's healing. We need to be careful to not hurt their hearts but to help them forgive those who hurt them. When they tell their stories to us, they need to know we empathize with them. And they need to know someone understands their experiences.'

I resonated with her goal to understand these women and to support them with empathy. I was struck by her pure heart and her rare quality of not wanting to bring harm to those who were already crushed and bruised in every way.

\* \* \*

I had visited Kunming in 2011 with the goal of staying for more than a week in a shelter for survivors of sex trafficking. This was a year before my infamous alley incident mentioned previously in the book. That first time staying in a shelter, I had no idea what to expect. My previous trips focused on my philanthropy work with some interviews with survivors. All I knew was that I wanted to document stories of modern-day sex slaves for my book on the voices of survivors of historical sex trafficking and the forced prostitution by the Imperial Japanese military before and during WWII, known by a wicked euphemism 'comfort women'. I had finished the first draft of this book—an effort of more than ten years. I was considering writing a last chapter on how the cycle of sexual enslavement never ended in Asia.

The first person I met at the shelter was a woman named Ying Yue, a timid and shy woman who was living there with her young son. Ying Yue gave me short answers to the questions I asked her. Her responses were no different even when I communicated with her through a translator. I was worried that I wouldn't be able to write her story. Over a week, and after repeated sessions of chatting and eating together and observing one another, I learned she was from a minority tribe and struggled as a single mother of a hyperactive three-year old boy. She didn't know who the father was. By looking at her fair-skinned son, we could deduce that the father was Chinese.

I felt sadness when talking with her. She was uneducated and did not have any other job prospects when she first went into prostitution. When the translator was not around, I tried to communicate with her using my limited Mandarin vocabulary. Her mother tongue was a minority dialect. The living room had a TV, and some of us sat around to talk, including the house mother. Despite the limited language ability, we got to know each other through our actions and eyes. We were able to transcend language and connect with our hand gestures and with our hearts. It was a unique connection. She seemed to understand that I cared enough to come and hear her story.

I felt sad and teared up when she cried and shared with me how her father had abandoned her and the lack of financial support from her impoverished family. Her husband became violent too. That's how she ended up selling her body in the brothel. She had heard about the shelter through a friend. This shelter saved her from an early death. If she had stayed on at the brothel, she would have either contracted STDs or become addicted to drugs. She understood how blessed she was. I resolved to donate some money to her by the end of my stay. We had a bond, and it's something that I often feel when I connect and interview a traumatized survivor of enslavement. I had learnt to be patient and create a safe place for them so that they could open up to me and share their experiences without pressure. Her son was very hyper but he would stay still enough to receive candies from me. I reflected on Ying Yue's future and whether she would be able to marry well. I had heard from another staff member that there was a man in her life. I felt a maternal pang and was protective of her.

I also visited another shelter with more young women. More than a dozen stayed in that house. When I reached this shelter, it was time for dinner preparations. I helped set egg and tomato dishes and rice bowls and chopsticks on the round dinner table. There were also fried vegetable dishes and boiled eggs.

I volunteered to do Korean-style egg facials on each person. I had learned the recipe for the facial from my mother—egg yolks, yoghurt, and cucumbers, that's all it took. The women seemed to really enjoy anything related to Korea due to the popularity of Korean dramas and pop stars. It was a profound moment for me to serve these women and bring beauty and joy to their lives, even if for a day. Earlier, I had felt I wasn't bringing anything useful to them because of my limited Mandarin. But I was perplexed over why anything Korean was so popular among these women. This was a remnant from my childhood identity issues when I earnestly desired to be a blonde girl to fit in with the rest of my classmates. I told the girls that I was a 'banana', yellow or Korean on the outside but inside, I was 'White' or very Westernized. But their blank faces told me that they couldn't grasp as to why I didn't want to be Korean—a cultural phenomenon that they found to be very hip.

In my basic Mandarin, I spoke with each of them and learnt more about their family backgrounds and how they got there. I had lived in Mainland China for more than six years and was very comfortable interacting with the locals, especially women. Because of my Korean heritage, the women seemed to be much more interested in what I had to say, and some asked me about Korean dramas and how to say certain Korean words. I was amused. They couldn't understand why I would reject being Korean. They helped me feel more comfortable with my identity.

Most of the young women were in their twenties and had broken relationships with their fathers. Many had broken connections with their mothers too.

All of them had an orphan mentality of being resigned to looking after themselves. With this mentality came a lack of trust in others and a stubborn poverty mindset of selfishly putting yourself above all. They fought with one another often.

That week, I spoke every morning with a group of about twelve young women in the jewellery workshop. I spoke of how I learnt to honour my father and mother and forgive them for disappointing me in the past. Though my parents had provided practical support, they had not been emotionally nurturing to me. But I was now healed of the burdens of my childhood. I spoke to the women in such a way that I was able to also convince them of my healing. The forgiveness message seemed to resonate with each person. I led them in a prayer of forgiveness for those they couldn't forgive. The tears flowed, and I hugged a few who sobbed bitterly. I empathized with them as I too had been in that state of unending weeping. What stood out to me was that most of these women were either fatherless or came from broken families. I was also struck by how each woman spoke of their need for more money.

The staff leader of the shelter, named Xuxu, was a sincere woman with a mousy exterior. She was the polar opposite of the tall, broad-shouldered, and bold Amy. Xuxu had a round face and small eyes. She was meek, but after spending time with her, I realized that she had a will of steel. But not everyone would perceive her inner strength. Xuxu was an introvert and not a real talker. She spoke in simple terms. Xuxu seemed to have a high tolerance for the drama inside the shelter. Several women were constantly fighting with one another; there was an unending stream of gossip and jealousy. I interpreted it as women with unhealed trauma responses triggering one another. I could see the tension between some of the women during meal times, and it reminded me of the catfights some young women would get into in high school. A few of the women left the shelter to get away from the strict rules, only to return.

I met Xuxu twice—first for an interview in 2009 when I was there on a trip and then again in 2011, when I had visited the area for work. One of Xuxu's colleagues told me that she knew everything about each woman in the shelter. Xuxu also told me that she had become a Christian at a young age, and she still attends a house church. She used to work as a cook in an international restaurant called Wicker Basket but felt exhausted with the daily grind of work; she also felt that it didn't help meet her full potential. Several colleagues were ministers at their church, and she also wanted to minister but felt her minimal education was a limitation in this regard. Most of all, she also believed that her faith in God was mediocre. So, she began to pray for a new opportunity because she didn't want to be a cook anymore. She found her opportunity when Amy met the restaurant staff for a talk on sexual exploitation of young women in the city.

Soon after, Amy approached Xuxu and asked her to work for Door of Hope. Xuxu told me, 'When I asked Amy, "why did you ask me?" she told me that "while I was praying, I saw your face in a vision."' I too knew that Amy had a gift of being led clearly by God, and she had an unusual ability to pioneer this rescue work in other cities and nations despite her being your average housewife. Years later, she was the first person to perceive that my future husband and I would make a great match, even before I began dating him. Amy had seen us together at a meeting. I sensed that I was connected with Xuxu and Amy, not by chance but serendipitously. There was a higher purpose, but I didn't know it at the time.

I asked Xuxu which story had touched her the most, and which girl had changed the most. She said, 'Gu Yang has changed the most. She once said to me, "Many people looked down on me when they found out I was a prostitute, but here I feel real love, and no one looks down on me."' Gu used to live with her boyfriend. A team of volunteers encouraged her to stop this because they felt he could be 'using her'. As a new Christian, she was advised to marry rather than live-in with a man. She took a big decision to leave her boyfriend, who then broke up with her.

Xuxu also mentioned another young woman, Gao Li, who had changed a lot. After getting baptized, Xuxu encouraged the women to live a holy life. I was impressed by how deeply she cared about each one of these girls as if they were her own children.

She also told me about Li Jiang, who came to the shelter and then moved in with her boyfriend. So, Xuxu rebuked Li Jiang and told her to stop sleeping with her boyfriend because God is not pleased with premarital sex. Li Jiang conceded and returned to the shelter. Two years later, he pursued her and asked her to marry him when he realized that she had transformed into a wholesome person. Once at Bible class with fifty attendees, Li Jiang gave a powerful testimony on leaving prostitution. It was an extraordinary moment because of the huge stigma surrounding women in the flesh trade. Everyone prayed for her, and for many, it was the first time they listened to a former prostitute share her testimony. She was totally healed of shame over her past.

Xiao Liu's husband always beat her. She went into prostitution because of a deep sense of worthlessness. When Xuxu first met her, she was scheming to meet a man with HIV so that she could give it to her husband. 'If I have the chance, I will kill him!' Xiao Liu had told Xuxu. 'A Christian sister said to her, "Do not do this. Stop this thought." Xiao Liu decided to leave prostitution and heard about the shelter for exploited women. She has changed a lot. She's a Christian now. She has shared the gospel with her mother. She's been a part of the ministry since 2007,' Xuxu said.

In a self-deprecating manner that's common among the local Chinese, Xuxu downplays her work and describes what she has done as 'a little bit of work, but I cannot see the fruit'. What motivates Xuxu to keep going in this tough line of work, despite discouraging reports of women who willingly go back to prostitution, is that she hears the girls saying they haven't forgotten about Jesus. Of all the staff at Door of Hope, I was the most impressed by Xuxu, her quiet confidence and genuine humility and love.

Amy suggested that I ask Xuxu about her prison ministry as it was amazing. Xuxu has been doing prison ministry since August 2006; she is ministering and showing acts of kindness to dozens of women in jail. 'I've met with 120 prostituted women in prison. On Christmas Day, we gave the guards and women prisoners gifts of clothes. There are many prostitutes and pimps in prison. There are prostitutes who are over fifty years old. The oldest prostituted woman I met is sixty years old,' Xuxu informed me.

I know how challenging it is to get access to prisons in China; it was nearly impossible to minister in one as a Christian. I asked Xuxu how she managed to get unprecedented access. This is what she told me. 'Several years ago, the boss of the barbershop in my apartment asked me to help him find the three women working in his shop as prostitutes. Prostitution is illegal. He said the police took them away. We asked the police, and they said they were sent to prison. A friend told me how to get to the prison. This is how we began this prison ministry.'

'It's not just a prison but a rehabilitation centre to train women to find other work. They learn computer skills and make ethnic minority clothes that are sold. They're given classes on HIV awareness and STDs,' Xuxu explained.

Xuxu was more than happy to share more stories of some of the women she helped. Her memory was astounding as she spoke incessantly.

'I met a girl named Li, and we tried to convince her to leave prostitution. She left, but her good friend was not willing to leave. Her friend doesn't believe in God. She wants to make easy money.'

'I went to prison to pick up one girl. Her mother was there. I asked her if she was there to pick up her daughter. She abused me verbally. "You hurt my daughter! I'm going to tell the police!" And she called the police. They knew me, and said to the mother, "She's a good person. She will not hurt your daughter."' Another woman named Xi Xi used to gamble on the computer, and I encouraged her to stop. This woman quit gambling. She couldn't admit she was a prostitute though. She became pregnant, and before she left for the hospital to give birth, she shared with me that she was prostituted.'

'Everyone is ashamed of working as a prostitute. But after believing in Jesus, she felt uncomfortable in telling me a lie, and that's why she told the truth. She'll come back to our ministry later. I met her in prison, and she said to me, "If you didn't come to visit me in prison, I don't know what my life would be like now." She even asked for a Bible. But when the guards discovered it, they forbade me from visiting. But Xi Xi talked with the guards and convinced them to allow me to visit her again.'

It was a lack of self-confidence and her frustrations at being stuck in a dead-end job as a cook that left Xuxu wallowing in feelings of worthlessness, not unlike the women she was helping at the shelter. 'God totally changed me, and I could face my insecurities and do this ministry for the last three years. Many times, I didn't know what to say to people, but the Holy Spirit leads me. Many times, I wanted to give up,' she said. Their work is so emotionally taxing; it is painful to hear the stories of abuse.

I asked Xuxu why she thought women get involved in prostitution. Without skipping a beat, she said to me, 'Some are cheated by others. They think they're going to work in a good job. They work in a massage parlour or barbershop, and their boss forces them to sell their virginity. Another girl was raped by a man, and he brought her to a brothel when she was fifteen. One woman's aunt ran a brothel and introduced her to work there. Others told me that their workplaces were in brothel areas, and they were lured by the naive prospect of earning a lot of money.'

'Mei is an orphan, and no one wants to care for her. She told me once, "No matter what happens, I'll make a lot of money and wear beautiful clothes." She sells her body to three different men. She smokes all the time. Several days ago, she left early in the morning. I went to look for her with another volunteer. We found the barbershop's door open. Mei came out sheepishly. Sometimes the man gives her 100 RMB. I don't know how to deal with girls like Mei who are deceptive.'

'What else do the girls need?' I asked.

'No one has finished their skills training. The girls decide to drop out early on. We've supported them to study art or to learn make-up skills, but they don't finish. I have experienced a lot of heartache, and sometimes I feel happy knowing that God is here. But sometimes I feel sad. I pray to see the girls' lives totally changed. Five girls recently went to a Christian camp run by a house church.'

* * *

Ai Jin was a staff member of Door of Hope, and we had a natural rapport. We became fast friends and connected by Skype once in a while over the years. She was around twenty-seven years old when we first met and had a spunky personality, wore black-rimmed glasses and her square jawline was framed by poker-straight hair. She was single and longed to get married—we bonded over this same desire.

Whenever I visited Door of Hope, I would let her know in advance and we would catch up. Ai Jin told me that she and two other young women from Door of Hope got together every Tuesday to pray before their outreach. Then they walked the streets of a red-light district to tell girls as young as thirteen that they could quit being prostitutes. Ai Jin said, 'Eight years ago, the average girl working in brothels was twenty-five. Now it's fourteen and fifteen. I think it'll get worse since it's becoming harder to find jobs, especially for girls from poor families with no education. They desperately need money. At my church, my pastor told me that what I'm doing in reaching out to prostitutes is what Jesus did. That touched me and encouraged me a lot. Before I started work at Door of Hope, I didn't want to shake hands with prostitutes thinking their whole bodies were dirty. Every day, I prayed for more love for these women. Now I can treat them like my own family.'

Ai Jin and her peers see their work as part of a contribution to building a civil society, unlike some underground church members in the past who have traditionally steered clear of community service because of persecution. 'Social work is a new area in China,' she said. 'Most people don't want to help prostitutes because they feel prostitution is just a job to make money to support themselves. Others don't want to get involved because they don't want to get in trouble with the mafia and pimps who control the girls.'

God's love compels Ai Jin and others in their ground-breaking work. These believers are a picture of what is happening in the urban house churches of China. Slowly, Christians are wading into anti-human-trafficking work, preaching about God's love to the afflicted, mending broken hearts, and proclaiming liberty to the captives and freedom to prisoners.

It is clear that Ai Jin feels a sense of calling to her work, but she has one other reason: her fourteen-year-old cousin is a prostitute. She told me with tears in her eyes, 'When I found out that my own cousin was working in a brothel and wasn't willing to leave, I was so upset that I wanted to quit the ministry. But God said to me that if I quit then other families will ask me, "Why didn't you help my daughter?" This makes me believe that God called me here. If God is calling me, then I want to do this ministry for the rest of my life. It's an honour rather than a duty to work here.'

I cried with her when she told me about her cousin. How heartbreaking. I wondered what if I was in her shoes? Would I live differently? I'm documenting the stories of the survivors using my skills as an interviewer and writer, but should I be doing more? I wrestled with this thought, and I knew that Ai Jin deeply understood the debate I had within. We were exposed to inhumane suffering and how could we not take action? We couldn't turn away. No man is an island, and these women languishing in the prisons of modern-day sex slavery were our cousins, our sisters, our mothers, our daughters, our family.

Ai Jin helped reinforce that ordinary people can do extraordinary acts of heroism. She was the first to admit that she was weak and often wanted to quit. But her tenacious belief in God kept her going out to the world of sex trafficking and prostitution, and that challenged me. She inspired me and told me to continue writing.

# 3

# Poverty Fuels Trafficking

Over the years, the one thing I have come to believe and I firmly stand by is that human trafficking in China has been and will continue to be exacerbated by the country's now-abandoned one-child policy. By 2010, the sex ratio at birth in China was 119 males to every 100 females. It is estimated that China is missing more than sixty million girls and women. China's one-child policy, in place from 1979 to 2015, helped create this monstrous imbalance, as millions of couples were determined that their child be male.

It is commonplace in countryside hospitals to see rows and rows of blue blankets for baby boys, and not a single pink baby girl blanket. This eerie sight is a striking visual of gender discrimination at work. Though it's illegal to determine the gender of the foetus, there are countless parents willing to pay for this information; once they find out it's a girl, they abort.

This centuries-old discriminatory mindset is partly responsible for societal or cultural acceptance or lack of moral outrage for continuing this disgraceful practice. It is widely acceptable for women to be bought and sold as brides like cattle or family-owned property. The rural areas of China have been frozen in time in their way of life along with their attitudes towards women. Boys are favoured because they carry the family name and represent social security for their aging parents, while girls are raised to leave and marry into another family. A Chinese proverb aptly describes this mindset in these words: having a daughter is like pouring water onto another's field or married daughters are like spilled water. If I had been born in Korea eighty years ago, around the time my grandmother was born, I would have faced a similar fate of gender discrimination. In fact, my own grandfather virtually ignored the children of his first daughter and instead lavished attention on his son's children because they carried his family name. In impoverished families, girl children are often neglected and held back from school with all the family resources carefully and strategically invested in the sons of the family and their education, as a kind of insurance policy that they would be taken care of in their old age.

The effort of desperate parents to find wives for their single sons has led to an increase of trafficking of women and girls, both internally and from countries such as North Korea, Myanmar, Laos, Vietnam, Indonesia, and Pakistan. These nations also have a shortage of women.

Back in 2011 before my television documentary filming trip, I visited Door of Hope's shelter to interview some of the survivors and learnt that two of the thirty girls there had been sold as brides to poor farmers but were able to escape. I spoke with one of these young women, Mei Li, who had an aloof, tough demeanour, seemed sceptical of my intentions. She was short and portly and had caramel highlights in her chin-length hair. She wore eyeshadow and lipstick on her heart-shaped face that made her look older. When we first met I tried to earn Mei Li's trust. Amy had said that Mei Li is a walking miracle. I had the feeling that Mei Li's transformation gave Amy the strength to continue in the face of pressure, challenges from the slow-healing process of the girls, and the difficulties in raising funds for this kind of rescue work. I sensed Amy was very proud of her as she gave me a brief outline of her story. Mei Li was sold as a fourteen-year-old bride, then locked up in chains like a dog by her elderly husband and contracted HIV later when selling her body. My heart felt heavy but I braced myself for the sad re-telling of her tale.

We sat down in a room of Door of Hope's centre, and I introduced myself and asked her a few general questions. I asked her if she wanted to ask me anything and gave her the room to control our conversation. Then she needed no more hand-holding and willingly opened the faucet and poured out her pain without much prodding from me.

'I was angry with my father. He flatly refused to pay my high school tuition fee. I was in middle school and yearned to go to high school. This is an all-too-common story in China where sons are favoured over daughters for many reasons. My parents, like most parents in the countryside, did not see value in investing in the education of their only daughter. "No, you will stay at home and work in the fields, Mei Li. You're not going to school anymore," my dad bellowed to me from the kitchen table, not even bothering to look up at me as he finished his late dinner.'

I nodded with empathy and interjected telling her that I too had experienced a similar painful rejection by my father and grandfather for being a girl. The baggage is lifelong, and most Asian women have experienced the same. She resonated immediately and continued sharing, 'I burst into tears and ran straight to my best friend's house. "What happened to you?" she asked and put her arm around me. I poured out my frustration. "My parents won't let me go back to school. They said they're saving money for my brother to go, but not me. I have to help my parents do farm work and then get married," I told her between heaving sobs.'

Mei Li continued her story.

'There was a woman with long hair in a glamorous outfit at my friend's house. She nodded sympathetically. She was a friend of the family and heard my disappointment. Her kind eyes and nodding head made me feel instantly understood. "Why don't you come with us? We're going to the city. I can pay for your meals. You're so pretty, I can buy you a nice outfit that will make the boys in your class chase after you," she said with a laugh. I didn't notice at first that there was a glimmer of excitement in her eyes. I couldn't put my finger on it, but I felt a twinge of uneasiness at the way she looked at me.

'I hesitated for a few minutes. My father expected me to be home soon to help with the housework. Then an image of him sitting at the kitchen table yelling at me flashed across my mind. The angry feelings rose up in my chest, and that's when I made a decision. I'll show my dad. He'll really know that I'm mad at him, and he'll be sorry that he hurt me. "Okay, I'll go."

'We went to a nice restaurant and hit the shopping areas. The woman bought me a nice black and white striped dress. "Really?" I squealed when she said she'd buy it for me. After wandering around downtown, the excitement wore off several hours later. I began to feel guilty about my rash decision. All I could see was my father's concerned face filled with fury at my open defiance. I feared his fists and the punishment of working longer in the fields for a while. The woman was talking on her phone while my best friend and I sat on a bench. She was on the phone a lot and looked at me several times.

'That night, instead of going back to my family and my village, I was taken to a tall building. The woman said my best friend had to pick up something for her family, and she went into a taxi with another man. I said goodbye to my friend but felt a sense of something ominous in my gut. This woman then walked with me to the building's stairs, and we went up three flights.

'I stopped at the top of the first set of stairs. I sensed something was not right. I was uneasy and said I wanted to go home and turned around. The woman grabbed my arm and held on really tight. I struggled, and then she slapped me. I was in shock and left speechless. She had been so nice earlier in the day, just like an aunt.'

I was dumbfounded, and I didn't know how to react to Mei Li's story. I tried to imagine what if it were me in her shoes. Would I have so blindly and naively followed this older woman to my detriment? Perhaps I would have in my rebellious teen years. I could feel Mei Li's palpable pain as she spoke. I simply nodded and felt sad for her.

With tears in her eyes and almost as if she were having traumatic flashbacks, she told me about what had happened next.

'She knocked on a door on the third floor. A man with a cigarette in his mouth opened the door and eyed me up and down. She said, "Here she is, she had dinner a few hours ago." And then she walked away towards the stairs. I called out, feeling desperate, "Auntie, where are you going? I need to go home!" The man was wearing a black turtleneck and grey pants. He pried me from the door and forced me into a room and locked the door.

'I panicked and couldn't breathe. I screamed for days. There was no clock, no phone. I looked for food and water in the closet. There was nothing. "Let me out, let me out, I want to go home," I shouted and pounded at the door. All I could hear was the television and smell the cigarette smoke. "I'm hungry," I shouted, but my voice was strained. I was starved for days, and later learnt that I was there for two weeks. I was given water occasionally and had to use the wastebasket to relieve myself. By the time a few men came in the room, I could barely move from the floor. I was in a foetal position on my side. "Help me," I whimpered. "I need to go home."'

I was gripped and was in shock for her. How could this happen in our day and age? Are there monsters out there who would trick and kidnap a girl like this? But there was an evil familiarity, a sense that I had heard this same story before. The faces of the elderly women survivors of Japanese military sex slavery, euphemistically known as 'comfort women', flashed before my eyes. Most of these women were Mei Li's age—fourteen or fifteen years old—when they were deceived into thinking they were going to work as a nurse or factory worker. Instead, they were taken to a brothel and raped repeatedly. The cycle keeps repeating with no end in sight. I felt this was a profound moment for me like a confirmation of my calling as a documenter of these atrocities and human rights abuses against women.

'These old men came in and stared at me for five minutes. They lifted my arm and saw that I had no strength. It seemed like they were, oddly enough, inspecting me. I was confused by why they were looking at me rather than helping me.

'It was a cold transaction. Days later, a man in his sixties came into the room. I looked up outside the door and could see that the man with the turtleneck was counting a stack of bills in his hands. This man wore a short-sleeved shirt and smelled of sweat and grime, like he hadn't washed himself for weeks. His thinning hair was greasy, and his eyes were on me.

'I wondered if he was here to help me, and I said to him, "My name is Mei Li, and I need to go home to my village in the north." He tried to lift me up and then had a second thought. He hit me in the face and began to beat me, punching me all over. "Why? Why? Why?" was all I could shout as I covered up my face and tried to protect the parts of my body where he was hitting me with his clenched fists. Finally, he said, "I have to take you home, and I don't want you to run away." I was weak, dizzy, and thirsty. I had been locked in that room for two weeks, and it was full of the stench of human waste. Yet he beat me mercilessly.

'I choked out, "I won't run, I won't run away, stop beating me . . . you're hurting me." I sobbed. I don't know if it was my promise to not run away or my wailing that stopped his hands. I could taste blood in my mouth. I was dazed.'

It was hard to write on paper about the violence she experienced. It was unbearable, and I could see the pain in her eyes. I hoped that there was some kind of release and healing as she unburdened herself. But it felt like I had taken her yoke, and it was crushing. I told myself that I had to really stand in her shoes in order to be able to write her story with power—this gave me the motivation to keep on going.

'I was fourteen. Only when I went to this man's small and musty home—this man who was old enough to be my grandfather—did I realize to my horror and disgust that I had been sold as a bride to this wretched and violent man. He was a farmer, and we all knew that men like him couldn't afford to marry the traditional way. And besides, as a poor man, who would want to marry him? Us village girls were always talking about running away to the city to find a handsome working man there.

"'I've paid for you. Now you're my wife," he grunted. He chained me like a dog in one of the rooms. He unchained me when he wanted to use me.'

I had interviewed dozens of traumatized women survivors of sex trafficking of all ages by this point and by far, this was one of the worst stories I had ever heard. I felt physically sick and teared up after hearing that she was chained up unless he wanted to use her. Mei Li must have felt safe with me to divulge these details, and I wondered if it was because Amy asked her to speak with me. I pressed gently and asked her exactly how old this elderly man was, but she didn't want to talk about it. I could sense shame around his age. I waited and let her know that she could decide if she wanted to continue or not. This was her story, and it was an honour for me to hear it and bear witness. I made it clear that I was there for her.

Mei Li continued.

'Months later, I found that my body was changing. My stomach became bigger. I was fixated on my growing stomach and with a sense of dread. I wondered if I had a disease. He told me with a crooked toothless smile that I was pregnant. I had no idea what to do or how to handle this news. I cried for days. One day, the pain intensified, and I felt the weight of my stomach drop. I couldn't stop breathing hard, and that's when I gave birth to a baby girl. I felt so conflicted towards her. I loved her and also resented her. I felt overwhelmed by this bundle, and felt panic that I'd have to take care of both of us when I could barely survive myself. What if he hits her too? I was only fifteen. I named her Wen Tong after my mother.'

Since I had no children, I couldn't imagine what it would feel like to be a mother. But I thought of my mother's unconditional, extravagant, protective love towards me and my sister and brothers, and then I felt her conflict and panic over the thought of her elderly captor abusing her young daughter. Mei Li seemed the most disturbed when talking about this period. I could sense a turning point was coming.

'The abuse continued. I tried to shield my daughter as best as I could. Though I was kept chained inside the house after the birth of my daughter, I had a bit more freedom. I also began to develop an attachment for the old farmer.' Amy mentioned that many of these girls develop Stockholm Syndrome or an unhealthy bond with their pimps, abusers, and traffickers and begin to develop a kind of love for them as if under a wicked spell. Mei Li seemed to suggest that it was normal for her to feel this endearment towards her captor at the time. However, it was clear to me that in the present moment, she felt nothing but disgust for him.

'When I was sixteen, I couldn't handle the beatings anymore. I ached to see my family again. I knew instinctively that I wouldn't survive another year in this home. I began to think of ways of escape, and after picking a date I began to count the days. The day came when I was not chained and left alone in the house while the old man went to work in a nearby field. With my heart pounding in my ears, I grabbed a bag of clothes, some dried food and some coins that I had hidden under the bed.'

'I hugged my baby one last time. My tears streamed onto her like steady rain on a drum, beat after beat. She cooed at the salty water and didn't realize this would be the last time she'd see her mother. I kissed her soft cheek and said goodbye. "Please forgive me," I whispered to her. I tried to stop the visions of the old man taking frustrations on her. Weeping, I ran and ran and was too scared to look back. I found a bus and hopped on board. I couldn't stop crying on the bus.'

My body hunched over in grief as her pain and tears deeply impacted me. I wanted to feel her suffering so that the words would flow authentically through my fingers as I scribed her experiences. Back then, I didn't put up any defences, which may be the reason why I often experienced secondary trauma after interviewing survivors such as Mei Li.

Her story echoed the testimonies of the North Korean bride trafficking victims I had met and interviewed several years before. Their stories were effectively all the same: elderly husbands in China—thirty or forty years older, physical and sexual abuse and rape, and the women sold for the cost of an iPhone or a luxury bag. For years, even to this day, I couldn't bring myself to buy a luxury bag for myself as I would associate it with what it would cost to buy a human from a trafficker. My bags are hand-me-downs from my thoughtful sister. How could I indulge in materialism when I've seen with my own eyes, the abject misery of people bought and sold and exploited like merchandise. I asked Mei Li how she managed to escape.

'When it looked like we were in the city, I got off after an hour and a half. I looked around as I stepped down and sat on the ground by a small tree. I felt lost. About ten minutes later, a woman approached me, handed me some tissues, and asked if I needed help. I nodded my head. She promised me a job.'

Out of sheer desperation and the fact that she didn't want to sleep on the streets, Mei Li willingly followed a stranger for the second time, even though she paid a huge price for her mistake the first time around. I concluded that she was still a teenager, and so wounded by years of abuse that she didn't know any better.

'I was taken to a brothel. The woman was part of a group of traffickers who actively searched for girls to sell into sex slavery. I was numb. I couldn't think for myself anymore. I felt I didn't deserve anything good. I had left my baby girl with an abusive man I hated. I was dreadfully guilty. So I decided to take up the new "job". I told myself that since I had already prostituted myself with the man who bought me, I could now earn a living off of this.'

The worthlessness that Mei Li felt was very common among all of the young women I had spoken with. They all felt a crushing sense of low self-esteem. I wasn't surprised that she went out of one frying pan into the fire. Her cycle of trauma and pain wasn't broken yet. That part was yet to come.

'I had to deal with dozens of men, and some of them reminded me of that "husband" on the farm. Some were nice though and gave me treats. Others were drunk and slung nasty words at me. I have cigarette burns and some scars on my heart from this time. The men were mostly married with children. I asked them if their wives knew what they were doing, and usually they laughed and told me to shut up. A few of them opened up about their wives and what they couldn't stand about them or how they were too "cold" to try new things. I took drugs to dull my pain. I couldn't function without a hit of heroin. It wreaked havoc on my skin, and I began to look fifteen years older.

'A year later, I was taken to get a medical check-up. My pimp thought I looked really sick. The doctor told me I had contracted something called HIV. I had never heard of the disease and didn't realize the seriousness until the doctor told me that I could die from it. That's when I began to cry. No one had taught me how to protect myself from STDs. I was taught how to seduce, but no one mentioned HIV/AIDS. Sometimes, other prostitutes told me about condoms, but they didn't demonstrate how to use them or how to convince clients to use them.'

'I sunk down on the floor of my room one night and wanted to take my life. I was actually eager to die. I thought of my daughter, how I missed her. I used to try not to think of her since it brought me so much pain. I had to take more drugs to forget. What was she doing? She was three years old by then. I wondered if the old man was taking good care of her. I wept for hours. I pounded at the wall with my shoe and yelled, "God, if I'm not out of here by tomorrow, I'll slit my wrists!"'

One night, some volunteers from Door of Hope came into her brothel to share information about free medical treatment. They told the women in the brothel that they could leave this line of work and find a safe place in their shelter that rescues trafficked women forced into prostitution.

Mei Li finally left the brothel. She was nineteen but had already lived several lifetimes of anguish and loss. When she met Amy at Door of Hope, Mei Li sobbed into the shoulder of the older woman.

Mei Li continued her story. 'I was a mess and didn't know where I began and where these men's souls ended. It was as if a trail of dirty souls tailed me wherever I went. I was their object, their toy. I had no control over my body, and it was hard to conceive that I could take my life back and not have to answer to my pimp every night.'

'I told Amy of being starved for two weeks, of being sold to the old farmer, of the beatings and the rapes, of being taken away from my family and all that was familiar and then abandoning my baby daughter. I had lost so much that it felt the sorrow would never end, that the tears like a running tap would never stop.'

\* \* \*

Without the work of frontline social workers, Mei Li would still be trapped at the brothel. She had been broken down by years of abuse by her older husband, the farmer, and developed a kind of Stockholm syndrome towards him. She had fallen under his controlling spell—a strange cycle of psychological abuse. She also had symptoms of post-traumatic stress disorder (PTSD) from years of cumulative pain from being sold, raped, beaten, and torn away from her family and all that was familiar to her.

A group of dedicated women volunteers supported Mei Li emotionally to help her find hope in life again. She has undergone a long process of healing through counselling and sharing with those who care for her and have the skills to help her. She has gone through stages of anger and self-blame—all part of her healing process. Mei Li would often ask 'why did this happen to me? why was I angry with my father?' and so on. To these questions, Amy would gently explain to her, saying, 'Other people chose to have this happen to you. You were caught in a web of deception—you did not choose to be sold and forced into sex slavery.'

The journey of healing has been messy, and Mei Li has expressed great anger and depression. She adopted the Christian faith and that has helped bring a sense of peace and a redemptive purpose to her hardships. So far, she has had no physical manifestations of HIV. 'This is a miracle,' said Amy.

Mei Li's is a sad story, but her pain has been transformed into joy and a newfound hope for her future. Once suicidal, she has found a renewed reason to live. She has decided not to reunite with her daughter or her father and family; however, she has not ruled out a reunion either. This young woman who was once chained like a dog is now thriving and wants to see others come out of sex slavery.

Many more women like Mei Li—hundreds of thousands of young, uneducated, poor girls from the countryside—will be deceived or forced and sold into sex slavery in China as they migrate to the cities in search of work. I also believe that bride trafficking will rapidly increase with the looming crisis of millions of men outnumbering women. Most of the women I met had been trafficked into forced marriage multiple times.

Between the years 2005 and 2010, I had the privilege of getting to know many migrants in Beijing through my work that involved managing funds for an organization involved in helping migrants and humanitarian aid in the region. China is experiencing one of the largest migrations in history. At least 150 million people from the countryside have moved to cities in search of jobs and a better life for their families. I learned through my research and by speaking with on-the-ground NGO workers that each year millions of women leave their villages, migrating to bigger cities in search for employment. It is the only way they can hope to support their poverty-stricken families or ailing parents. Yet, only a few women find decent job opportunities because they lack education and contacts, and they have difficulties adjusting to city life. Many find themselves working for $50 a month in menial jobs, while others are lured into higher-paying jobs by pimps. I have observed that migrants, their children, the fatherless, and orphans are at highest risk.

A common story among young migrant girls is that their parents refuse to pay for their tuition. Given the scarcity of resources, these families prefer to send their sons to school than their daughters These rural girls often discontinue after the compulsory school age of fourteen, and their parents force them into jobs to support their brother's tuition. Because of this, some get trapped in the hands of traffickers in the cities. 'They're very naive and give themselves to prostitution after they go through a violent "breaking in" by traffickers forcing them to submit to sex slavery,' said Amy. 'They come to conclude, "My life is ruined. How do I justify this? Well, at least I'm helping my family, and my little brother is going to university and something good is coming out of this." These trafficked women have this self-sacrificing mentality once they have experienced a "breaking in" by traffickers and brothel owners.'

While meeting with NGOs that helped migrants living in slum-like dwellings during my time managing the migrant workers fund, I met Lijuan, a twenty-one-year-old from a small village in Yunnan province. She became the face of young migrant women for me, and her quiet dignity and resilience left an indelible impression. I was eager to learn more about this courageous group of people who take on the 3Ds of jobs—dirty, dangerous, and demeaning—and I wanted to do something to help bring dignity and the support they needed. I helped conduct one of the first baseline surveys of a migrant community by mobilizing an army of student volunteers, and I wrote a white paper on migrants in the city, working on it day and night.

Lijuan helped me to better understand the struggles they faced in the city. She was on the short side and had blunt shoulder-length hair and a smooth, flat face. She spoke quietly and could easily blend into crowds like an invisible woman as if she herself didn't want to stand out and rock the boat.

Even though she had only completed junior high, Lijuan bravely moved to Beijing by herself, travelling a long distance by train in the crowded, inexpensive carriage where passengers bring their own tiny plastic seats. She risked everything because she felt that moving to the capital city was the best chance she had to find a job with a higher salary than what she could make in her hometown. Despite feeling intimidated by the big city, she pressed on and found small freelance jobs. To her amazement, she eventually found work at a hair salon, earning less than 600 RMB a month. As a migrant in Beijing desperate for work and without a support system and with little education, she was very vulnerable. I felt protective of her. I was so relieved that she hadn't experienced any kind of exploitation. She may have been discriminated against but thankfully, she was not deceived or tricked into sexual servitude.

Like most migrants in bigger cities, she sacrificed more than half of her earnings to support her family by wiring money to them every month. Lijuan was their lifeline, their ticket to survival. She felt shy speaking with me, a foreigner, yet she seemed to feel excited to spend time together. Our interpreter was an NGO staff, a young Chinese university graduate. Their destinies couldn't have been more divergent even though they were similar in age.

We first met Lijuan at the subway station's street-level exit in a remote part of Beijing's outskirts. It is where mostly migrants live because of the cheap rent. She led us through a maze of old apartment buildings to her place. She lived in a cramped, refurbished closet in the moist basement of an old apartment building. She opened her door to what seemed like a closet or storage space that was turned into a tiny apartment. Cardboard boxes with a fabric covering the top held her life possessions. On top of the boxes were several pieces of preserved sausage. I felt suffocated and was heartbroken to see her living conditions. I wished she could have lived in a better place. I tried not to let her see that I felt sorry for her. So I smiled more broadly and listened extra attentively.

The communal toilet and washing area was filled with a dozen people using buckets to pour water over themselves. They looked up at me with curiosity and surprise when I walked by, speaking English with my young interpreter. Lijuan, with dignity, led me out of her hallway and into the sunlight. I said through the interpreter that she was a very exceptional young woman. I tried to encourage her as much as I could. However, she ended up encouraging me. Her determination to financially help her family was incredible. Years later, I still tear up when I think of her and wonder how she's doing.

Another migrant woman Hong, whom I met in Beijing through my work, shared her story of poverty, crushing medical debt, and quiet desperation. I thought of her for a long time after our meeting.

She was a pretty woman with alluring eyes and long lashes, a full figure, and a dark complexion. I could imagine that she had been a great beauty in her youth. Hong spoke with a coquettishness that pretty girls learn early on to wrap others around their fingers.

While still in the countryside, Hong signed up for free vocational training through Xin Zhi Guang, a social enterprise in Beijing. She had read of many news stories of women who were sexually exploited by sham businesses or trafficking rings. She wasn't even sure if Xin Zhi Guang was a legitimate organization or not. Despite her strong sense of self-preservation, she went ahead as she had no way to support herself and her family. Hong decided to travel all the way to Beijing to sign up for the training.

She told her story with her large brown eyes brimming with tears. She gripped my hands. She became destitute and wounded when her husband suddenly left her and their son. Racked with anxiety and debilitating pain from divorce, Hong had to find a way to support herself and to help pay for her mother's mounting medical bills. Her mother had a terminal illness and couldn't live on her own. Hong's enormous debt to the hospital is a common story in China. Many cannot afford their inordinately large hospital bills, and they end up paying these bills over a long time, like indentured slaves or they become bankrupt.

I could not find one organization that helped pay off medical bills for the poor in China. I had read news reports that medical professionals routinely take bribes, and that the best care goes to those with deep pockets. It is a tragedy, and I hoped that a tycoon could take on this issue and offer free cancer care or medical services. This is one of my quests in the near future—to help find a way to help those in medical debt.

Thankfully, Hong received good training to be a domestic worker. The social enterprise helped her get a stable job. Her desperate risk ended up saving her from destitution and exploitation.

Unlike Hong's good fortune, one Chinese girl at Door of Hope's safe home was trafficked into Myanmar after a woman told her, 'You'll have great prospects, a great husband, and a better life than what you have here.' The girl naively agreed and ended up in a violent situation. She managed to escape—one of the very few victims that did.

* * *

For my documentary, I prepared to interview Hua, a survivor of sex trafficking, at the Door of Hope centre. I towered over her and hunched down to look at her face to face. She was a petite, shy woman with an almost invisible presence. She looked as if she wanted to hide in the shadows. When she smiled, her entire face lit up. She came from a village called Jindong. I was unsure if she would be able to clearly and boldly articulate her story. Soon after I introduced myself, I tried to ensure that she felt safe and secure. I gave her assurance that she could control our conversation. She looked relieved and a will of steel emerged as she spoke.

The cameraman placed her to stand at the window so we could film the back of her head in order to hide her identity. I asked her some simple questions to warm her up. Then I asked her how she came to the Door of Hope shelter. This is Hua's story.

'My family was the poorest in the village. We had a very hard life. My parents loved me. One day, my father was cooking some eggs when I did something wrong so he beat me. A little later, he said, "Come. Let's eat eggs together." I told him I didn't want to eat because you beat me. My father threw all the eggs away, and my family couldn't eat. I knew my father loved me. If I didn't want to eat, then my family couldn't eat.

'My parents valued me even though I was a girl. We worked in the fields together. I have five sisters in my family. The first, second, and third didn't have a chance to go to school. I remember this one time it was snowing and very cold, and I didn't have shoes to wear. Even on a hot day, I wore ripped clothes. I was very young and had to work with my parents in the fields.

'In the process, I grew up and experienced love and hate. Before I came to Kunming, I experienced a lot of love in my family. The hate began when I came to a town near Kunming. I began working as a kitchen waitress. At that time, I noticed several girls, who were also working as waitresses, would sometimes go out at night and then come back counting a lot of money in front of me. I admired them, but I didn't know what they really did for the money.'

Hua was deeply loved by her family. It was sad to hear that her slippery path to sexual exploitation was mainly due to her naiveté because she was deceived by other girls—her predatory colleagues. It was horrifying. 'These girls tricked me. They had told me they were doing a cooking job. But they were in prostitution. And they got extra money for recruiting me deceptively. I followed these girls and went out at night to the nightclub. From that time on, I experienced hate. In that nightclub, I met different kinds of men,' she said with a hard tone of anger in her voice.

'After one week, they forced me into prostitution by locking me in a room with a man. I couldn't run out of the compound since the gate was closed. The top boss beat me with a leather belt if I didn't perform. There were several men. They were the boss's helpers, like the mafia, and they watched the girls.'

Hua said these co-workers who recruited her were not remorseful and were motivated by greed. There were more than twenty girls from China forced into prostitution along with her. One girl was just fourteen years old. Most of them were tricked by the men in different ways and lured by the promise of fake jobs with inflated salaries—I've already mentioned previously that migrant women are especially vulnerable to this method of sex trafficking.

As time went on, Hua learned more about the other trafficked young women and how they were forced into the flesh trade. 'They also tricked girls from Vietnam. There were four or five Vietnamese girls. There was a thirty-year-old woman the others called older sister. At first, she was tricked by a man. Then she went back to Vietnam to trick other girls.'

As an Asian scarred by racism in my childhood in Canada, I'm particularly incensed by racial discrimination. I asked Hua if there was a racist caste system among the women as is common all over the world with White or fair-skinned women bringing in more money from johns while darker-skinned women were at the lowest rung. The same racist system was behind the sexual slavery system of the Japanese military during WWII, and I had exposed that in my speeches and articles.

Hua believes that racism fuelled the gross mistreatment of Vietnamese women who were treated the worst and beaten more than the Chinese and ethnic minority women. 'I remember one sixteen- or seventeen-year-old Vietnamese girl—she was very beautiful. When the boss forced her into prostitution, she didn't want to and resisted. They used a leather belt to beat her.' Hua then went on to elaborate how the traffickers had many vicious dogs around to control the girls and prevent them from escaping the homes where they were imprisoned. Yet, they didn't want the dogs to bite the women and damage their 'goods', which would make them less attractive to their johns.

'The girls were very afraid. The boss ordered the pimps to rape the girls first. Then they couldn't resist and had to do what they wanted them to do. I was like a sex slave. I wept at night. Every girl lived in fear. Even while sleeping, the girls cried and were scared. First they beat and raped me, then they forced me into prostitution.'

Hua looked traumatized as she was re-living that agonising time of sexual servitude, and she began to cry with shoulders heaving. I ordered the camera to stop rolling to give her a private moment. I reached out to touch her shoulder and reassure her gently. It was a sacred moment, and I dared not move. It seemed like her pain hung in the air over us like a heavy blanket. After five minutes, her sobs subsided, and I asked her if she wanted to go on or not. After a few deep breaths, and another moment, Hua nodded her head resolutely. I asked her how old she was at that time.

'In 2002, I was locked in that building for two months and couldn't leave. I was twenty-one years old at that time. There were many brothels in this village. When the police came, the dogs barked. Some girls were locked upstairs. One night, I knew the police had come, and some of us girls went downstairs and ran out. The pimps could not catch us. The brothel boss tried to find us. The police caught two pimps but not the main boss.'

'The whole person is almost torn down from this horrific treatment. I was always afraid. I was worried that if I fell asleep, a man would rape me again. When I was young, my parents told me that I couldn't even hold hands with a man or I'd get pregnant. During that time when I was locked in that place, I was raped every day. I was so afraid and full of hate for the men. I felt like collapsing at that time.'

Hua escaped the pimps and hid in another village for two months. After that, she found her way to Kunming. She found odd jobs working in restaurants and making artificial flowers. But when her father fell very ill for several months and needed a new heart, an operation that would cost hundreds of thousands of dollars, Hua made an extremely painful decision to sacrifice herself to work as a prostitute to support his medical bills. I was utterly shocked because I knew it was a living hell for her to be raped by strange men. Desperation had driven her to such a terrible fate. Hua didn't clearly answer me when I asked if her parents knew how she was sending money. Perhaps they could guess, but was she sacrificed at the altar by her parents because of poverty? Would they have allowed their son to suffer so much?

But Hua's life took a turn for the worse. 'I was hired by a married man for a week. Later, I found out I was pregnant with his child. I struggled over whether I should abort the baby because my village would shame me for having a child out of wedlock. I decided to keep my baby even though the father abandoned me and tried to force me to have an abortion. He had a child of his own.'

In 2003, her father fell down in the field and passed away. That's when she stopped selling her body. It was around this time that her boyfriend from her days in prostitution also disappeared for a month for no reason. Hua had become suicidal.

Her friend told her about the shelter and job opportunities at Door of Hope. She had told her that the bosses are foreigners, and they teach morals. No dirty words are allowed there. Hua decided to stay at the shelter and sought a job making jewellery. Soon after, her boyfriend also reappeared suddenly and they reconciled.

Experiencing kindness and care from the Door of Hope staff helped Hua to open her shattered heart to begin the trauma healing process. 'When I came, I began to experience love again. In the past, I had many bad experiences and hatred in my heart. One time, I wanted to have a cup of water, but I was afraid to ask. A woman gave me water. They took care of me, encouraged me.'

Hua was initially concerned that she wouldn't be able to work during her pregnancy but the staff reassured her they will care for her and her baby. Hua had felt relieved and profoundly touched by their unconditional love for a stranger and found herself slowly changing. Soon, she was able to reconnect with her mother and after her son was born, her mother came to support her for a year, staying with her at the Door of Hope shelter.

The biggest transformation came when, against all odds, Hua chose to forgive her traffickers, the girls who recruited her into forced prostitution, and even the men who raped her. She was also able to forgive the married man who fathered her son. Now she prays for her former enemies and feels joyfully liberated from her past prison of hatred and bitterness.

'Last year, I forgave the men who raped me. I thought I'd never forgive them. I forgave my son's father too. I was set free. Initially, I felt that I could not do it. But I decided to forgive. It is meaningless to hate. My son's father is not good. My friends told me to give them the address of the father of my son so they could beat and kill him. I didn't want them to. After being transformed by love, I was able to forgive those who hurt me deeply.'

Hua dreams that her story will help other women trapped in forced prostitution. 'I hope girls who are tricked into prostitution will walk away earlier. It's scary in that kind of situation, and even in your sleep you're crying and in fear. I hope the women will leave earlier. If you're not lazy, you can do any kind of job and have many other choices. I regret working as a prostitute. I regret that I was attracted by my friends and that I stayed in that dark environment.'

Miracles do happen and just like the lotus flower blossoms out of mud, some of the women at Door of Hope are also able to find good men and get married. Hua told me with excitement that she'll get married in a month. A new family life awaits. The last image of Hua that is etched in my mind's eye is of her delicate frame set against the window at dusk, gently playing with her adorable son.

# 4

# Reaching Out to the Pimps

In my search for understanding modern-day slavery, I learnt from Hua—and the other survivors of sex trafficking I had interviewed—that women are considered expendable due to culturally acceptable gender discrimination, which espouses they are inferior to men. This discriminatory attitude has made girls and women more vulnerable to being bought and sold for more than a century in China. I also discovered something new from the frontline NGO workers I met in Kunming during my trips to southern China. I learnt that there are more small operations with regular people selling women than there are large-scale, sophisticated operations run by organized crime syndicates like those in Hong Kong.

'There are mafia bosses, but mostly people are selling women as a business to make a lot of money quickly because there's no moral foundation here in China,' said Amy. She was referring to a lack of a Judeo-Christian moral base in the country. 'When I tell them that what they're doing is morally wrong, they respond with a "why?". They don't get it. They're not evil people who enjoy exploiting women,' she said. It reminded me of the time I spoke with a young Christian woman doctor who told me that she and her husband, also a doctor, both took bribes at the hospital for several years, even after her conversion to Christianity. She said that it was a widely accepted practice among medical professionals in her province, and no one in her family or at school had taught her that it was wrong or corrupt to take kickbacks on the side. Only when someone addressed the topic at church did she realize that it was morally unacceptable to do so. I was taken aback at how one could be so unaware of moral ethics but then again, this nation was closed off from the rest of the world for so long. When I first moved to Beijing in 2004, I was told repeatedly by several journalists and diplomats that Pyongyang's infrastructure and way of life was not unlike how Beijing was twenty years before.

The strategies of traffickers are constantly changing. A woman or a couple used to go to villages, and through a contact they would meet low-income families with pretty daughters. They would take these girls and hold their ID cards. However, most of these girls ran away after three or four months. It was a logistical nightmare for the traffickers because they had to watch them all the time and keep them locked up.

Traffickers also often hire 'loverboys'—good-looking, uneducated men who recruit young women on QQ, a popular social media platform, or through websites. They are trained to woo these girls, and by sending their pictures to the girls and writing love notes they manipulate the girls to fall in love with them. They then bring the girls to the city and live together for a week. Soon, the loverboy cries and says, 'I'm in trouble. I have this debt.' Or, he'll say, 'We need to buy a house. I know a way to make money really quickly.' The girl prostitutes herself and justifies the act by telling herself that she's doing it for her boyfriend—for love.

The loverboy tactic makes the girls more resistant to leaving the brothels. Amy told me, 'I say, "Is this really love? That he lets you sleep with ten to fifteen men a night and you give him the money?" They say, "Yes, we're earning money for his gambling debt or for his sick dad." It's so evil. These lover boys twist love in horrible ways.'

Amy rarely kept to a routine schedule, so I did my best to ask her as many questions as I could whenever I could catch her at the Door of Hope office. It took some time to earn her trust but after a few heart-to-heart sessions about our hopes, dreams, and personal challenges, we warmed up to each other. In one of our conversations, Amy talked about an encounter during her routine visits to the brothel areas a few years back. On that occasion, she saw a two-year-old baby girl in the arms of her father in a brothel. The young man's name was Guo—the former trafficker Amy and Door of Hope befriended. Back then, Guo was a *la keren*, which meant he had a role in managing the girls at the brothel and lining up their customers. The baby, named Chun, was walking in and out of the brothel and was at risk of being abused and exposed to clients. She was also mimicking her father and said to passing men, 'Pretty girls inside, pretty girls inside . . . come inside.'

Amy sensed that caring for Guo's daughter was their long-awaited open door to a deeper relationship with him. She boldly approached the father and said to him, 'This is not right for your daughter to be here. Please let me take her.'

He asked, 'Why would you do something like that?'

'Because I believe in God,' replied Amy, who went on to explain what she meant by this.

Guo was visibly touched by the offer and began to cry. 'I felt that God didn't want to know me anymore,' he said. He thought he had sinned so much that he was now beyond redemption. He explained that the mother of his daughter was a fifteen-year-old prostitute who had run away. Amy recalls that this encounter was a special moment, a turning point for this young man, this brothel manager.

Amy took his daughter to the shelter, and her sweet face soon radiated with contentment and peace. Door of Hope helped Guo find a new vocation, and he obtained a long-distance driving licence so that he could create a different life for himself and his daughter.

He began attending a men's group to receive prayer and support. His life was changed, and his daughter's life was transformed as well.

Door of Hope discovered that Guo, like many of these young men working as pimps and traffickers, was once raised in a Christian family that mixed faith with Chinese tradition. Many of the young men working at the brothels would respond tenderly to Amy whenever she shared her belief in Jesus Christ. 'I see such a hunger among mafia people and pimps, and such a desire to get out of this work,' she said.

\* \* \*

Over a period of several years, I was able to know Guo better myself. But this was after I had quelled my inner disgust at a man who exploited women, even underage women for a living. I witnessed his transformation, listened to his inner struggles and later, his fall from grace. I was intrigued by him, and I must admit there is a part of me that gets an adrenalin rush from investigating traffickers and narcissistic criminals and delving into their twisted motivations. I especially love tough-interrogation-style interviews to trip someone up when it involves a person who has done something egregiously wrong and is trying to cover it up and hide. I had to hold back on Guo though, and it went against the grain of my pit bull interviewing instincts. Instead, I had to use a gentler approach on him to get him to open up to me. I forced myself to keep an open mind towards him even though all my inner instincts wanted to put him away in jail forever. I have to say that he really helped open the curtain of the underworld of human slavery, and by doing so, helped me gain exceptionally rare insights into this dirty business of the modern slave trade in this region. The fact that this racket had a mom-and-pop local family business tinge to it was reinforced as Guo later introduced me to his cousin who was still a working pimp. Guo also admitted his other family members were involved in this business of exploiting young women.

Guo was a short, goofy man in his mid-thirties with a dark complexion and a hairstyle that almost qualified as a bowl cut. He dressed in sloppy fashion with his shirt outside his jeans and sported worn-out running shoes. He had a kind of sneer when he smiled. Guo looked like a Chinese version of Sean Penn. When I mentioned it to Amy, she laughed and said, 'Yes, I agree!'

When I first met Guo a few years earlier during a previous work trip, he seemed unhappy and stressed. He had no other options but to live off the earnings of the women and girls he had lured and deceived into forced prostitution. He had a scary ability to hook women and reel them in. Amy called it a 'luring spirit', and it was obvious when Guo turned it on. I would later learn through my conversations with Amy, other frontline workers, and the victims that the women who were most vulnerable to such 'luring' were those who experienced sexual abuse in the past and girls from fatherless families.

A good example of his skills in action was when he spoke with Sarah, who translated for me when I first met him. I wanted to interview him to understand why traffickers do what they do.

As Guo turned on his luring charm on Sarah, I could see her face change visibly like she was being drawn into his web of control. This may have been her first meeting with a trafficker. He used his eyes to make longer-than-usual eye contact in a seductive way used to charm women, and he turned on his smile and fake charm and lowered his voice in a manly way. His total focus made Sarah feel as though she was the only lovely one in the world. Her eyes lowered, and she responded in a flirty way. Alarmed by their interaction, I said to Sarah, 'Remember we need to meet the others later.' I began asking Guo questions to divert him from her. I wasn't lured in by him; perhaps, my anger and disrespect for his line of work helped guard me from his charm offensive. I also didn't like Sean Penn. Although I didn't know Sarah well enough, I wanted to protect her.

I noticed that Guo had an amiable personality, but he could be pushed around and bullied too, even by women. I noticed the

Door of Hope staff were very firm with him, and soon I began to adopt that approach as well because we weren't sure if he was going to follow through. I wondered how he had survived as a pimp. He told me he had been beaten up by violent clients before. I wasn't surprised. I wondered what happened to the women if even men were hurt by these johns? I shuddered and stopped thinking about it.

Guo was a child labourer who worked on a boat before becoming a pimp at seventeen. The exploitative conditions at his workplace were akin to slavery. He was also a victim of enslavement and I began to feel more sympathy for him. His brother had been a pimp and a trafficker of women and girls for ten years. He invited Guo to work with him.

At the height of his brother's work as a trafficker, there were a thousand prostituted women in the neighbourhood. But for reasons unknown, his brother left the world of trafficking and exploiting women a year ago. All of the girls working for him had left, and there were only about twenty to thirty girls remaining in the brothels.

Amy asked Guo if he would be willing to do a TV interview with me for a documentary. To my surprise, he agreed. I was thankful for getting uninterrupted time with him to ask him some hard questions. He also asked his cousin, a pimp trafficker, to interview to join us. To give both Guo and his cousin a private and safe setting for the interview, they suggested that I book a hotel room for our camera set-up. So the cameraman, Guo, and I sat together with the camera rolling. He looked rather comfortable and almost proud to share his story on camera. I lobbed the first simple question, 'How did you become a pimp?'

'My education level is too low. And even if I could learn, I wouldn't have got a good job. I don't know how to use a computer, and I don't know how to do office work. I don't know Putonghua very well. It was convenient to be able to take care of my child while on this job. I make more money compared with office work. A day in the office with ten hours of work, you only earn 30–50 RMB.'

It always comes down to making money and sheer greed. I asked him about the daily operations of pimping out women, and how he recruits johns, which is something the average person would never know anything about. He was eager to divulge his trade secrets and said, 'I gave my name cards to the guests. If they wanted a girl, I would bring them to the hotel. I took a taxi. The guest paid the cost of my taxi. I brought two girls, and the guest chose one of them. I worked with some married women. Some husbands knew, some didn't. I seldom worked with women under seventeen. The boss understood that it's illegal to have sex with minors. Some clients wanted younger girls. In another town in Songming, they have many underage girls. There's a girl only thirteen years old. The boss kept her at his home and didn't let her outside and forced her into prostitution.'

I pressed him about underage girls, and if he had trafficked them He insisted he did not; however, I sensed that he was lying to protect himself legally. He wasn't entirely stupid I thought to myself. I said that the NGO staff told me that pimps use violence to control the enslaved women. Guo responded, 'Sometimes the girls steal things from the guests like their mobile phones and money. For that, they get beaten by the boss. In these areas, I've heard of a lot of very bad situations. For example, if a client beats the girls, the boss will beat the girls too, or he will ask others to beat them. It's a very dangerous place.'

I asked him if he used violence. He denied it. 'Maybe my cousin forced girls when he did this pimping work, when there were a thousand prostitutes in the neighbourhood. I didn't. I wasn't the boss,' he said.

I wondered if Guo would admit on camera that these girls were forced against their will into sex slavery. I asked him first how these women were lured into prostitution. He denied they were forcibly recruited but later admitted that they were tricked into it. 'The girls introduce their friends to this kind of business. The boss's relatives or friends introduce the girls to prostitution. Or sometimes on the internet or on QQ, they'll say come and join and earn big money. They are not forced but rather *attracted* to go into prostitution.

'Some handsome boys called Romeo pimps make money selling girls. They attract the girls and become their boyfriends because they're handsome. They promise to marry them. The girls are seduced by these men, but in reality he tricks them into prostitution so they can earn for him. These handsome guys are swindlers, making a living off of women. I know people like this.' In one area, at least seventy to eighty per cent of the women were deceived by Romeo pimps. I'd estimate at least a thousand women were tricked.'

I asked Guo if any of the pimps feel remorse for the women? He didn't respond to the question directly—not this time or in our previous talks—but he told me the girls are very sad, especially when they lose their beauty with ageing and cannot earn enough money. He also mentioned that sometimes the girls would be upset when the men would cheat them out of their life savings. Guo did not seem to have any kind of deep empathy for these women.

He explained that each woman's situation was different from the other. He said, 'Some women are willing to work for the men. Some still want to marry them.' Many assume that the girls are willing to prostitute themselves for their boyfriend traffickers. There are women who are desperate to provide support for their families, and some cannot leave the brothels because they have no other work options or family support.

Then he shared a piece of information that was weighty because it suggested that there is a widespread, well-organized sex trafficking operation that runs along the major road arteries in the province and beyond. I listened to every word he shared. 'Women are smuggled by car. In Yunnan's south, east, west, and in Huidu, where there is a major highway that runs through, there are many prostitution places. The girls stay in the hotel. Almost every hotel has some women in prostitution to drink, dance, and have sex with clients. The girls drink with the men, play with the men, and sleep with the men. They may even be in this hotel.'

When he mentioned that sex trafficking victims were in the very hotel we were conducting the interview, I knew it had to be true. In almost every hotel in China, single men are bombarded with cards featuring photographs of sexy women and their phone numbers, which are slipped under their doors. These are actually the 'business cards' of the pimps so that the guests can call for women, if they please. Sometimes, the guests are also directly approached and asked if they want a 'massage'.

I cannot remember the exact question but I might have asked why a large number of women were deceived and trafficked into prostitution. Guo's answer was frightening because it rang true. 'The clients have many, many requirements. Some like fat women, some like slim, some like plain or big women. Some want variety. Different requirements too—some want blow jobs, some want big breasts. Some want a girl with good manners. They have many requirements. Some have high standards. Some would fight us when the girls didn't meet their requirements.'

'If the girls don't want to do the work, then what do the traffickers do?' I asked.

'If she just hangs around with other girls and doesn't do the job, then the boss will beat her. If she still doesn't want to, he'll charge the girl a fee, and then let her go. If she doesn't have money, he'll beat her and let her go.

'The boss recruits the girls and trains them in prostitution and how to have sex. The boss doesn't force the girls. Some girls are willing to go into prostitution. Some girls also run off with the client and don't give the pimp his cut of the deal. When the pimp tracks down these girls and their clients, he will beat them.

'The girls are used to that kind of environment. They like working in these environments because they can earn more money. They work for about twenty days and can earn 6,000 to 7,000 RMB or even 10,000 RMB. They earn a lot more than working in a regular job.'

I was livid when he said the women like this work for the extra money. But I bit my tongue. I needed this interview. 'Why do men buy and sell women? Is it purely for the money?' I asked.

'There are numerous reasons, but I think the main thing is the money. Some girls were hurt by their boyfriends, and their hearts are broken, so they go into prostitution to release their hurt. Some divorced women are lazy, and it's easy to make a lot of money.'

'There are many, many rich people who want virgin girls. They'll pay 3,000 or 5,000 RMB for sex with a virgin girl, and they'll ruin her whole life. I feel sorry for these girls. Some superstitious businessmen think that having sex with a virgin will bring them luck and help them earn more. That's why they try to find virgins. Some girls are not virgins but claim to be. Deep in my heart, I pity these girls. They are so poor. I feel that even though they are paid so much, their whole life is ruined.'

This was the first time I heard Guo say that he felt pity. Did he suppress his empathy in order to carry out his pimping work? I concluded that he had to. It was the only way to survive; it was his coping mechanism.

According to the staff and volunteers at Door of Hope helping Guo, his three-year-old daughter, Chun, was the product of his short-lived relationship with a fifteen-year-old girl lured into forced prostitution. Guo had told me that he hardly dealt with underage girls and that he had met Chun's mother after she graduated from middle school. He was working at a fruit shop at the time, he said, and they began dating. She became pregnant. He asked her parents for their blessing to marry. 'They forbade us,' he said.

Her parents asked Guo for 200,000 RMB, but he did not have a steady job at the time. After Chun was raised by her mother's parents for a year, they sent her back to Guo and told him to raise her. Chun's mother continues to live with her parents.

Guo never went into detail about why Chun's mother abandoned her own child. She stopped responding to Guo's calls. His eyes turned away when he said, 'I feel I'm a failure in my relationship, and it's a burden to me. I think my ex has a bad heart. Why did she leave me? Both of us should raise our daughter together, earn money together, and be a family together. That would be a happy life for us. I feel very hurt because Chun is growing up without her mother.'

Chun grew up spending most nights in her father's arms as he continued to pimp women for a living. On the streets, Chun heard cursing and witnessed all kinds of fighting and rough behaviour that a child should never be exposed to. I could tell she did not have a regular upbringing. This girl seemed far too hardened.

By the time she was three, she was fluent in curse words and had an ability to manipulate people that scared me. She was sweet one moment and then would look at me with the corners of her eyes and say words in a rough tone to get her way. Amy was shocked that a toddler would manifest the crude behaviour of the underworld that she had been immersed in.

Soon after Amy's encounter with Guo, she found a foster mother for Chun and placed them in one of their smaller shelters. Guo was on friendly terms with this foster mother, and it was clear to all that Chun was in a safe and nurturing environment that was so much better than the red-light district. After spending a year bonding with her foster mother, an older gentle Chinese woman, Chun softened and became more like a little girl. I spent a few afternoons with her and bought her candy and ice cream. Her tiny hand held mine, and we walked around the neighbourhood of the shelter, a five-bedroom apartment that was about fifteen years old. I could tell she was resisting forming an attachment with me, and I didn't try to push since I was leaving within the week. Her round eyes looking up at me reminded me of the terrible cost of innocent children born out of forced prostitution. Countless babies have also been aborted by women and girls forced into sex slavery, and countless children are abandoned or are being raised in dysfunctional families. But Chun's restored innocence also reminded me that broken lives and hearts can be restored through loving care.

When Guo left the world of pimping, he was broken by the viciousness of the red-light districts. I asked him why he made the decision to leave.

'One reason I left this job is that it's dangerous. I was arrested five times. The police would keep me in prison, fine me and charge me money. In the last three years, I didn't earn any money. I had to borrow money to buy a car. Another reason is my daughter— she is growing up. Many people told me that when she grows up, she'll despise me because of my work as a pimp. Also, this kind of job has many troubles and problems all the time. It's very dirty, and I felt very dirty. It is tiring. When I was doing this pimping, I hardly earned any money. When I left this work, I still hadn't earned money.'

He still has financial pressures and worries about his future, but he now has more peace in his heart and his daughter is well cared for. 'For example, earlier I was constantly worried about being chased by police. Now I don't have this worry. One of my best friends, I call her elder sister, lent me money to buy a car to become a driver. She told me, "Your daughter is growing up. If your daughter goes into prostitution, how will you feel?" I was haunted by that thought, and it was the other reason why I left.'

Guo is now thirty years old, and he pointed out that he doesn't have a house or car. He wonders how his daughter will view him, and whether he'll be able to find a stable job that pays more than pimping.

One regrettable outcome from our documentary filming trip in 2012—when we faced off with the thugs after I filmed in the brothel alleyway—was Guo's fall from grace. I felt responsible.

Guo had become a Christian in the last year and was cleaning up his life. He had left the shadows of the world of exploiting women for profit. Many encouraged him to start a small business as a driver for hire.

For years, I had heard of the trafficking of Vietnamese women and girls into China for forced prostitution in brothels or forced marriages with poor Chinese farmers. I wanted to document that this was happening, and we asked Guo to help. The plan was that he'd wear a small camera to document these girls in the brothels where they reported to work.

It was here that Guo met a young Vietnamese woman when he was filming a mama-san asking him what kind of woman he wanted to buy for the hour.

Sadly, he ended up having relations with the Vietnamese woman. He admitted it over the phone. I felt sick about it. I wanted to give up on the filming. Amy was deeply disappointed in Guo even though he said sorry the next day. I wondered about the power of media. Though media can bring change, it can also cause havoc as it did in Guo's life at a time when he was leaving his work in the red-light districts. He caved in to temptation and went back to his old ways simply because I asked him to film in a brothel and interview a prostituted woman. I felt a heavy sense of responsibility that I haven't been able to shake off ever since.

* * *

In the same hotel room where we filmed our interview with Guo, he introduced me to his cousin, Wu, a working pimp. In my quest to get the most up-to-date information about human traffickers, getting a chance to spend time with Wu was a big deal as a journalist. It is next to impossible to get a pimp to speak on record, let alone be filmed on camera. Wu was younger and slicker in his dress and hairstyle. His intimidating mannerisms conveyed that he owned the room as he walked in. He had an arrogant air. Unlike Guo, he was a successful Romeo pimp or the stereotypical 'bad boy' that many vulnerable girls are drawn to, and he had a mildly attractive face that some women might find appealing. I felt like he had a 'luring' spirit that could easily reel girls into his deadly web, more sinister than Guo's. I didn't sense any hint of compassion in this young man and the two cousins were polar opposites in demeanour and confidence.

I was shocked that he was willing to speak on camera, albeit with his face darkened. Was he that cocky? Was he a narcissist who wanted to share his exploits for the world to hear? I was terrified of this working trafficker and made sure that the cameraman was always nearby. We had two chairs set up across from another, and I sat barely two feet away from him. I had a knot of anxiety in my stomach and wondered if it was safe to be in the same room with this pimp. My wild imagination filled with unlikely Hollywood plots went berserk.

The cameraman signalled that the camera was on. I took a deep breath and hoped that I could get honest answers, but something in my gut told me I might not get the entire truth. Wu was too conceited and seemed to have an agenda of some kind. I was intent on uncovering what that was.

I complimented him on his blue dress shirt and nice hair. He preened and looked smug. I wanted to catch him by surprise and jumped right in and asked what motivated him to start pimping and trafficking women and girls into prostitution. I watched him carefully for any signs of nervousness or self-consciousness; there was none.

'I am not educated. Doing this job is better than working for other people. I only work at seven or eight at night. If a john or guest needs girls, I'll bring the girls out. The rest of the time, I can hang out with a group of people who are doing the same job. We play cards and chat and have lots of free time. Every day it's the same. I send the girls to the guests. Chatting with friends is my daily work. After I finish work, I surf the internet.'

I then asked questions that revolved around what the girls were suffering and if he felt any concern. His response was utterly shocking, and I had to stifle a laugh in disbelief. 'I think they are quite happy because about every ten days all the girls go to the Karaoke Television (KTV) and sing songs and dance. They enjoy their lives. But for us, we have to work hard for a living. Some customers even scold us. I suffer more than these girls. Sometimes, the guests blame us and insult us and are angry with us. We have to go to different places to bring the girls to the guests, so we're busier than them.'

I wondered aloud about the use of violence to keep enslaved women in place, and asked him if he beat the women to get them to comply. 'It's up to the girls. If they don't want to do this job, they can't earn money. We have seven or eight girls, and we have other girls too that we can use if someone doesn't want to do this work.'

'You've never beaten any girls?' I asked incredulously since, to me, he had a hint of anger and the air of someone who could hit a young woman. He denied it. 'I haven't beaten any girls. It's free for the women. They're doing their job and get money. They pay their rent by themselves. They're free and not a slave to their boss or to me. In these two years that I've been doing this work, I haven't heard of any pimp beating the girls.'

Wu says the girls are not forced because they're paid. This is a common line of argument used by the traffickers. While there are women who feel empowered to go into prostitution of their own free will, the survivors I spoke with felt otherwise. They were not willingly selling their bodies.

When I asked Wu about money, he said, 'We don't care how much they [the women] get. We only care how much we get. We charge each customer 150 RMB—my boss gets 130 RMB and I get 20. We don't know how much the girls make from each client.'

His view on women seemed dismally low, and I wondered if his girlfriend knew about the nature of his job? It was hard to believe that he even had a girlfriend—a bit of normalcy in his criminal lifestyle! 'I think a girl who is doing such kind of prostitution is not a good person. I feel they are bad. My girlfriend doesn't know what

I'm doing. She doesn't know the details. If she calls me and asks me what I do for a living, I won't answer the question.'

I asked him directly if he was a Romeo trafficker. He denied it, but said that drawing in women and making a living off of the sale of their bodies was his main job. 'No. Only girls can approach girls to do this job. Most of the time, men don't do this. It does not work if men want to cheat these girls. They will ignore us. I'm planning to do this for one more year. Then I'll get my driver's licence and become a driver.'

I earnestly hoped he was being truthful about his plans on becoming a driver. I wanted to know how he felt when the girls were beaten up by their clients. Was his mind only on the money or did the safety of the women ever cross his mind. He didn't catch on that I was trying to entrap him to share honestly. 'We don't always know what happens or how they treat the girls. Sometimes, the girls call me crying. Then it's my responsibility to find out what's happening. Usually, the client is drunk, and he'll beat me up too. About once every ten days, I'll get beaten. I care about the girls. I'll even go and let them out. If the john is still angry, he'll release anger at me. Even if I suffer. But it's fine because my boss will pay me extra. I'll protect the girls.'

I concluded the talk by thanking Wu profusely, and he asked when the documentary would air. I told him that he would be able to see the film at Door of Hope. I had a hunch that he would be keen to watch.

* * *

Previously when I was working as a philanthropy fund manager, I often travelled to Yunnan province and the Myanmar border areas. In between hosting conferences for strategic planning for non-profit organizations and site visits for projects on HIV/AIDS, our NGO hosts would drive us to remote villages deep in the countryside to treat us to mouth-watering ethnic minority food. These were hole-in-the-wall outdoor restaurants but to me they were food heaven.

During these trips, I met several beneficiaries of the NGO programmes funded by our donor clients, and my eyes were opened to the limitless depth and breadth of suffering of those trapped in sex trafficking and forced labour. I learned about the vulnerabilities of borders, and how humans were trafficked along with drugs from country to country. Through these visits, I was further inspired to help—even if it was just one thing that I could do as a privileged professional woman to help those who could not help themselves would have meant something.

During one such visit, we spent time in Ruili, a sleepy border town. I was there to visit Chen for the second time and check in on her programmes on behalf of a donor. Chen was the director of an outreach centre for prostituted women and drug addicts. She was a tall woman with a confident gait, and she had a tanned heart-shaped face that could pull off a helmet-like short hairdo. She was direct and matter of fact in her speech, and I respected her deep commitment to alleviating suffering in the area. Chen was the one who first told me that we could go to any café along the border and find a well-dressed man in a crisp white suit who could sell us a human being for as little as 300 RMB. I shivered.

She lined up a small group of former prostitutes from Myanmar that I could speak with. Chen's NGO was supporting them with job training, counselling, and emotional support. They came from impoverished backgrounds, and all of them said that they did not willingly enter the flesh trade.

Two of these women, who were in their late twenties or early thirties, had got into prostitution in order to cover the room and board costs at their sons' schools. We were in touch with a New York foundation to see if they would cover the school costs on the condition that these women agree to get out of that line of work permanently.

I tried to connect Chen and these women with Door of Hope
so that they could learn jewellery-making as a way of alternative
employment, but they did not form a partnership for reasons
unknown to me.

Another non-profit that I helped select for funding had an HIV
prevention programme for prostituted women and drug addicts on
the Myanmar side of Kachin state. Bangyuan Wang managed the
programmes. He was a stout young man in his early thirties with deep
thinking and a compassionate heart. Quiet and observant, with a witty
sense of humour, he didn't speak with me in detail until my second visit.
I sensed that I had to earn his trust and he was still determining what my
motivations were. Bangyuan was the hub of the NGO community in
the region. He knew everyone and was respected by all. He later allowed
his passion to flare up when he didn't agree on something related to
the HIV prevention programme. But overall he was a mild-mannered
person, and it would have been easy to overlook and underestimate
him. I formed a friendship with Bangyuan and came to realize that he is
an unsung hero who has worked selflessly in some of southwest China's
poorest regions. I felt honoured to know him.

Bangyuan was willing to go to the farthest reaches of the border
areas with Myanmar and often crossed over into that nation for
outreach to emaciated wild-eyed drug addicts who were at risk of
contracting HIV. A thin river, which looked more like a stream in
some parts, divided China and Myanmar. Many Chinese crossed
back and forth for business. Some of the girls were forced into
brothels, while others were involved in the murky world of drugs,
either partaking or trafficking; it was hard to distinguish. For some
reason, my host Bangyuan couldn't make the return journey with
me and went back to China through another route. I crossed the
border on foot along with one of his staff members, a young Chinese
woman. The border was guarded by armed Chinese soldiers. I had
held my breath the entire time and tried to look carefree, but inside
I felt panicky.

We also travelled to the capital of Kachin state, Myitkyina, and we were taken to a few shady brothels. I learned from frontline workers and from Human Rights Watch that traffickers prey on girls and women in Kachin state to lure them into forced marriages in China, sentencing them to a life of sexual enslavement. Some women have reportedly been sold for $3,000–$13,000.

One time, a giant of a Chinese man, at least six foot five, approached us to ask what we were doing there. He was one of several thuggish-looking enforcers. I put on my brightest smile and responded to him in my simple Mandarin that I was a Korean-Canadian tourist visiting from Beijing. Our host said something to him about HIV/AIDS awareness. He seemed satisfied and allowed us to walk away.

This was a village area stuck in the 1960s. The dirt roads blew dust when the occasional motorbike or ancient bus blasted by. The buildings looked rickety and run down. And there was no mall, not even a small one, in sight—only outdoor markets with mystery meats splayed on wooden tables. We were staying in a decrepit hotel nearby before driving to other villages the next morning, and I worried whether we were safe. Suffice to say, I didn't sleep soundly that night.

In this village, I interviewed women in wooden shack like brothels lined up side-by-side and learned that beneath the smiles, they felt trapped and longed for a better way to make a living. But they had no education, and there were no other job prospects in the region. One woman who seemed under the influence of drugs said she wasn't happy. In front of one of the balcony areas of the brothels, I saw two boys under three years of age, bathing. My heart felt heavy for the rest of my time in that neighbourhood. I took a photo of them and posted it on my blog. I hope that these two boys, who must be teenagers by now, are flourishing and studying in school. But, somehow, I doubt this is their fate.

We walked over to a seedy strip of storefronts with a huge casino as the crowning jewel at the end. It was known for having a large number of prostituted Chinese women. I had a camera with a large lens around my neck and surreptitiously pressed the button to take a flurry of photos of the women walking around; some were waiting for johns to approach them. My host had told me that it would be dangerous if I was caught taking pictures but I took my chance and clicked dozens more and stopped when we arrived at the casino.

Later, we were led to another brothel to interview a pimp and a young Chinese woman. The pimp was predictably smooth and calloused towards the plight of the women. Out of the blue, I was jolted with a revelation that I was in a brothel talking with a man who trafficked girls and women and forced them to be sex slaves. Bangyuan and the NGO workers were used to mingling and chatting with the pimps, traffickers, and exploited women and it was normal for them. But for me, it was very unusual.

In the midst of our conversation, it suddenly dawned upon me that it was quite risky to be speaking with the pimp. He seemed so normal, yet it was as if a light switch had been flicked on as I realized the horror of who he was. I couldn't trust his eyes. There was something so dark and wicked about the way he looked at me. I was completely creeped out.

Instead, I quickly asked to speak with the pretty young girl with short curly hair who looked sixteen or seventeen. She admitted that she took hard drugs with her clients. She said it was fun to do so, and it helped her make more money. I didn't detect any hint of regret in her; maybe, it was all an act for her pimp who was sitting close to us. After we left that dark place, I thought about her limited future and hoped that she would not contract HIV/AIDS like many of her young, naive peers.

Walking through this area was a monumental experience for me—a watershed moment that impacted me deeply in my journey towards justice, and again, I felt that I could no longer turn away and live a selfish white-picket-fence life. This was one of the turning points in my journey.

On another trip, my manager Brian came with me to Myanmar from America. We were hosted by the Kachin military at their compound. I cannot remember how this invite came through. As we drove into the treed area, I saw cages of wildlife, including scruffy-looking black bears that were probably being illegally sold to Chinese medicine producers. Several soldiers with large machine guns walked around the building. My simple room with a bed and desk looked spartan. As I sat on the bed for a moment, I felt something was not right; I suspected hidden cameras in the room. Immediately, I left for a site visit of an HIV/AIDS programme that one of our donors was funding. My boss felt jet-lagged and stayed behind in his room that night. When I returned later that evening, I wore my swimsuit in the shower and changed clothes with a jacket on because I sensed there were eyes watching. I was reminded of a story I had heard about a hotel for foreigners in North Korea, where the mirrors in the bathroom and bedroom are two-way, and officials watch your every move.

In the morning, I was awoken by a pounding on the door. I had slept with my clothes on because I had an intuitive feeling that all was not right, and I leapt out of my bed to open the door. Brian came in, face flushed and panicked, and said that the soldiers had come into his room and interrogated him for hours. I felt dread and immediately began to say my prayers because I thought we were not going to make it out of there. I called our host Bangyuan who came rushing over, and after discussing it we concluded that the head soldier probably wanted to practise his English with Brian, and they could have been toying with him, sensing his fear. Brian was possibly the first American man the soldiers had seen. We decided to leave for the border earlier than scheduled.

My trips to southwest China were life-changing. *I spent time with blind people, AIDS orphans, prostitutes,* and drug addicts with HIV. I fell in love with these people and the region.

A great passion lodged itself in my heart to do what I can to help channel more resources and mobilize others to go as well. I want to see that region transformed by compassion and strategic services. I know it will take a lot of work.

*  *  *

Mary, the volunteer who was with me on that night when we were surrounded by the gangsters, told me stories of hope and wrenching despair, including the grim killings of vulnerable girls in the very areas where Door of Hope does its outreach.

'Every visit to a red-light district is memorable, but their stories are so sad,' she said. 'They tell us about how they were sexually abused as children or raped as eleven- or twelve-year-old kids. There are fourteen- and fifteen-year-old girls with absolutely no understanding of the danger they are in. Since we started our work, three young girls have been murdered. Some of them were beaten by customers and left in a desolate place. Still, they return to the streets. They believe no one cares.'

The work done by Door of Hope is transforming other parts of the city as well. They are challenging local churches—a potentially formidable force to fight against sex slavery and abuse of women—to capture a vision of bringing God's love and hope into society's darkest corners and to come alongside as volunteers in the rehabilitation centre for trafficking victims.

But it has taken some time for them to lend their support. In the initial pioneering stages of Door of Hope, the local church leaders Amy spoke with said it was more strategic to focus on professionals and university students. 'Prostitutes and the mafia are beyond redemption,' they said, 'so how can they contribute to China's future?' This is a common mindset of Christians, perhaps a throwback to the Cultural Revolution days when family members and neighbours betrayed one another to the government, so people had to look out for themselves and trust became obsolete.

Door of Hope workers have been instrumental in showing local churches that prostituted girls and mafia are not garbage or second-class citizens, and that their lives can be restored. Their staff try to make personal connections with the pimps and gang leaders through dinners and continual dialogue about their families and lives. They begin to care for these hardened people and their families. 'We tell them, "We love you, but we hate what you do." When the time is right, I ask them, "Why do you continue to do this? You're a clever man or woman or couple. You have business sense, you're good with people." I use the verse from Proverbs 19 that says treasures gained from wickedness do not profit,' said Amy.

They try to convince these brothel owners to leave the business by breaking down the fines they pay to the police after their girls are arrested. They are fined at least 2,000 RMB per girl. 'Some police earn money off arrests. They're getting their cut from prostitution,' said Amy.

The streets where Door of Hope staff members do outreach are notorious for their violence. People have been shot, stabbed, and had their throats slit in the area where they regularly interact with the brothel girls. One night, a local mafia boss saw Amy with her team of foreign and local women, and asked, 'Why are they not afraid?' He was struck by how they were smiling and giving gifts to the girls. That night, he went to sleep and had a dream. The dream disturbed him so much that he sent his people to get Amy and her team the next morning.

Amy and her team were ushered into a Chinese teahouse setting, which was a front for the brothels, where the mafia boss was waiting for them. He said, 'I need you to help me. I asked this question in my heart: Why are the foreign women not afraid to be out in this dangerous neighbourhood? And that night I had a dream. I saw you walking down the street in this area, and standing behind you was a very tall, eight-foot figure dressed in white, and his wingspan touched either side of the street. He was walking behind you. I want to know who that man is.'

'The amazing thing is that these mafia people really understand protection and the hierarchy of who's protecting you,' said Amy.

'We preached Psalm 34, where it says the angel of the Lord encamps around those who fear God, and God delivers him. I told him this is why we're not afraid. We met with him once a week for three weeks. He received the Christian faith.'

The mafia boss immediately closed both brothels and went back to his hometown. 'God saved this man through his dream,' said Amy. 'And through this pimp's dream, God encouraged my heart so much and reassured me that His protection is always there. We don't have to walk in fear or be afraid. If we fear, we won't be effective in our work.'

Early on in my trips to this part of China where we were meeting the heads of villages, it dawned upon me that I was walking in the shoes of my ancestors. Ancient village systems still exist in China and Korea, and when I met with city and village heads in different cities in my philanthropy advisor role, I had a flash of insight that my great-grandfather and my grandfather who had formal leadership roles must have carried out similar meetings long ago. My great-grandparents also loved and served the poor with free meals at their gated home and gave away clothes and even money to those in need. This was an illuminating revelation that helped me accept my Korean identity, and know that I am included in a long generation of Koreans and a part of a rich tapestry of a justice legacy to give back to the community. This is what my mother received from her grandparents and instilled in me naturally through example without using words. It was ironic that I had to immigrate to China from Canada to find out who I am and to appreciate my roots.

I reflect back on this formative threshold season of my life with gratitude. Personal pain had driven me to desperately search for meaning and purpose. In meeting unsung, humble heroes like Amy, Xuxu, Ai Jin, Bangyuan, Chen, and many more, I had found a North Star of sorts—shining examples of a noble sacrificial lifestyle that helped rescue so many out of enslavement. They exemplified what

William Wilberforce, the leader of the movement for abolishing the slave trade in Britain, had once said: 'If to be feelingly alive to the sufferings of my fellow creatures is to be a fanatic, I am one of the most incurable fanatics ever permitted to be at large.' And, I too wanted this for myself.

# Part II

# Wartime Sex Slavery

# 5

# Generational Pain

The time I had spent observing Door of Hope's mission of rescuing women from forced prostitution reinforced my belief that a historical and horrific form of sexual trafficking still exists today. My experience was eerily reminiscent of my work uncovering wartime sex slavery and sexual violence by the Japanese military that was sanctioned by the government of Japan and systematically carried out from the early 1930s until the end of WWII. The girls and women were euphemistically known as the 'comfort women' because their sole role was to comfort the Japanese soldiers on the frontlines of war. Sadly, however, from the ashes of the end of a world war, the untold suffering of girls and women in sex trafficking continued on. Modern-day sex trafficking included the same hallmarks of recruiting techniques, the same undercurrents of racism, gender discrimination and cultural issues throughout the Asia Pacific.

I was fifteen when I first learnt of this issue from my mother who shared with me what she read in a Vancouver-based Korean newspaper article about a survivor of Japanese military sex slavery. We were eating at the dining table, and I remember feeling shocked and giving her my full attention. During this first account, I learnt that the elderly Korean woman survivor was of my age when she was forced into Japanese military sexual slavery. I remember having a sinking feeling that it could have been me had I been born at that time in Korea. I immediately identified because we were a similar age and she was Korean too.

I had never heard of the historical tragedy of these young girls in slavery and felt deep dismay that I hadn't learnt of it in my Social Studies class at school. My mother said it was a painful chapter of history that most Koreans know about as it happened during the colonial occupation of Korea by the Japanese. She also conveyed that it was wrong that the Japanese government was denying they forced these girls.

The woman featured in the newspaper article was Kim Hak-soon, the first Korean survivor to speak to the international media. Hearing her story fired up in me a desire to uncover the truth behind these atrocious war crimes against girls and women; this was the first glimmer of human rights activism that sparked in me. I vowed to myself that I would fight for and do something for these women. I was filled with a sense of purpose and a fiery drive came over me in my studies. I would wake up early, often hours before I had to go to school to excel at my homework. Nearly a decade later in 2001, I wasn't able to forget this vow, and I began to research further on this egregious war crime.

I learnt from various accounts that on 14 August 1991, a slight, pepper-haired woman in a white traditional Korean dress took the stage at a press conference in Seoul, Korea. With a brooding intensity in her wrinkled face and hollow eyes that belied her ordinary appearance, sixty-eight-year-old Kim Hak-soon did something completely out of character for women in her culture. She testified tearfully that as a seventeen-year-old, she was forced into sex slavery by the Japanese military in northern China. She was raped by up to thirty Japanese soldiers a day in Manchuria during the Japanese war against China.

Several months before her press conference, Kim saw on the news that the Japanese government was denying that young Korean women were forced to be sex slaves. Japanese ultra-nationalists and Right-wing conservatives called Kim and others like her voluntary prostitutes when they bore witness in the media about being forced into sexual servitude for the Imperial Japanese military before and during WWII. Kim refuted that she was a willing prostitute.

'How did I become a public witness? When I read newspapers and watched the news, Japan kept denying the truth,' said Kim. 'They took us forcibly, put us directly in the military compound, and turned us into comfort women.'

Kim suffered profoundly with her secret for fifty years before breaking her silence. You could say Kim led the very first 'Me Too' moment in Asia, decades before the movement took hold of the West.

Born in 1924 in Manchuria, Kim came from an impoverished family. It was a time of political instability in Korea under Japanese colonial rule, and her parents had fled to China after the infamous massacre on 1 March 1919 when more than two million Koreans protested for independence from Japan.

Kim returned to Korea with her mother after her father passed away, and everyone around her seemed to think that she had been born under a curse. Her father had died because of her bad luck, they whispered. Because of such superstitions, she became a scapegoat for all of her family's misfortune. After her mother remarried, her stepfather adopted her at the age of fourteen. She wasn't very happy with her new family dynamic and often ran away from home. Instead of ensuring his stepdaughter's marriage prospects, Kim's stepfather sent her to a *gisaeng* school for female entertainers who were taught the styles of Japanese geisha music and dance.

After graduating, Kim's stepfather took her to China to earn money as a *gisaeng*. On their arrival, Kim was abducted by Japanese soldiers and taken to a large, empty house near the military barracks. For the next four to five months, she was confined to a tiny room and repeatedly beaten and raped.

The only relief she had was the presence of three older Korean girls at the house. She didn't know their Korean names, as they were forced to go by their given Japanese names. Kim was the youngest one at seventeen; the oldest was twenty-two. In this cold, deserted house, all the Korean women were required to speak Japanese and entertain the men with Japanese songs. The soldiers referred to them as *chosenppi*—Korean vagina—or other racially charged, derogatory Japanese terms. By day, on meagre food rations, the girls were forced to run errands, deliver ammunitions, cook, do laundry, and work as nurses to tend to injured soldiers. In the evenings, they were confined in their rooms to serve as sex slaves. At the slightest protest, Kim and the others were beaten and dragged around by their hair.

The long curse over her life seemingly ended when she escaped with the help of a Korean man who ran a pawnshop in Shanghai's French concession. It was an unlikely war romance. They were married in Shanghai, and by the end of the war she had borne a son and a daughter.

Eventually, Kim and her family made their way back to Korea. Life, she recalled, was filled with misery and tragic accidents. Her husband made a living as a military supplier for some time. After the Korean War ended in 1953, he died in an accident, leaving her a widow. Then, her daughter died of cholera and her son drowned in a swimming accident when he was only ten years old.

Years later, alone, with her secret past as a Japanese military sex slave locked in an internal vault, she hesitantly considered revealing her experiences. One small step away from life on the streets, Kim eked out a living as a housemaid and a peddler on the harsh streets of Seoul. Her experiences in the Japanese military rape camp continued to haunt her.

Even long after, in order to keep my heart tender for what these women suffered, I kept an image of Kim in my mind's eye, standing forlornly on the streets selling small cheap goods on a blanket to survive. The sorrowful twilight years of her life illustrated how her experiences as a sex slave for the Japanese Imperial military destroyed her and snuffed out her future as a wife, mother, grandmother with a caring family.

Kim suffered profound, debilitating shame for fifty years before bearing witness and revealing her secret. She also compelled many other survivors of Japanese military sex slavery in several nations to break their self-imposed silence of shame and self-hatred, and the issue soon gained worldwide recognition through the United Nations and the international media.

When Kim and others bore witness in the media about being forced into sexual servitude for the Japanese military before and during WWII, Japanese ultra-nationalists and Right-wing conservatives labelled them as voluntary prostitutes. Kim strongly refuted that.

In contrast to the horrors experienced by the victims of the Holocaust during WWII, I found absolutely no mention of 'comfort women' or 'Asian women' in the indexes of any history book in my high school library in Vancouver. I didn't understand at the time that my curriculum was Eurocentric. I felt disturbed by what seemed like the erasure of the suffering of young Asian women, many of whom were mere teenagers like me when they were enslaved. In this case, it seemed like these human rights violations had been whitewashed from world history. Much like how I unconsciously whitewashed my own ethnicity, my Korean language, my identity as an Asian woman to fit in to a largely Caucasian or Anglo-Saxon Canadian society. Asian women, even in the West, struggle with being silenced by their culture, and it is often self-imposed.

From my research of court documents involving survivors of wartime Japanese sex slavery, academic papers, books, and interviews with leading experts, I couldn't find one comprehensive source on Japanese military sex slavery and survivor accounts in those years. I learnt from a variety of sources that it is estimated that between 80,000 and 400,000 women and children were trafficked into sex slavery camps throughout the Japanese Empire in the Pacific Theatre from 1931 to 1945. They were forced into this system for the sole purpose of satisfying the sexual needs of Japanese soldiers. It was thought that these rape camps, known as 'comfort stations', would make the soldiers less likely to rape the local women, thereby reducing hostility in occupied areas, stopping the spread of venereal disease and averting potential espionage. There were more than a thousand 'comfort stations' in China alone. Some call it the largest-known trafficking of women and children in modern history.

These women were trafficked and forced into sex slavery in military comfort stations all over China, Indonesia, the Dutch East Indies, the Philippines, East Timor, Singapore, Vietnam, Cambodia, Laos, and other occupied territories that became part of the Japanese Empire during WWII. The victims included Koreans, Japanese, Dutch, Taiwanese, Chinese, Eurasians, Filipinos, Burmese, Malay, Vietnamese, Thai, and Pacific Islanders.

They were 'conscripted' through deception with promises of jobs, and often by physical force, coercion, and kidnapping. Many were sold as merchandise to keep the 'comfort stations' running. Collaborators and brokers from their native countries often assisted the Japanese military. Victims reported being taken on military vehicles and boats and gang-raped by the soldiers on board. Girls as young as eleven years old were forced into the rape stations on the frontlines of war and attacked by up to sixty soldiers a day in military brothels. As Japan expanded militarily, the need for more wartime sex slaves dramatically increased.

It was after decades of silence that a few dozen elderly women began to speak out about their experiences in sexual servitude for the Imperial Japanese military-run forced prostitution system. The numbers of survivors are dwindling, and it is likely that many will never emerge from the shadows to testify.

\* \* \*

My parents immigrated to Vancouver when I was two years old. I have no recollections of my brief time living in Korea. I have been told that my parents left me in my great-grandmother's care for many months while my mom went back to school in another city. As a caregiver, I'm told that she was very doting and I was spoiled with love. The day she returned, I looked at her as if she were a stranger for several minutes, then I began to cry in recognition. Somehow, I felt this memory was a significant one during the most formative years of my life and had left a tinge of fear of abandonment in me.

When I was growing up, I held my Korean identity at a distance and imagined myself to be a Caucasian blonde woman with blue eyes or an African American hip-hop dancer. It didn't help that I could see no Asians that looked like me on TV or in positions of authority in society or on the teaching staff at school, and this fed into my lifelong inner conflict over my ethnic identity.

As a sixteen-year-old, I sat in front of the TV in our family room, transfixed and horrified by the images of the Los Angeles riots of 1992: billowing smoke from burning buildings, Korean American snipers guarding their businesses, and rioting youngsters ransacking businesses. The LA riots left a deep impression of racial hatred between ethnic communities. When my African Canadian friends made a comment about Koreans shooting African Americans in the riots, I shrugged and looked away. I had no easy answers, and, in that moment, I felt ashamed to be Korean. I sensed their seemingly irrational blanket resentment of Koreans. It felt racially discriminatory but I didn't speak up about it.

The historical LA riots brought my inner conflict over my racial identity to the surface. I felt like I didn't belong anywhere—I was neither with one group nor another. I was stuck on a bridge in between cultures and people. The riots would also sear the collective trauma of the Korean American community into my memory. Several families lost their loved ones during this riot, and some of them bear the scars to this day. It changed me and my generation forever; I would no longer tolerate racial discrimination. I realized that racism is a hidden undercurrent and that anything could be a tipping point to ignite it. Racism can manifest in seemingly innocuous words that are really an onslaught of micro-aggressions. Psychologist Derald W. Sue who wrote two books on the topic defines it as, 'The everyday slights, indignities, put downs and insults that people of colour, women, LGBT populations or those who are marginalized experience in their day-to-day interactions with people.'

Learning about the mass systemic sexual exploitation and enslavement of girls as young as eleven triggered in me an irrational feeling of resentment towards the Japanese, much like my African Canadian friends' anger towards all Koreans. It was as if my generational DNA were awakened and feelings and resentment that my ancestors held towards their colonial oppressors in the Japanese erupted and pulsated through my veins. I became wary of the diminutive Japanese man with friendly eyes and a ready smile who rented our basement with his cheerful wife and two daughters.

I had grown up in a Caucasian neighbourhood in Burnaby and was the only Asian girl in my grade. In my teens, I felt no connection with my Korean heritage because I was haunted by the humiliation of racial discrimination that I'd experienced. When some schoolmates came over to play, they looked inside our fridge and were frightened by the big jars of kimchi. 'Eww, what *is* that?' they asked while scrunching up their noses as little girls do. I burned with shame and felt like disappearing into the floor, even though kimchi was my favourite dish and our meal-time staple. One year, a few White girls in my fifth-grade class would say 'Chink you' instead of 'Thank you' to me. I wore these blue chequered shorts that had been made for me out of the softest material by my mother's friend, and I had no idea that she had sewed them out of bedsheets. My classmate said with glee that she had sheets just like my shorts as she chortled with a mean glint in her beady eyes. I never wore those shorts again, so afraid I was of other people's opinions.

I hated the Asian face that stared back at me in the mirror. I demanded that my mother only speak to me in English and never address me by my Korean name, Saejung. She stayed silent and turned her pretty porcelain face away from me. I wondered if her heart broke at those words.

As an adult, I gazed at photos of myself and my parents taken just before we hopped on the plane. Soon after, my parents divorced, and my father drifted out of my life. I cried myself to sleep for a long time after that. Insensitive adults at church would ask mockingly, 'Where's your dad?' At the time, we were one of the rare families with divorced parents, and this seemed to magnify the turmoil that I, a depressed and highly sensitive child, felt about being the only Asian in my class.

Yet, I cried at seeing the Hyundai Pony, the first mass-produced South Korean car, on the streets of Canada in the 1980s. As an eleven-year-old, I seethed with anger as I watched a play at church in which the grown-ups enacted the true story of a public execution of a pastor in Korea during the Japanese occupation. This pastor, played by my friend's grandfather, walked on a wooden board with long nails. With every step, he had a surreal look of peace as he looked up towards heaven. With bloodied feet at the end of his walk of pain, with weeping churchgoers around him and Japanese soldiers looking on, this pastor thanked Jesus and died peacefully. His face was radiant as he looked heavenward and passed heroically. This was a true story from the Japanese occupation of Korea when the Japanese language and Shinto religion was forced upon Koreans, often with brutal violence. There was not a dry eye in the large church sanctuary. I cried too, with something stirring in my soul. It was an ancient pain that was left to rot—an unhealed wound that could've been closed decades ago had these atrocities been recognized and acknowledged with a healing apology from the Government of Japan. Instead, the wounds and torture inflicted by Japanese colonialism were left to fester in a way that would impact later generations that had spread to the four corners of the world.

Resentment towards the Japanese festered even in church circles where we were supposed to forgive our enemies, and it was here that I learnt the most about it from the chatter of the children of first generation Koreans. Young teachers in their late teens and twenties and friends at my Korean immigrant church later relayed in bits and pieces what they had heard from their parents—that the Japanese were cruel to the Koreans, and that they tortured and killed, especially Christians. We didn't have an opportunity to take a Korean history class in school so we received most of our information through oral history. I expressed my wish to learn more as it seemed like a black hole in my understanding of history, and in response, my thoughtful mother immediately bought several Korean books for me to read. These books had been translated into English by Christians who were eventually martyred, and they contained stories of persecution by the Japanese colonialists. Their palpable passion and radical commitment to God, even in the face of death, was inspiring. Some spoke of forgiving their enemies; something that I could not fathom and that would come to mind when I met a Japanese Christian reconciliation group years later.

For the overseas Korean community, the church was the central point for social gathering; my faith has ultimately shaped my social justice awakening in profound and unseen ways. As a lifelong Christian who grew up in church, I questioned my faith in the face of peer pressure and a dissatisfaction with the rigidity of Sunday school classes at church. It felt as though we were playing religion but there was no heart and no God in our midst. Our Sunday school teachers looked bored themselves and lacked that infectious spirituality. One young man who occasionally led the worship was a serial womaniser. The adults would sometimes get into heated arguments to the point where scuffles would break out.

My friends at church were rebellious and couldn't be bothered with God. They were the children of pastors and elders, and they were pressured to look good and be good. As fourteen-year-olds, we would regularly go joyriding in my best friend Sylvia's parent's silver Hyundai Pony along the tree-lined streets of our church's rural neighbourhood. Sylvia was two feet shorter than I was and a year younger, and we were inseparable for years. She was called 'little Sylvia' and I was 'big Sylvia' because I was tall and lanky for my age. We were considered the terrors of Sunday school, and no one wanted to take on our class. I formed a girl gang—a clique—in the fifth grade with four girls from Sunday school and I said we were all required to wear black clothes.

One thing my childhood church did well was outreach to forgotten elderly people in senior homes and hospitals. These experiences left a great impression on me. About once a month on Sundays, a group of us accompanied our pastor to sing for elderly men and women who were wheeled into a room. Often their mouths were drooling or their vacant eyes stared elsewhere. After our performance, we lined up to shake their hands and say a blessing or something encouraging. I wasn't sure if they could hear me when I said, 'God bless you' or 'Jesus loves you.' When I was in the seventh grade, a teenager named John was suddenly fired up about Jesus and was experiencing a 'revival'. He organized trips to do street preaching in the Downtown Eastside, an area commonly referred to as the 'poorest postal code' in Canada. In 2010, the BBC dubbed the area as having the 'worst drug problems in North America'. When I was twelve, Sylvia and I walked around to talk with people, and we met with one senior Japanese Canadian man. We asked him if he believed in God. He said no, because he and his family were forced into an internment camp. His face has been etched in my memory all these years. He looked so bitter but was intrigued by the sight of us children wandering the streets on our own. Years later, I realized he was referring to the unjust treatment of Japanese in Canada during WWII.

Going on a humanitarian mission trip to Tijuana at fifteen was a most sobering event. Sylvia and I signed up to go with a group of mostly college-age youngsters and one adult pastor. Right before I decided to go on this trip, my old Sunday school teacher, Peter, came over to visit, and he wanted to share something with me. He had just returned from a mission trip to South Africa and spent the entire time crying and urging me not to be so materialistic. I was taken by surprise and wondered what he meant by materialistic. After spending nearly two weeks in a poor area of Tijuana and playing with poor children while the older ones shared Bible stories, I had a better idea of what materialism was. All of the parents were waiting for us at the church to take us home when we returned to Vancouver. I sobbed into my mom's shoulder and said it was a life-changing experience. My awakening to social justice was just beginning. I had heard about the first survivor of wartime sex slavery during this year.

It was also around this time that I stopped attending Sunday service until I hit nineteen. I had a borrowed hollow religion in my teens and was bored of church service. These were years of pushing boundaries, sneaking into nightclubs, dancing on the tops of stereos, shoplifting earrings and make-up with friends, and exploring friendships with boys.

I didn't truly comprehend God and the depth of my faith until years later as I was facing personal challenges.

My mother's faith, however, was awe-inspiring. She had a ministry to the poor through her church for more than thirty years and sacrificially used the money she earned from her business to help others much like a social enterprise. She would be frequently helping people in our home, counselling them, and hosting dinners for large groups of people. She called lonely elderly single women from her church to check in on them. To help her persevere in her work and deal with my teenaged rebellion, she cried out to God in her prayer closet, sometimes with tears. She often also cried with people who were deeply hurting and would relay their stories to me. One particular example was unforgettable when her friend's husband was hit by a car and had an arm amputated which affected his ability to work for a living. My mother provided home-cooked meals for them.

My mother's grandparents, who raised her, had used their influence and wealth for the good of others. They would open their home and hearts to love and feed the poor who came from far off places to be nourished. They gave away coats, money, even the long johns they were wearing to those begging in the winter, so moved were they with great compassion for those in dire need. In my thirties, I began to appreciate my mother more and her noble example made me want to carry on my fourth generation blessings of social justice work.

An unspeakable damaging wound on the Korean people that continues to affect me in subtle ways occurred when Korea was colonized by the Japanese from 1910 until 1945. It was a time when several generations of my family line were forced to speak Japanese. In every aspect of life, they were stripped of their Korean identity, their dignity, and their ability to control their lives. They were made to feel insecure and anxious in their own homes. During the war in Manchuria and later during WWII, it was as if Korea has been plundered and used like a rag to wipe the Japanese war machine. Even shiny metal cutlery was ordered to be given up to be made into weapons. Countless men, women, and children were mobilized into the war effort as free labour and many girls and women became sex slaves on the frontlines of war.

As I interviewed relatives—a pulling-teeth kind of exercise because Koreans are known for taking secrets to their grave—I discovered that this was an extremely traumatic time for all Koreans on the peninsula and is part of our collective memory, as a generational trauma, even to this day. As a result, I have a certain radar and sensitivity to racial discrimination like an unhealed trauma response. I feel a certain level of discomfort when I meet Japanese in Japan or Japanese in other parts of the world who have racist attitudes that have gone unchecked since WWII towards Koreans and Chinese. I can sense it keenly, and I know that I'm not imagining it.

I recalled that one relative spoke fluent Japanese but owned no Japanese electronics and vowed he would never buy a Japanese car. He drives an American car to this day. He grew up during the Japanese occupation and experienced unjust treatment from the teachers at the Japanese government-run school he attended.

I've heard multiple stories of older members of Chinese and Korean communities who distrusted the Japanese. There were whispers that no one wanted to date Japanese men. While the Chinese and Koreans intermingled and freely dated, it was unusual to see a cross-pollination with the Japanese. It was as if they had been erased. Even in Hong Kong, the Chinese and Korean communities rarely mix with the Japanese—my friends and I have intentionally tried to bring everyone together at social gatherings, and it is very touching to see unity overcoming division and suspicion.

I've witnessed outright discrimination towards the Japanese in North America and in Asia. Perhaps there was an element of self-erasure of their Japanese identity in Canada too after the tragedy of their internment experience. It was wrong to imprison Japanese Canadians and Americans during WWII for being the 'enemy'. I empathized with them and was pleased when they received an official apology from the Canadian and American governments.

I began to explore 'generational pain' in the Holocaust literature and asked some Japanese Canadians if they had experienced this kind of pain passed down from ancestors who were forced into the internment camps. They said yes. My parents, like other immigrants in the 1970s and 1980s, experienced racism too. Their journey was a part of the cloud of experiences that shaped my spirit.

I felt an inexplicable, almost obsessive, compulsion to document stories of survivors of the Japanese Imperial military sex slavery system. I wanted to write a book that I had wanted to read all those years ago when I first looked for information on the topic. I sense this drive has its origins in feelings of being discriminated against in terms of both gender and ethnicity. It was also a search for who I was—my identity. I was so lost for many years. I was bi-cultural, straddling two cultures and worlds, but could never be defined by only one. It was my experience of racial cruelty and being rejected and hurt that led to a passion for standing up for those who have been marginalized. When I learned about the 'comfort women' Japanese military sex slaves of Asia, a profound generational anger that must have been running through my DNA latently rose up. It made me realize that I cannot deny or reject my ethnicity.

The 'comfort women' issue and the denial of the Japanese government propelled me on a journey to meet these women and document their stories. I wanted to know how they were able to survive these experiences. It has led me to take several trips to Seoul, Tokyo, The Hague, Washington DC, Los Angeles, San Francisco, and across China, and it culminated in the publication of my book *Silenced No More: Voices of Comfort Women* in 2015. It was the English-language book about Japanese military sex slavery that I couldn't find in libraries as a teenager.

Since it took me so long to finish writing this book—more than fourteen years—I felt deep remorse for not being able to publish it before many of the victims passed on. I still feel guilty about it to this day. Several of the elderly women I interviewed asked me to tell the world about the truth of what had happened to them in forced prostitution. But most of them were not around by the time my book was published. They never received the official, healing, and sincere apology from the Japanese government that they've fought for.

# 6

# Elderly Sex Slavery Survivors

After my exposure to sex trafficking in China, I became a journalist specializing in stories that covered human rights, women's rights, and modern slavery. In July 2001, during my first few years in the profession, I heard that Kim Soon-duk, an eighty-year-old survivor of Japanese military sex slavery, would be speaking at a press conference at the US State Department in Washington, DC. She was travelling all the way from her home in a suburb near Seoul, Korea as part of her quest for justice.

She was inspired by Kim Hak-soon's brave public testimony and a year later, she came forward to testify of her ordeal in Japanese military sex slavery in 1992. Kim was not legally married to the man she lived with. Now dead, he never knew of what she called her 'shameful experience', and neither did their three children. She waited for him to die before coming forward. Three months after his death, she asked her cousin and niece if she should testify. Both of them told her to keep her secret. She testified anyway, and they were infuriated.

In a matter of a few hours, on a whim, I spontaneously booked a ticket for the next flight and drove straight to the airport to meet Kim Soon-duk in Washington, DC. I planned to write a freelance magazine story on Kim's ordeal. I felt a rush of adrenalin as I sped down the highway from Vancouver to Seattle. I hadn't even booked a hotel room; I would think about that when I landed.

When I arrived at the State Department building, I felt like pinching myself and was dizzy with naive excitement. It was surprising and unexpected for me, as a junior journalist and a Canadian, to be inside of this impressive building that housed the heart of foreign policy. In a corner of the large wooden panelled room, I saw an extremely petite lady wearing a pink traditional silk *hanbok* dress and short jacket. More than half a dozen photographers were gathered all around her clicking away furiously. Her eyes darted around the room and did not rest very long on anyone. As she settled into her seat, her shoulders seemed to straighten with a certain determination, and she appeared very comfortable in the spotlight. When it was Kim's time to speak, she walked up to the podium and began telling her story with a raw childlike simplicity that seemed out of place in those formal dark-wood-panelled surroundings with the prominent American flag.

When Kim was young and living in a remote village, she had dreamt of going to a city and attending a big school. As a young girl, she had worn her long hair in a braid and had shoes made of straw. She had two older brothers and one older sister but was closest to her mother and younger sister. Her family endured hardships under Japanese colonial rule. They, as Koreans, were forced to change their names to Japanese ones. Neither were they allowed to speak in their Korean language. The soldiers confiscated their metal kitchen utensils and dishes to make weapons. Her father, a distinguished man of customs and discipline, always wore an immaculate white outfit, as was the tradition of the day. He was mocked by the Japanese, and they shot at his clothes with a black ink gun. Shortly after, Kim and her family moved to another village to avoid persecution.

In 1937, when Kim was sixteen years old, some Japanese people came to her village and told her that she would work as a temporary nurse in Japan. They selected one girl from each family in her village. She found herself on a boat with fifty other girls between the ages of fifteen and seventeen. As they struggled with seasickness, they consoled each other with stories of their families.

They ended up in Shanghai and were taken to a military brothel where they were immediately separated and placed in individual rooms with thin partitions. No one informed them of what was about to happen. Kim recalled seeing a long line of Japanese soldiers outside of the rooms. One after the other in steady succession, the men raped the girls. Some screamed and fainted, some cried, while some tried to run away. Those who ran were caught and killed to intimidate those who stayed behind.

Kim began three years as a sex slave servicing Japanese soldiers. She was raped countless number of times while being subjected to the most abhorrent living conditions. Many girls committed suicide. Kim attempted thrice.

'Every single day, the war soldiers lined up,' she said. 'There were so many, we couldn't count them. I was very sick. I couldn't sit down. I was bleeding so badly. When the military moved, we all moved with them. I wanted to die. The shock was so great, it is beyond words.'

Kim had no idea where she was in China and had no means to get back to Korea. All she could do to survive was think of going home. When one high-ranking Japanese officer treated her with a special kindness, she appealed to him to allow her to return. Later, he was able to obtain permission for her and three other young women to return to Korea in 1940. Too ashamed to go to her family home, she went to Seoul instead where she worked as a maid and in other odd jobs. The cultural ethos demanded that brides were virgins when they married. Kim never married as she was unable to overcome her feelings of shame and impurity, believing that her experiences would be too much for a man to be able to accept and love her unconditionally.

Kim concluded her testimony by calling on the government of Japan to sincerely apologize to all survivors and issue reparations. Her story was similar to Kim Hak-soon's; both felt crippling shame and yet overcame it to go public as survivors of sexual violence.

I also thought of a Holocaust survivor who had spoken at my school years ago, and I connected the dots with Kim, a fellow survivor who suffered unspeakable horrors during WWII. I was frustrated that these elderly women survivors of military sex slavery were not as supported in the same way as Holocaust survivors were, and that this crime against humanity was not as widely known. The inklings of wanting to do something about it sprang from this first meeting I had with Kim.

During our one-to-one interview after the press conference, Kim disclosed what she wanted most at this point in her life. 'I want the Japanese government to apologize first and make reparations to us.' Her voice drifted. 'That's all I want. And that this kind of inhumane history of sex slavery will never be repeated.'

'Are you hopeful of receiving an apology in your lifetime?' I asked.

'We'll have to see. We won't know until we try,' she said.

Slavery had long-lasting effects on Kim's body. She suffered physically and mentally every day, and when she thought of the past, she was unable to sleep. 'I am still suffering today. If I hadn't been taken, I would have led a happy life with my family members,' she lamented. 'I'm separated from my family now. They finally got to know the truth, and it was a big shock to them. They couldn't imagine that such a thing could happen to me.'

Kim said that she still had nightmares, including a recurring one in which soldiers' legs were chasing her. Yet, she didn't harbour any prejudice towards the Japanese. 'We have to recognize in Japan today, there are many good citizens. I do not hate the younger generation,' she said.

At that time, Kim was living in a care facility in Seoul for survivors of Japanese military sex slavery called House of Sharing.

Every month, about 150 Japanese people came to visit her and the other survivors—many of them bearing gifts and offering tearful apologies. One young Japanese woman volunteered for a year as a caretaker and cook at the home.

When asked if she had ever been in love before, Kim briefly mentioned her relationship with a high-ranking Japanese officer. When pressed for more details, the confession of her love for the officer emerged. Kim longed to reunite with this general and had even looked for him during her trip to bear witness in Tokyo for the landmark Women's International War Crimes Tribunal for the Trial of Japan's Military Sexual Slavery in December 2000. I wondered about the effects of Stockholm Syndrome on a person, even more than half a century later.

Kim also became a celebrated artist. Her work depicted her pain far deeper than her words. One painting titled *Kidnapped* was of a young girl with terror-stricken eyes as a Japanese soldier's hand is grabbing her tiny hand and taking her away from Korea. 'I feel better when I do art exhibitions,' she said. An art teacher showed Kim and the other survivors at their home how to paint, in the hope that it would release some of their pain.

Kim hosted a travelling art exhibition of her work entitled *The Quest for Justice: The Story of Korean Comfort Women as Told Through Their Art* in several cities in the US and in fifty venues across Japan. It featured the artwork of fellow survivors Kim Bok-dong, Lee Yong-nyeo, and Kang Duk-kyung. In one of the paintings, a closed bud of a flower rested against a young girl's cheek. This bud never bloomed; it represented her stolen youth. In *At That Time, at That Place* Kim painted a naked girl hiding her face in a foetal position as three Japanese soldiers hovered menacingly against a dark background. She said it depicted her first rape in Shanghai by a Japanese soldier who had stood in a long line.

Lastly, Kim described a day in her life at the House of Sharing. She moved in when it was opened by Buddhist supporters in 1992.

Most of the women who resided at the facility had come from Mainland China, where they were stuck, with no way of returning home to Korea after the war ended. 'I do some farming, and I talk to guests. Sometimes I seek out doctors for medical care,' she concluded.

\* \* \*

In my search for understanding of the Japanese military sex slavery issue and to interview actual survivors for my book project, in March 2003 I attended a conference called 'Preventing Crimes against Humanity' at the University of British Columbia in Vancouver. Hwang Geum-joo, another sex slavery survivor, was to speak at one of the seminars, and I was moved at the thought of spending time with her. I also felt anxious that I wouldn't get enough time to speak with Hwang.

Before the conference started, Hwang stood outside of the main hall, looking out of place with her traditional blue and white *hanbok*, rubber shoes, and peppery hair pulled back into a tight bun.

When Hwang was twenty years old, her father fell ill and her family became destitute. She volunteered to work in a military supply factory, believing she was going to make a lot of money for her family. Instead of being employed in a factory, she was placed in a comfort station in Manchuria.

'The Japanese dragged us away during the annexation of Korea, and we had to obey,' she recalled. 'All high school boys were forced to join the Japanese military and were conscripted as soldiers. Unmarried young women were forced into sex slavery, including myself. The comfort women in the military unit were not treated as human beings. We were beaten almost every day. I was particularly rebellious and earned more beatings than the other girls. Even now, my ears go fuzzy sometimes, and I can't hear for long periods of time. I have magnetic strips attached to my knees and hips. If I take these off for a bath and forget to put them back on, my knees and hips swell up and I am unable to sit down.'

Hwang had been forced to get a '606 injection', which was commonly used to sterilize the women and girls in the military sex slavery system.

When asked if she could, one day, forgive the Japanese military and government for the suffering she had to endure, she responded emphatically, 'I cannot forgive the Japanese.'

On the day she was to return to Korea, I gave her a goodbye hug. It was apparent that she was not used to being hugged, but she sweetly smiled anyway.

During one of the trips when I had spent time interviewing elderly survivors at the House of Sharing—I had the opportunity to stay at a shelter for the survivors in Seoul. My stay was arranged by the Korean Council for Justice and Remembrance for the issues of Military Sexual Slavery by Japan (Korean Council), and it was at this place that I got to know Hwang Geum-joo better. At first, she did not remember me from our Vancouver meeting, but then her memory was jogged. She was wearing a denim button-down shirt with a pair of shimmering copper-gold pants that flared out and narrowed at the ankles. She donned an embroidered beige vest on top of her ensemble. Her black and white hair was tucked in a bun. Her feet were tiny.

'I have no uterus,' Hwang confessed with a flippancy one would expect from someone who was discussing the weather. She was a straight-shooter and did not mince words or waste time when it came to sharing her opinions. She had rough hands, and she was as tough as nails. 'That Kim Dae-jung . . . he promised that the first thing he would do as president was to resolve the comfort women issue. That son of a bitch didn't do anything. I had lunch with him. He promised,' she spat out.

She had been raped by up to forty men a day, yet she never seemed depressed about her life. This time, she even said that she forgave the Japanese and did not blame the younger generation for what she experienced. I was taken aback by her willingness to forgive and wondered about the reason behind it since she offered no explanation for her radical new stance.

'I've travelled to so many cities, and I wear my *hanbok*,' she said. 'People go crazy over my dress. I once touched Abraham Lincoln's statue in Washington, DC. No one else could. Just me.' She beamed as she spoke of meeting President Bill Clinton and shaking his hand. She also brought up the topic of sex when she spoke of the impact of her slavery ordeal. She remained afraid of men.

Hwang had not had a mother figure since she was sixteen years old, yet she was surprisingly nurturing despite her rough edges. Many of the elderly survivors I met were unusually tough and resilient. Out of the hundreds of thousands of military sex slaves, only a small fraction, the strongest of them all, survived. Hwang was the only one of the girls at her 'comfort station' who attempted to return to Korea.

'I walked,' she said. 'It took four months to get to Seoul, and I travelled with other refugees. I wore a soldier's uniform. I begged for food and slept on the streets. It was a very painful time. When I returned, I learned my father had passed away. I had no desire to go home. I didn't try to find my family. I couldn't tell anyone what happened as I was so ashamed, but when I saw Kim Hak-soon's public interview, I decided to come out too.'

Following the Korean War, Hwang continued to endure sharp pain and discomfort related to a venereal disease she had contracted from being subjugated to forced sex. She remained single and adopted three orphans, one of whom died as a child. Hwang raised and supported her son and daughter through school by running a small restaurant near Seoul University. Her children had families of their own and still visited her. The activists grew very close with her. Beneath her gruff exterior, she had a soft heart.

* * *

During another trip a year later in September 2004, my friend Helen and I visited the House of Sharing, which was a two-hour drive south of Seoul. We had planned to stay there for a few weeks to interview the women. Helen was my translator and travel companion. I was driven to meet these women after meeting Kim Soon-duk in Washington, DC and Hwang Geum-joo in Vancouver. I knew that time was running out since these women were in their seventies and eighties.

At this time, I was in transition having left a TV journalism job to travel and tour China for the summer and to research Japanese war crimes, including an interview with a Chinese survivor of Japanese military sex slavery. I was anticipating a move to Beijing after I fell in love with the city. I knew it would be a tectonic shift in my life to leave behind my comfortable lifestyle in Canada to immigrate back to Asia for an adventurous life overseas. It was a nerve-wracking time in my life as I deliberated over the big move and debated the pros and cons of leaving job security.

The House of Sharing consisted of two dormitories for the residents with a few spaces for overnight guests, as well as a temple and an office building with a lounge. In the front, there was a haunting statue of a young girl with her hair pulled back in a bun, wearing a traditional *hanbok*.

Beside the dormitories was the History Museum of Japanese Military Comfort Women, which was established on 14 August 1998. The museum consisted of two floors with five different sections depicting various experiences of the military sex slaves and multimedia presentations of survivors' testimonies. In the 'experience room', one could stand in a creepy model of a bare room in a comfort station. Standing in the spare dark room, I dared not sit on the flimsy bed that had the look of an army barrack with a single metal bowl for washing. I teared up and felt suffocated. I briefly imagined how the girls were tortured in these tiny cubicles. I couldn't bear the thought of it after a few seconds. What a profound immersion that helped me to identify more with the enslaved girls and women who had no way of protecting themselves; it was more terrifying and real than reading words or watching a film.

There were nine women in their late seventies and eighties living at the House of Sharing. They looked like vibrant crotchety grandmas, and I was surprised they didn't have a different look. I would later learn that my expectations were way off.

Everyone got up at dawn in the House of Sharing, and I heard windows opening and water splashing onto the ground in a nearby bathroom in staccato procession. The morning air was crisp and chilly enough for layers and layers of clothing. Helen and I stayed in one of the rooms on the bottom floor. We got up and folded up our musty bedding every morning. In our guest room, we had faded flower print blankets and thin mattresses with covers.

One morning, a survivor named Kim Gun-ja walked into our room suddenly. 'The others are angry that you haven't returned two of the mugs,' she said smugly before quickly walking out. We had taken the mugs into our room for a drink of water the night before. That morning, the missing mugs were the biggest controversy to hit the home. It was as if we had stolen a family heirloom! Apparently, they counted them every morning and were quite perturbed when they found that two were missing. They also reprimanded us for missing breakfast. I profusely apologized to each of them.

When I first arrived there, I learnt the sad news that Kim Soon-duk had passed away earlier in the year. She was eighty-three at the time of her death. I stopped for a moment and felt guilt wash over me that she had died before I finished writing my book. I was further motivated to keep persevering, despite how difficult it was to travel to different countries and line up interviews through an NGO and secure a reliable translator. Sometimes I wondered if I should pack up and end the research to live a regular carefree life.

One of the caregivers, Ms Sohn, looked like your typical Korean *ajuma*, with short curly hair framing near flawless skin. She was stout and had a steely demeanour and was standoffish towards me and Helen.

She quickly explained that the women forgot people easily, so it was like starting over all the time. She listened to the same stories. 'Yes, grandma. Yes, grandma,' she said, mimicking her responses to them. The women would pinch her and hit her in a strange kind of affectionate way when she reacted like this.

One resident was nicknamed 'Ghost Grandma' because of her habit of appearing suddenly and seemingly out of nowhere. Her real name was Ji Dol-yee, and she was quite striking with her snow-white hair and powdery pale skin. She had Alzheimer's disease. Ji only conversed in Mandarin, which was the language she inherited when she was stuck in China after the war ended. She ended up marrying a Chinese man and had a daughter and a son who continued to live in China. I was set on trying to pin down Ji to ask her a few questions, but she remained elusive until the end of our trip. Whenever she entered the room, I gazed at her with fascination, staring at the pure whiteness of her hair and aura.

Another resident, named Bae Choon-hee, had an identity crisis and wished she was Japanese. She married a Chinese man after the war ended, and her son and daughter lived in China as well. She was unfriendly, almost suspicious of our intentions. I made a note to tread carefully around her. I was hopeful about our time there and had high expectations about the information I could gather about their lives before they were taken to the rape stations, about their anguish, and recovery time. I was especially curious to document how they felt towards the Japanese today, and whether they had forgiven all the men who hurt them so deeply.

Kang Il-chul was very warm for a few days, but that did not last long. She stopped talking and avoided my eyes. It was as if I had ceased to exist in her world. Once, as I snapped a photo of her at a group event when the women were taking a day trip to the city, she blocked her face with a piece of paper. Perhaps she was tired of being documented by strangers. I was sad to see that the impact of trauma was affecting her even after nearly sixty years.

One of the volunteers later explained why the women at House of Sharing were so reticent with newcomers: they didn't want to become attached to people.

I yearned to bring joy to the women that I had read about for years and wanted to connect with at a deep level. One evening in the TV viewing area, I brought a bag of scarves with me to give to the women. 'Please choose one for yourself,' I said aloud. About seven of them dove into the pile of scarves, and one complained that another had stolen the pink scarf from her while she was deciding between two colours.

I tied a scarf around Bae Choon-hee and said, 'Look in the mirror.'

'Why should I? I'm too old,' she replied. She had turquoise eye shadow and her eyes were rimmed with heavy black eyeliner. She had on a brown wig too.

'You have pretty eyes,' I told her.

'You're lying!' Bae cried and said a word in Japanese that sounded like it would be censored on TV. Her flash of anger hinted at a troubled soul. I was hurt by her reaction and shocked at how these women were so different and so much tougher than what I had imagined them to be like. But why would they be shrinking violets or demure women when out of all the victims across the Asia Pacific, they were the most resilient and survived against all odds. Feeling disappointed by this rude awakening and a loss of my idealism, I reminded myself that they had survived hell and lived to tell about it. This thought made my heart harden for the better.

After that, a sad drama about lost love came on the TV, followed by another one about a love triangle. Some of the women had tears in their eyes. They were all riveted. Their simplicity and girlishness had somehow been preserved after all these years.

Kim Gun-ja was the first resident at the house with whom I felt a connection. She was a loner and when we were watching TV she made wise cracks about the drama that everyone else ignored. I thought she was charming in a dark, jaded way. At dusk, we walked down a twisting road as the sun was setting. She was wearing a dark track jacket and had a blue and turquoise scarf tied closely around her neck. Her leather shoes were striped with light brown, olive and white. She had a bad back and walked slowly with a stoop, using a cane.

I asked about her past. 'I'm Catholic,' was all she said at first. 'Do you know why we grandmothers live together?' she asked slyly. 'Do you know what happened to us?' She was testing us to see if she could trust us with her deeply personal experiences. She knew why we were there, but she wanted to evaluate how we'd respond.

'Yes, I've heard,' I said gently. 'We wanted to see you *halmonis*.'

Then she started to open up. Kim Gun-ja suspected that her foster father, a policeman, sold her to a Korean broker for money or promotion at the age of seventeen. This Korean man had rounded up many Korean women and girls for the Japanese traffickers, and they were taken by train to Manchuria. There, she was raped systematically by 'cruel and violent' Japanese soldiers every day for three years. She was severely battered and lost hearing in one ear. Kim's heart and life were shattered, and after the war ended, she could not marry. She lived in poverty until she moved to the House of Sharing. She couldn't forgive the Japanese soldiers and had a deep hatred for current Japanese politicians. Like the others, she wanted an official apology and compensation.

It was emotional to hear her story, and we held her arms on either side of her. We showed our love and support and hoped she could feel our sincerity. Helen and I were equally honoured to be there, and to see Kim's resilience was awe-inspiring. I asked her what happened after she came back from the frontlines of war and if she managed to return home.

She was only twenty years old when the war ended. This was three years after she was first taken into captivity as a sex slave, and she was finally able to leave China and the confines of the military brothel behind. She said, 'It took me one month to get back to Korea. I took the train, and I walked a lot during that month. A few years later, the Korean War began. Then, someone I loved took drugs and died—that's why I never married. So a Catholic person visited me regularly to give me support.' I couldn't imagine the double heartache. I asked her if she had a faith to help her persevere through the hard times.

'In 1996, I realized that Catholicism was the way to heaven. I used to be a Buddhist before I converted. I have peace now, and I don't feel sad. Kim Soon-duk died, and I'm not afraid. She lived right beside me. My will to live is strong,' she said. I mentioned that I had met Kim Soon-duk too and that I was really upset that she was not here. There was a silence that resonated, and it felt like the air was pregnant with Kim Soon-duk's tiny lithe presence as we walked slowly in lockstep with Kim Gun-ja's lumbering steps.

She went on to describe the other two Catholics and one churchgoer at their house run by Buddhists. She also told us why she takes a walk every night. 'I don't want to be bedridden. Another grandma asks others to help her, give her meals. She just looks to see if anyone will help. The Chinese grandma has dementia. She says her husband wants to take her while she's watching TV,' she said.

I asked her about her family background to discern if girls from impoverished families were more vulnerable to being enslaved. Kim Gun-ja said, 'My two other sisters and I were orphaned. I had no parents to arrange my marriage. That's what they did back then. My dad died when I was ten years old, and at sixteen my mother died.' I wondered about her present health as I had heard Kim Soon-duk talk about her serious health ailments that were directly linked to her horrendous experiences in sexual servitude.

'I had an operation on my leg. I have arthritis. I had a thyroid operation, and that's why I sweat so much. I can't go anywhere because my health is weak. The other grandmas went on a day trip. They also went to China. I couldn't go. They're going to Japan.'

'Why are they going to Japan?' I asked

She responded in a fiery manner. 'To fight of course! You'll meet other grandmas tonight. Say hi and give them gifts. They'll be happy.' In hindsight, Kim Gun-ja may have been the gatekeeper in the House of Sharing, a quiet wise sage with a rational approach to communal living and the constant stream of foreign guests including Japanese tourists who came out of sheer curiosity.

We also spoke with Kang Il-chul in her room before she began to ignore us. She spoke of her life in China after she was 'freed from hell'. She became quite animated and spoke with passion. 'Seven years ago, I came here. I was living in China before. I had married a North Korean man who died during the Chinese war, during the Communist takeover in 1949. I had a hard time with my mother-in-law. I hate North Koreans, and I hate the Japanese. I worked as a support staff person at an eye and ear clinic—not as a nurse, but I did similar work. I can speak Mandarin fluently. I can turn it on at will. I have two sons, two granddaughters, and two grandsons. Both my sons work in companies in China. I went to Full Gospel Church and became a Christian when I was seventy-three years old.'

Kang married a North Korean man out of a sheer desire to survive. She hated him. But without him, she would have been sleeping on the streets. Her room was adorned with many photos of herself, as well as a picture of Jesus with a scripture verse beneath it. The most striking photo of all was a large, recent image of her standing prettily in a wedding dress, holding a bouquet of scarlet roses. Her large red lips, the most prominent feature on her face, stood out. She had taken that photograph recently because she had never had a formal wedding. There was no groom in the photograph—perhaps it was to show she didn't need a man or didn't want one. Perhaps her marriage to the North Korean man was intolerable. Many survivors have expressed their hatred for men and sex. More than anything she had shared, this photo conveyed a deep sense of loss. She still longed to have a real wedding ceremony and to wear pretty things. Her youth had been stolen from her, and she was trying to reclaim it through a solitary wedding photograph.

I offered her a scarf and tiger balm cream. 'Please take one of each,' I said.

Gifts had to be distributed fairly among the residents. She took the tiger balm cream and put her index finger to her lips. 'Shhh . . . I won't tell the others,' she said as she revealed a bruise and a Band-Aid on the back of her left knee where she would apply it.

'Do you pray,' I asked, looking around at the many Christian pictures.

'Yes.' She closed her eyes and folded her hands in front of her. With a hushed voice, she prayed, 'Why, O God was Korea under Japanese oppression for thirty-five years? And why were we taken and made to suffer so much? God, why did you allow me to be a sex slave? We still suffer and hurt. Why? God, in scripture, you said you bring justice. I know you will bring justice to this situation. I trust you and put my faith in you. Because we are poor and pitiful—that's why this young woman came here. Thank you for this day trip celebrating ancient Korean history and culture.' Then she prayed the Apostles Creed.

Her prayer was the most sorrowful thing I had heard at the House of Sharing. Did she feel that God had failed her? I was too fearful to ask her that hard question. I too was almost wondering why God let such an egregious crime against humanity to take place. A heinous war crime against countless girls and women who would later be accused of being voluntary prostitutes by the very Japanese government that made the sexual enslavement system all happen! I heard nothing but silence from heaven.

Kang put her finger to her lips again and said, 'Shhh . . .' That was the last time Kang would say a word to me. The next day, after what I thought was a bond we shared, Kang ignored me. Even as I approached her and said hello in the dining area, she hurried past me. I was disappointed but I thought it might be the impact of her deep trauma and that she was too tired to share with us anymore. I hoped that she would find healing someday.

Then there was Bae Choon-hee, with the identity issues I could relate to. Her dramatic appearance and edgy personality stood out. She explained how beautiful Japan was. She had lived in Japan as a stage singer for thirty years and sounded like a native speaker. She sang haunting songs for everyone in the house. They were very dramatic and almost comical at times.

Moon Pil-gi was the sweetest and the most gentle. In the beginning, we did not press her for much detail on her experiences. She invited us to her room where we ended up talking. It was an easy interaction with her, and we felt a bond. Helen and I talked about Moon in the evening before going to bed. She was our favourite.

Moon was forced to quit school early because her father felt it was a waste to educate girls. That was the Confucian mindset of that time. In 1942, when Moon was just fifteen, a Korean man lured her with prospects of an education and earning lots of money. She didn't say whether he was a stranger or family friend. Shortly thereafter, she was taken by train to northeast China and forced into a rape station. It was painful for her to re-tell her story to us as we cried and held hands together.

'They tried to rape me,' she said. 'They were forcing me. They were treating me as a slave, and they kicked me and hit me when I was not very good to them. They burned my skin. There was a red, burning, scorching, iron bar, and you know I still have a scar underneath my arm.'

Moon said it was mostly soldiers who raped her. The military comfort stations were surrounded by barbed wire, and she was under guard constantly. She feared she would be killed if she tried to escape. She was forced to stay at this station until the end of the war.

Like most survivors, she complained of sleep disorders and terrible nightmares.

A few days later, the women went out for their weekly demonstration in front of the Japanese embassy. They sat in chairs and wore bright yellow vests with printed banners and sashes demanding an apology and compensation from the Japanese government. Seventy people attended the weekly Wednesday demonstration, and a majority of them were Japanese tourists. Younger activists gave impassioned speeches with the aid of a megaphone. I gave a short speech calling on the Japanese government to stop treating these elderly survivors as violent protesters by having armed guards stationed in front of the embassy, but instead apologize sincerely and bring them the much-needed closure. I urged the Japanese tourists in the crowd to go back to Japan and tell others the truth about military sex slavery and this dark chapter of history in their nation.

When it was time for us to depart the House of Sharing, Moon Pil-gi cried, and so did we, as we said our goodbyes. Although a few of the women were charismatic and open to strangers, most of them had been cagey and standoffish. This was most likely a long-term impact of their experiences. They were tired. They were ageing. Morale was low. I was sorely disappointed that the women were not as talkative, and later a volunteer told me that I should have 'forced' each survivor to talk. I was shocked by her suggestion, and I was uncomfortable with the idea of making traumatized women open up against their will. Yet, even months later, I wondered if I had used the wrong approach by being too gentle and was regretful. Ultimately, the precious time I had with them was one of the most formative experiences of this season of my life as a single woman in search for a new purpose in life.

* * *

I met another survivor, named Lee Young-soo, on that trip to Seoul in 2004 at the same shelter for victims of Japanese wartime sex slavery where I stayed with survivor Hwang Geum-joo. Lee was fashionable, very smart, a natural politician, warm, and childlike. A few years after our meeting, she became a superstar spokeswoman, touring the US and speaking before politicians about the need for the Japanese government to issue an unequivocal apology and compensation to military sex slaves. I was particularly taken with Lee because she was from the same city as my maternal grandmother who must have narrowly escaped the same fate. Her porcelain oval face and features were eerily similar to my grandmother's. I was immediately comfortable with Lee and our rapport was easy, like we had known each other for years.

Lee was born in 1928 in Daegu, Korea. Her impoverished family of nine, including her grandparents, lived in a cramped house. She only had one year of formal education, but her ability to grasp complex information and communicate it in an eloquent way was an innate talent. At the age of fifteen, she was drafted into the Voluntary Labour Corps. In the fall of 1944, when she turned sixteen, she was lured away into military sex slavery with her friend Kim Pun-san. The women usually described Korean middlemen or Japanese soldiers who did the luring. I always feel gutted when I hear that they were fifteen or sixteen—those are the years of carefree self-exploration, the puberty years of awkward interactions with boys, and personal awakenings unique to youth. All of that was stolen from Lee and the others.

On the way to a Taiwanese rape station, she was beaten and tortured. 'It was my first ride on a train, and I vomited,' she said. 'I called for my mother because I was sick. The Japanese soldier came, pulled on my ponytail, and banged my head on the floor. He did this to the other girls too. And to this day, I can still hear a noise ringing in my head. I told the older girls I missed my parents and wanted to go home. I longed to see my mother. That's what I said. And the Japanese soldier hit me again because he said I was using Korean. The older women advised me to use actions rather than words.'

Before they were ordered onto the boat, Lee knelt down and desperately prayed to God for help. 'As I was praying, a Japanese soldier came and kicked me. He followed us all the time. He kicked me as I was praying and weeping, and if my friend hadn't caught me, I would've fallen over into the water,' she said.

On the boat ride to Taiwan, Lee was raped for the first time, and the attacks continued. She blacked out for the rest of the voyage. When the time came to disembark from the ship, she could no longer walk properly. She was struck in the head and lost consciousness during a bombing of the underground shelter she took refuge in with the other women and the comfort station proprietor. They were soon moved to another bomb shelter where she was forced to serve soldiers. She caught a venereal disease and was given injections of compound 606 to sterilize her.

Despite the harsh conditions, Lee eventually made it home to her family. No one asked her about her experiences. Lee suspects they could guess what had happened to her and their hearts were broken over it. Her mother overcompensated by lavishing her with extra attention and love, treating her like a child in a sheltered life. They lived together until her mother died when Lee was forty-eight years old.

Lee managed to eke out a living through sales work, and I could imagine that she excelled at it by charming customers. She hiked at six o'clock every morning and maintained a wide circle of friends in different parts of the world. An avid shopper, Lee's wardrobe was filled with expensive and beautiful clothing. Compared to the women I met at House of Sharing, Lee seemed like she had worked through most of her pain.

When asked if her *han*—the Korean word for everlasting woe and resentment—had been eased at all, Lee replied, 'I meet a lot of young people, but I can't ask young people to relieve my *han*. The Japanese government has to resolve my *han*. If I have *han* or nurture it, it ruins my health. So, in some ways, I don't want to resolve my *han* for the younger generation. It is a fighting strength. Some *han* is released by talking to people or going to protests and seeing many younger people. When I speak with young people like you, my *han* is released a little. I believe it'll be healed by the younger generation continuing to fight for justice and by the legacy we leave. I don't think it'll be released while I'm alive. There has been a hint of relief through the Korean government as they are trying, to some degree, to resolve the redress issue with the Japanese government. But the Japanese government has not done anything to relieve my pain.'

I believe this unresolved never-ending *han* is what I carry too, an intangible trait that reminds me of a line from a Jewish psalm that describes 'deep calls to deep'—something that has been passed down generationally and now, we as a people collectively possess and grapple with. And perhaps it is what I felt, an awareness that hit me like a lightning bolt, when I first heard about the wartime sex slaves.

* * *

It was after meeting Kim Soon-duk, that I committed to writing *Silenced No More: Voices of Comfort Women*. As part of my research for this book, I met many survivors from other countries, including China, the Netherlands, the Philippines, and Taiwan over a ten-year period. Their stories were heartbreaking and had tragic parallels to those told by the Korean women such as being stripped of their identities and given Japanese names, being trapped in a prison at the military brothels, and experiencing long torturous line-ups of soldiers waiting to rape them. The soldiers had comfort station tickets and condoms in hand which implies a very methodical and organized system implemented by the Japanese government.

Most of the survivors I interviewed have sadly passed away. But in China, shockingly, wartime sex slavery survivors are still coming forward.

By speaking with these women and the activists who are fighting to raise awareness, I am deeply convinced that the Japanese government must bring closure and healing to these survivors and their families while a handful of them are still alive through a direct unequivocal apology and by taking full legal and moral responsibility for enslaving these women and girls before and during the WWII.

These elderly women, in their twilight years, are like pine trees, known as the *sonamu* in Korea. The *sonamu* is unusually tough, and its leaves remain rich green through all seasons—harsh winds, scorching sunshine, and blustery monsoons. The *sonamu* will sprout in impossibly craggy landscapes, no matter what the season is. Its resilience has afforded it great significance as a national symbol of the Korean people who have endured attacks from invading forces over centuries. Ever unchanging, the *sonamu's* roots wind deep into the earth and give it strength. The survivors' strong will to live is the same. They are dignified, immensely strong, and stately. While they may never receive the long-awaited sincere apology from the Japanese government in their lifetime—an apology that brings closure and healing—their painful stories have raised global awareness of the horrors of sexual violence against women and children in war zones. They have shown the world that such crimes must not be tolerated or ignored.

# 7

# Repentant Japanese Soldiers

Some of the most inspiring moments I've experienced while researching Japanese military sex slavery for my book were during my meetings with three former Japanese soldiers—Waichi Okumura, Tetsuro Takahashi, and Yasuji Kaneko. I met and interviewed them in 2005, a year after my trip to Korea, when I travelled to Tokyo, Japan to gather information for my book. I felt it was the pinnacle of my search for historical truth to be able to sit down with former Japanese soldiers, who were perceived to be the 'evil' perpetrators. Of all the meetings I've had for my book, I was the most stressed about interviewing these men. For days, I deliberated over what questions to ask—way more than I had prepared for my interview with the survivors.

I learned from these men in separate individual meetings that following their repatriation to Japan from internment as war criminals in China, these three joined the Association of Returnees from China, often referred to as Chukiren, which was launched in 1957. One of the aims of this association was to promote Japan–China friendship and lobby for formal diplomatic relations between the two countries, which ultimately happened in 1972.

What was haunting me was a story my mother told me about my great-grandmother's younger brother who was allegedly a general in the Korean division of the Japanese military in the 1930s. This coincided with when the Japanese invaded Manchuria. Those were also the early days of when the Japanese began to systematically coerce and traffic girls and women into wartime brothels in Manchuria and other cities. This great-great uncle had graduated from Meiji University in Japan, so for him to be a ranking official in the army was a possibility but I wouldn't know for sure. I had no way to confirm his role, and I had mentioned this only to a few people I could trust. Later, he wrote and published his memoirs and my mother had a copy of it, but we couldn't find it during the time I was searching for confirmation. Before another trip to Korea with my younger sister Jayne, my mother asked this relative to give me an interview about *wianbu*—the Korean term for women forced into sex slavery for the Japanese military.

He agreed to it and looked forward to see me and my sister. But, to my utter regret even today, my great-uncle forbade me from going to see great-great uncle in Daegu, out of fear that he would die of shock from my pointed questions. I was very frustrated but the Korean side of me that respects my elders won out, and I submitted to my great-uncle's unilateral decision. Some months later, he passed away. I do believe he had witnessed these women and would have been able to share something substantial. However, I was grateful to have these meetings with the former Japanese soldiers, which were set up by an NGO though I cannot remember the contact. My great-great uncle's memory and my unanswered questions were the driving force behind these interviews with the three former soldiers.

These three Japanese men told me that for more than five decades they and other members of Chukiren spoke of their involvement in war crimes, even after the association dissolved in 2002. I sensed they were seeking closure, or perhaps forgiveness, before they died. They were looking for young people to carry on their legacy in Japan's peace movement. Each of these ex-soldiers had experienced a watershed moment, a turning point that caused them to confront Japanese cultural traditions and glorification of war. These brave men, who were eyewitnesses and perpetrators themselves, have become some of the most loyal and unexpected supporters of survivors of Japanese wartime atrocities. I was surprised I hadn't heard of them before, and I wanted the world to know about their wonderful support for victims of Japanese military sex slavery.

These three former soldiers were transferred to China after having lived in horrible conditions in a Soviet Gulag camp. At the end of the war, the Soviet Army captured Japanese soldiers in Manchuria and took them to prisoner-of-war camps in the Soviet Union. Tens of thousands of Japanese soldiers are thought to have died in the Gulags, and thousands remained in captivity until December 1956 before they were able to return to Japan. The Soviet Union used the Japanese as part of their labour force and held them for longer than the other Allies.

In what is known as the Miracle of Fushun, the Chinese at the Fushun War Criminals Management Centre gave amnesty to two of the former soldiers I met. This was an amazing turning point in their lives. During their time in Fushun, Takahashi and Kaneko scoured their souls to examine their own loyal worship of their emperor and the impact the war crimes by Japanese soldiers had on the victims and their families. They empathized in such a profound way that they were able to endure accusations by Japanese nationalists that they had been brainwashed by the Chinese Communists.

* * *

Waichi Okumura is one of the few Japanese who is critical of his country's prime ministers visiting the Yasukuni Shrine. I was impressed to learn during my research before our meeting that he had refused to see the deceased soldiers as gods. He was born on 13 July 1924 and conscripted into the military in November 1944. At the time I met him, a Japanese activist told me that he was a high-profile anti-war activist, a man on a mission to find the truth behind why he was forced to stay behind in China after the war ended in 1945. I found articles written about him and there is a film too. He was also an active supporter of survivors of Imperial Japanese military sex slavery, and I was particularly interested in this aspect of his life.

I met Okumura in a small restaurant with chic sixties-style furnishing and a cosy smokers' atmosphere. Dressed in a turtleneck and black jacket, he shook my hand as I did an awkward East–West mix of bowing my head and shaking his hands with both of mine at the same time. A friend of a friend, Keiko, volunteered to help translate for me. She brought along her good friend, Tomoko Hasegawa, who was piqued by Okumura's story and in my book-writing journey. She was touched by his honesty and his pain. Tomoko was a reed-thin woman in her forties who spoke fluent Mandarin and worked as a professional translator. This meeting turned out to be a huge inspiration and turning point for Tomoko who would later go on to meet Cindy Goh, a Singaporean businesswoman based in China. With Cindy's driving vision, together they would lead a group of Japanese that travelled to China to apologize to wartime sex slave survivors for what the Japanese soldiers had inflicted upon them. They called themselves Healing River-Rainbow Bridge and their work was powerfully healing for the survivors and their families.

Okumura was a meek man. I was expecting a charismatic alpha-type, but he was surprisingly timid. The first thing I noticed was that he could not look me in the eye. His eyes darted everywhere else and never met my gaze. I was troubled by this and thought that he wasn't used to a direct, strong Korean woman. In an attempt to put him at ease and lighten things up, I jokingly shared with him that I was a 'banana'—Korean on the outside but solidly Western in my mindset on the inside. This seemed to do the trick and Okumura relaxed a little and started telling his story.

He had been in Shanxi, China after the war ended and fought in the civil war with Chiang Kai-shek's Kuomintang against the

Communist forces led by Mao Zedong. He had never met a Korean Canadian woman before but told me he had seen many Korean military 'comfort women' in China, and he had heard the elderly survivors bear witness many times. I observed a softness and compassion in his eyes as he spoke of the women and my trust and appreciation for him grew.

Okumura wanted the atrocities committed by the Japanese military to be recorded truthfully, and he wanted an investigation into why a large group of Japanese soldiers were left behind in China after Japan surrendered. This impulse took him to China three times after the war. He had been featured in a documentary called *The Ants* which portrayed his efforts to expose the secret Japanese military orders that stole eleven years of his life and stripped him of his military pension upon his return to Japan because of his involvement with the Kuomintang. On official record, Okumura and the other soldiers were considered 'volunteers' in the Chinese nationalist military. They battled this claim in the courts to prove that the Japanese military had forced them to stay in China against their will. I admired his will of steel and willingness to sacrifice and take a gutsy stand.

The eighty-four-year-old said he had never killed or used sex slaves, but he had stood guard while other soldiers raped local women. I was looking directly in his eyes as he spoke about the sex slaves, and I could sense that he was aware of it and he expressed sorrow over their plight. He had met victims of wartime sex slavery in the comfort stations in China and spoke with soldiers who had raped them on a regular basis. He and 2,600 other Japanese soldiers were fighting against the Communists until he was captured by them in 1949. Then he spent the next seven years as a prisoner of war.

He was twenty years old in 1945 when the war ended. He said the Korean people—both comfort women and soldiers—were sent back after the war ended. The Kuomintang leader, Chiang Kai-Shek, separated Koreans and Japanese. There were 2,600 Japanese soldiers left in China, and they didn't know why they were not permitted to return home like everyone else. He eventually learned that they had no choice but to fight for Chiang Kai-Shek as volunteers. Years later, he learned that in March 1946, his name along with the names of the other Japanese soldiers were eliminated from an official list of soldiers in Japan. I could empathize with his obsessive quest for closure and to learn what happened to him that led him back to China several times. He said he was shocked when he finally learned the truth. 'I found out ten years later in 1956, when I finally arrived home in Japan, the government didn't want to admit they left their soldiers in China,' he said with disappointment and hurt in his eyes all these years later.

He then divulged a revelation that rocked me. He said that there were military sex slaves even after the war ended, and they were systematically raped for three years. It was incredulous, and I had never heard or read of this anywhere else nor could I find a second source to corroborate it. 'Yes, there were comfort women during the three years,' he confirmed.

The Japanese soldiers captured girls from neighbouring villages whenever they went out on the field to fight, Okumura further explained. 'The number of girls captured was usually much larger than the girls at the comfort station headquarters. When the Japanese troops gathered in a place, the first thing they did was build a comfort station. It was inevitable for the soldiers to get comfort women to encourage them to fight.'

'Why was it inevitable?' I asked, feeling a sense of outrage. 'Some Chinese girls were sold by their parents because they were very poor,' he said. 'Not all daughters were sold like that. Some were forced. In Japan, the same thing happened as it did in China. When the farmers didn't have much money but had a lot of children, they resorted to selling their daughters who were considered of less value and esteem than sons. It was considered normal to sell young girls into sex work. There was a military headquarters in Shanxi and an official comfort station where some of the women were sold by their parents.'

He confirmed the cycle of gender discrimination and what I had heard from the women at Door of Hope in China. Many of them were rejected by their parents for being female and that was one of a myriad of reasons that led to their sexual exploitation.

I asked him if the Communists used military comfort women? But he didn't know and had not seen Chinese soldiers rape local Chinese women. 'Some Korean women married Japanese soldiers and formed families. However, after the war, the Communist government couldn't accept that they were married and forced them to leave, thus separating husband and wife. The Communist military did not use comfort women,' he said.

On holidays, senior soldiers visited comfort stations. The generals and the captains of the military would use Japanese prostitutes who went to China to earn more money as it was deemed an honour to be able to serve the nation by 'serving' the soldiers. The next level below were officer types, and they could only use Korean comfort women. The lowest foot soldiers were given Chinese comfort women. This was an awful hierarchy based on racial discrimination that was imposed on the women in the military brothels. The Japanese women were set aside for the top-ranking officials while Korean and Chinese women, who were considered inferior, were offered to lesser ranking soldiers. In other countries, the darker-skinned women were mistreated the most and cost the least according to the tickets to the 'comfort stations' made available to soldiers.

Okumura confirmed that he met Korean women who were deceived and told they would be dancing entertainers for the military but to their shock they were raped and entrapped in forced prostitution.

Before this meeting, I resolved to understand how Japanese men in military uniforms could justify their rape of the women in the military brothels. Did they not see the young girls as human? 'How did the Japanese soldiers perceive the military comfort women?' I asked.

He took a deep breath and responded, 'In those days, there were brothels and prostitutes everywhere in Japan. It was perceived as normal for men, so soldiers did not think it was evil or immoral since it was accepted in our Japanese culture. Two condoms were distributed by the state health department to each and every soldier so they would not contract venereal diseases. The soldiers who used comfort stations knew nothing about the girls' poor backgrounds. They assumed these girls came for the money and were paid by the government, so they did not feel any guilt.'

'What else do you know of the military comfort women in your area?'

He paused and looked mournful. 'The soldiers were paid three yen a month. When they went to use a comfort woman, they had to pay 1.5 yen each time. They paid half their monthly salary for fifteen minutes with a comfort woman. Many soldiers grumbled after coming back from the comfort stations. Each woman had to deal with four men per hour. There were lines, lines, lines for this girl, that girl. There were highly favoured girls, and officers fought against each other to monopolize their favourite. I felt bad on hearing this. I also saw officers fighting and saying, "I want to take that girl." The troops who were far from the headquarters could only go to the comfort stations on holidays or special occasions, so they had to find and capture the women themselves. Those units of troops usually ambushed and kidnapped the local women. They raped them so they would not have to pay. The soldiers then brought them back to the makeshift camp where they built huts and used the girls until they were no longer able to have sex. I don't know about the number of girls. They just went to villages nearby and even raped old ladies.'

I was horrified to hear of the grandmas being raped too. It was inhuman. 'Why do you think they raped these women?' I asked with an aching heart, almost afraid of his answer.

'Lust drives them. Soldiers went to neighbouring villages to steal and loot, and then they sold the goods to finance their visits to the comfort station. When the Communist Party became stronger, the soldiers couldn't go to villages to pillage anymore, or else they'd risk getting killed. At the end of the war in August of 1945, we knew the war was officially over. Chiang Kai-Shek ordered us to stop all comfort station operations. But we were forced to stay behind and form a new army division. A comfort station was built, as usual, and more were established as the raping of locals continued. I've read many published diaries of Japanese soldiers. The first thing the Japanese military did when they arrived at a new location was open up a bar to offer liquor, and the comfort women or bargirls would be in the back. There were bars for soldiers everywhere.'

'How do you feel about the comfort women now?' I asked gently.

'We need forgiveness,' he said before falling silent for a moment. I was astonished by his mention of forgiveness and examined his eyes and face to discern if he was speaking from his heart. 'My words are not enough. There's a big difference between the way the Chinese and the Japanese view the war. In China, people can specifically say that "the war affected my family like this" or "the war affected my family like that". It is very specific. But in Japan, people say "Hiroshima and Nagasaki were bombed" or "Tokyo was bombed". The Japanese people do not talk about how the war affected their families directly. In China, they know how their ancestors suffered. It is important to talk about family matters. Then we can talk about war, and therefore take a closer look at the Second World War and wars in general.'

I resonated with his insights and believed that he hit the heart of the conflict between the people groups and their perspectives on war crimes.

In 2002, a male librarian in Japan introduced Okumura to Liu Mian Huan, a survivor from Shanxi province. The librarian wanted Okumura to financially support some of the former sex slaves.

'After I told her my story, Liu suggested that I share my experiences publicly,' Okumura said.

A tender and highly unlikely friendship formed between them. They were both survivors on opposite sides of the war in China. He met her again a few years later in 2005. Their beautiful bond helped each of them recover from pain and walk on the road to redemptive healing by forgiving those who hurt them unspeakably. In 2002, he also met Wan Ai Hua, a survivor and vocal activist from Mainland China, whom I had met in 2004.

'Wan Ai Hua was supposed to be doing farm work in the field, but it was too hot for her,' he said. 'She fainted when she realized the Japanese soldiers were planning to rape her and then put her in prison. It was so painful for her to remember the past, and when we went to the place where she was tortured, it was emotionally difficult for her. I had known of their existence because senior soldiers used these Chinese women as sex slaves, but it was when I met them in person that I began to really feel their pain. Wan Ai Hua was the sub-chief of her village. She was very talented and had power. She was also part of the underground Communist Party during the war with Japan. Now she is a very earnest Buddhist, despite the fact that Communism and Buddhism are totally at odds in beliefs and ideology. Marx does not believe in God. But she totally changed.'

It was fascinating to hear his precise recollection of Wan's story. I had interviewed Wan the year before in Mainland China, and yet he had more insight into her emotional state at different periods of her life and the conflict within over Buddhism and Communism. It gave him more credibility, and I believed that he sympathized with the survivors and even felt a burdensome shame and guilt towards them. Okumura, at eight-four, still had a sharp mind. He was easily underestimated because of his mild manners and diminutive stature.

I wanted to hear his perceptions on why the Japanese public and government were ignoring the Japanese military sex slavery survivors.

'It is because if the government admits all these facts, it means the government and the emperor are guilty of unsound acts. I do not believe the Japanese government will admit they ordered us to stay or that they forced women into sex slavery. If the government admits to wrong-doings, then it will collapse. Even after the war, the Japanese government insisted on using the same nationalistic anthem that praises the emperor, and they continued to use the very flag that flew over all their military operations as they invaded other nations. I think these things should be replaced by a new anthem and a new flag. All teachers and students are supposed to stand up when we sing the national anthem, but some teachers are against nationalism and do not stand up. Oftentimes, teachers who don't stand up to honour the flag are reported on. It is the worst in Tokyo.'

It dawned on me that he sees a parallel to his unresolved case and these women who have been grievously ignored. I asked if he believed that the survivors of Japanese military sex slavery would never hear an apology. He replied with passion in his voice, 'The government must apologize to comfort women survivors. This is an issue of human rights. If our mother was misused or disgraced, can we be silent? If our mothers were raped, we'd feel terrible. Wherever the Japanese soldiers went, almost every woman was raped in all of the villages. I wanted to have my own spontaneous truth and reconciliation commission, and I have come forward to testify on my own.'

'Have you forgiven yourself?'

'I've done things for which I cannot forgive myself,' he confessed. 'But I did not rape anyone. I guarded those who did. Everyone works together in a military unit, and each has a role. I feel collective guilt. It is not only the military but Japan itself. I am a member of this community. I'm an offender and also a victim. The Chinese people we fought against were also victims and offenders because they killed the Japanese too. That's what war is.'

Okumura's staggering honesty was impactful, and I admit I didn't expect it from an older Japanese man, let alone a former soldier.

He could not forget his first murder, so he made peace with his past during one particular trip in China. He returned to the killing field, where, in February 1945, he was ordered by his officer to stab and kill an innocent Chinese with a bayonet. He remembered clearly that was when he realized he became a murderer, and a Japanese 'devil', a term the Chinese used for Japanese soldiers. What intensely troubled him was that war could happen again.

'It is really dangerous,' he said. 'The spirit of militarism is rising. I want all the military bases to be out of Japan. I want the younger generation to know how miserable and evil it is in war. In war, it is justified to kill people. I want to bear witness and tell people how horrible war is. Japan should be totally independent. All the things we left in China are under the command of the American government. We're still under the influence of the US, and I believe the Americans and Allies must apologize to the Japanese.'

Like the former sex slaves for the military, he too was haunted. He was compelled to find the answer and some closure as to why he wasted eleven years in China. He kept asking himself why he had to stay behind. He filed a lawsuit in 2001 to sue the Japanese government with twelve other soldiers who were left in China, but he lost the case even though they had evidence of being left behind by a military order. The Supreme Court rejected the soldiers' final appeal.

'The order to stay in China is said to have come from the headquarters of troops, but I believe it came from Tokyo, and the government was in charge. I'd like to find the evidence. So far, I have paid 1.6 million yen for archival government documents. I haven't found anything yet. We want compensation for those lost years. But money is not the issue. I just want the Japanese government to acknowledge that they were the ones to order us to stay. But the government is indifferent to us.'

Due to years of smoking and drinking, Okumura has had two different kinds of cancers in his throat, and chemotherapy will not help. He laughs at the irony. 'I never had a fear of death during the war, and now I do after the doctor told me I have cancer. My body hurts. But in the past, I got shot, and I shot others too.'

We said our goodbyes and he humbly bowed. 'Okumura-san, I pray that you'll be released from your guilt and shame,' I said to him as I held his hand. His eyes were still dark pools. 'I hope you'll find true freedom.'

He bowed again humbly. Then, there was a visible impact on him, as if a weight had been lifted off his shoulders. He finally looked me in the eyes, and there seemed to be more peace. His eyes became still.

Because of our language barrier, I didn't have the honour of keeping in touch with my new friend. But I would occasionally look him up on the Internet. One day I learned of his passing and it left me feeling downcast.

Okumura passed away on 25 May 2011 in Nakano, Tokyo. What a loss for humanity. It was incredibly remarkable that a former Japanese soldier was one of the most noble and powerful advocates for the survivors of wartime sex slavery. He was a renegade in his own culture, who had faced his past and his demons, and transcended the prevailing attitudes of his country. His work lives on and can never be extinguished.

* * *

The next former Japanese soldier I met was Tetsuro Takahashi.

Before we arrived at his apartment, my translator Yumiko told me that there were three taboo topics in Japan: military comfort women, the Nanjing Massacre, and the emperor. She blindsided me with these controlling rules right before the interview. She was a connection from the NGO in Tokyo that helped set up these meetings with the soldiers, and I was taken aback by these sudden conditions during this interview. What was the reason for this? My mind raced and my heart beat faster. I could feel my stress levels rise. She was at least fifteen years older than me and exerted a Tiger woman vibe. I smiled demurely as my thoughts raced on how to ask about military sex slaves. I was intent on getting my information no matter what—otherwise, what was the point of the meeting!

When Takahashi answered the door, he was dressed in a grey sweater and slacks. He radiated intelligence and civility. He greatly reminded me of my mother's uncle. Both were tall, gazelle-like, sophisticated, and contemporaries. It helped me overcome any apprehension and feel comfortable with him. He asked his wife to get us some tea and snacks; he spoke kindly and was attentive to both Yumiko and me.

As soon as I pulled my recorder out, he said, 'I have no direct experience with Chinese and Korean comfort women. While in Jinan, I went to a restaurant called Sakura, and it was a comfort station. In another rural area, there were about ten Korean women in a comfort station.' I was astonished by his slick and direct answer from the get go that reminded me of an experienced public relations operator. He must have been interviewed by the media many times. Despite my translator's protests, he himself directly addressed the taboo topic of wartime forced prostitution. I was relieved.

I asked him if racism had a major role in the enslavement of Koreans and Chinese as Japanese military sex slaves. He gave me a direct and nuanced honest answer.

'Japan has such discrimination towards Koreans and Chinese, but it is not always overt. I was raised to have discriminatory attitudes towards Koreans and Chinese. Basically, Japanese children are educated to discriminate against them, and this still remains as an undercurrent in society. The military sex slavery issue is very much a result of this racial discrimination,' he said. 'In the Greater East Asia Co-Prosperity Sphere, the Japanese were superior among the Asians. As part of the basic policy, the Japanese government established a shrine in every colony and forced everyone to bow and worship the emperor.'

Takahashi was born on 15 February 1921 in Miyazaki prefecture in Kyushu. His was a typical childhood. After the end of WWI up until the 1930s was an era of economic depression. He said his studies, especially history class at school, and everything else at that time revolved around the emperor because he was considered to be god. It was the 'emperor religion'. He remembers that when a child was born, every family had the emperor's photo to pray to, and he compared it to the cult worship of Kim Jong-il in North Korea. 'But in Japan it was more intense than in North Korea because there was no information about anything else at that time,' he said. 'My parents prayed to the emperor every morning, and we did the same at elementary school. For history lessons, we studied the emperor's family tree and names of all the emperors. Everyone believed the emperor was the most important person. No one in the entire society doubted that.'

At twenty, he graduated from the Osaka Foreign Language University in 1941. At this time, he says that all Japanese men were conscripted into the military. He worked briefly for a trading company in China, but in February of 1944 he was drafted into the military and assigned to the 59th Division that was stationed in Shandong. That's where he stayed until 1959.

During this time, Takahashi also lost control of his life and his choices and he was 'conscripted' as a foot soldier against his will. He described this pivotal crossroads in his life both matter-of-factly and with the sense that it was a momentous time of crossing over from a regular civilian life into the frontlines of the horrors of war.

I wanted to know more of his role in the military. He said, 'I was trained for six months. In October of 1944, after the training, I joined the communications and propaganda department. I created musical theatres to promote the Japanese military to the Chinese as a way to counter the Chinese resistance movement. Right now, there's a Right-wing movement in Japan, and they say that Japan was not the aggressor. We need to learn the truth of our past history.

Without that, there will be no peace in Japan's future. This Right-wing movement is very dangerous.'

I was surprised to hear a former soldier express eloquently the need for historical truth. I asked him to explain if he and the Japanese soldiers knew they were raping the women and causing life-long harm at the military brothels or comfort stations, and he brought up the issue of gender discrimination and damaging sexist attitudes. 'At that time, women were discriminated against. They did not have voting rights. Personally, I did not discriminate. But the prostitution system was widespread, and it was not illegal to use a prostitute. During university, I visited prostitutes with my friends. It was part of the culture of the time. These prostitutes mainly came from the northern areas where many poor parents sold their daughters to brothel owners. The Japanese soldiers did not believe they were being aggressive with the women in the comfort stations or villages. They justified their actions. I personally did not know about rape at that time. The frontline soldiers frequently raped, and that was different from the comfort stations in their mind. It was legal for them to use military comfort women.'

Takahashi did not seem to think it was morally wrong to use prostitutes. That mindset is still prevalent today. Many men in Asia continue to use prostitutes as evidenced by the flourishing and widespread sex trade. I was feeling infuriated inside at his nonchalant response. After meeting so many women who had suffered the unspeakable and had their lives destroyed, I was in disbelief at his flippant answer. At this point, I challenged him but he couldn't detect my deep annoyance. It was a dead end, so I tried another tack and asked for his views on the Right-wing ideology of whitewashing the historical truth of Japanese military wartime forced prostitution. 'How is the Right-wing ideology dangerous for the future?' I asked.

'The fact that people deny and blame the comfort women as voluntary prostitutes is the most shameful point of this comfort women issue. The Right-wingers want to conceal that this happened.

To prevent repeating such aggression, we must learn the history of military aggression against China and Korea. I can understand what the Chinese and Korean survivors of Japanese wartime atrocities feel and why they cannot forgive the Japanese military. History should not be distorted. It should be corrected.'

Though I knew he was empathetic, his verbal expression of compassion for the survivors was truly powerful. I softened towards him.

For so long I had animosity towards the perpetrators. Meeting him helped lessen the hate I felt for Japanese soldiers. I wondered out loud what had led him to his extraordinary convictions.

He paused and then explained, 'After the war, I was detained for six years and then taken to Siberia for five years to do forced labour until 1950. I worked in a coal mine in Siberia. There were more than 2,000 concentration camps and 600,000 Japanese soldiers. It was a terrible experience working in such dangerous conditions. At least 60,000 soldiers died in the camp. We were treated very cruelly.'

It was hard to connect his cruel experiences with his now-serene expression. His hatred for his tormentors was tangible. I had to ask the obvious question to hear more, 'How do you feel about the Soviets?'

He responded calmly, but there was an underlying anger. 'I hate them. My time in Siberia was like hell. I have hatred for Soviets. It was awful. We had to work in construction of a railway line and a road. There were German and Polish soldiers in the camp too. Our prime minister will negotiate with Russia on Japanese prisoners of war in Siberia. I'm not demanding compensation on the Siberia issue, but there is such a movement in Japan.'

He told me that in 1950, the USSR sent Takahashi and 1,100 Japanese soldiers to a concentration camp in Fushun, Liaoning province in China. He remained there until 1956. The Chinese treated the Japanese soldiers well and humanely. By 1950, there were almost 600,000 soldiers repatriated to Japan from Siberia.

The time in China proved to be a life-changing time. 'We reviewed what we did in China and learned that Japan was the aggressor and realized how brutally we had treated the Koreans and the Chinese. We reviewed the atrocities that were committed. We learned these things in China when we were treated well. In Siberia, it was too cold at minus twenty degrees, and there was no time to think because of the forced labour work.'

The Japanese soldiers who experienced the Miracle of Fushun were surprised to be treated with dignity and given Japanese meals and medical treatment. They were 're-educated' by confessing their 'sinful acts' and reflecting on them. In 1956, military tribunals were held in China, and only forty-five were indicted. All of the former soldiers, including those convicted, were allowed to return to Japan by 1964. Charges against Takahashi too were dropped.

On returning, Takahashi and the others were able to do some soul searching and realize how they had brought so much pain on people like themselves. For Takahashi, this time in China was revolutionary and caused him to abandon his loyalty to the emperor, even though he had grown up worshipping him and fighting the war for him. He humbly divulged to me a transformative insight that reflected a remarkable self-awareness: he began to see that he was in 'bondage' to what he now deemed as the 'Imperial cult'. His worldview changed even more after reading the writings of Mao Zedong.

'This concentration camp period is a very important part of my life. I have spoken out against war and want to prevent war from happening again at all costs. Let war never happen again. We were placed into two camps in China: in Taiyuan, there were 100 soldiers, and in Fushun there were 960 of us. A total of forty-seven people died in both camps. There were 1,062 former soldiers who were able to return to Japan. I did not file a lawsuit in court, but I have helped Taiyuan soldier returnees for forty years.'

According to Takahashi, officials have re-opened Fushun as a museum. In the area of Fushun, more than 3,000 women and children were massacred by the Japanese with machine guns. In February of 1956, he had a chance to tour China and listen to the stories of massacre survivors during the war. 'It is a tragedy. There were some survivors who were ten years old at the time and are about seventy now,' he said. 'The survivors shared how they lost their parents, brothers, sisters, and children. We were totally shocked.'

We were on similar journeys of hearing survivors tell their truth after decades of being silenced or ignored. In 1957, after Takahashi and the other former soldiers who were imprisoned in China were repatriated back to Japan, they formed the Chukiren peace group. He was the former secretary-general of Chukiren.

In Kawagoe in Saitama prefecture, documents detailing the confessions by 300 Japanese veterans to crimes such as rape and murder of civilians are exhibited at the Chukiren Peace Memorial Museum. The museum raises awareness of Japan's human rights violations in China and other nations—a side of the war that is rarely in the spotlight in Japanese society. The Chinese Embassy in Japan provided more than 5,000 pages of handwritten testimonies by former soldiers in concentration camps in China. After Chukiren was dissolved in 2002 because many of its members had died, its activities were taken over by a new group associated with the museum with several members in their twenties and thirties.

'I support the military comfort women and their fight for an apology,' said Takahashi. 'It is important because more than sixty-four years have already passed. In Japan, the comfort women issue is not resolved as a war crime. It is critical to recognize war crimes and the need for compensation to victims in China and Korea. But this remains unresolved. Activists and survivors are trying to find resolution in court for individual claims. I think it is very natural for victims. It was the nation's crime after all.'

He demanded that Japan as a nation apologize and provide compensation to all victims including military sex slaves or those he referred to as 'comfort women'. I wholeheartedly agreed with him.

'Japan committed war crimes, so the government needs to apologize. This is very important and means reconciliation. The reality is that compensation is urgently needed for victims. We must consider their feelings and needs. But the Japanese government and the Right-wing want to see the war as meaningful and don't want to think that it was useless or that it was a bad war.'

I've interviewed countless Chinese across China on their attitudes towards the Japanese and whether war crimes from WWII had any impact on their views. Just about every person I spoke with unanimously expressed their racial hatred for the Japanese for denying that the women were forced into wartime sex slavery and their responsibility in massacres such as the Rape of Nanking.

He had noticed discrimination from the Chinese too. But in spite of the discrimination and lack of trust he sensed from the Chinese, the work of Takahashi and his Chukiren members persevered, and they were courageous in bearing witness and standing for peace. They were important early bridges of healing and conciliation with the Chinese, and their acts of confession and repentance were indeed worthwhile.

Building friendship between Japan and China was a major tenet of Chukiren. In the 1950s and 1960s, they drove the movement to return the remains of the Chinese victims of forced labour and to improve political ties between the two countries at a time when there were no diplomatic relations between them.

China's Cultural Revolution, which began in 1966, complicated matters. 'The staff at the camps who treated me and the other Japanese soldiers humanely were now blamed for their kind treatment of Japanese people, and were severely persecuted,' said Takahashi.

Takahashi strongly supported the Japan–China friendship movement, even when he experienced persecution for it. He continued to testify about his time in China and his regret over the atrocities inflicted on the Chinese. He also supported lawsuits filed by Chinese war victims in Japanese courts. He was responsible for

Chukiren's quarterly publication *Association of Returnees from China*, which fought against revisionist historians.

At the end of our interview, I expressed my wish for reconciliation as a Korean woman. I told him that God forgives him. I wanted to say more but I was aware of Yumiko's gaze on me. His eyes and entire face lit up. He looked like a different man from when we first sat down on the couch. His shoulders relaxed and a sense of peace came upon us. He thanked me several times and seemed to enjoy our time together. I wondered if I should have said more to him as I gave him a hug and a kiss on the face spontaneously as a cheeky Western gesture and said goodbye.

* * *

I was euphoric about my successful interview with Takahashi. I knew that his many surprising revelations would help enrich my book. Yumiko and I walked to the subway to go to our next venue, to meet another former soldier. I had been told in advance that our next interviewee had committed rapes during the war. Since I had met and interviewed and cried with some survivors of Japanese military sexual servitude, I was feeling enormous pressure over meeting a soldier who might have raped them. I had to quell the inner conflict and the deep unease within, and I resolved to push forward to tell the world about what happened to the women.

Yasuji Kaneko's hands had trembled when he was first ordered to kill. Over time, it became a mindless chore for him. When we arrived at his home, his wife gave us a sweet, polite smile and welcomed us in. She was aloof, and I sensed not entirely in total harmony with her husband's decision to talk about his past rapes. I felt sorry for her. I am certain that the issue of military sex slavery was a highly sensitive one for her because her husband had often visited the comfort stations.

We sat down on the *tatami* floor mat of their sitting room. I had to pinch myself for a moment because it was so surreal that I was about to interview Kaneko. There was tension but it could have been my concern over getting the right information. He seemed thick-skinned and ready to talk. I tried to discern if I could trust him and I sensed he was a simple, honest man seeking closure and the truth just like me.

I mentioned that we had just met with Takahashi, and I had interviewed Okumura the other night. These men had become very close over the years thanks to their shared experiences in the prison camps after the war. In order to try to break what felt like an iceberg in the room, I said to him, 'You're a hero for speaking out about your war crimes.'

He smiled shyly and did not respond. He was short in stature and had white shaggy hair and glasses. His legs hurt, so he could not walk for long periods of time. He pushed himself on a chair and began to tell his story.

'I was released as a war criminal in 1956 in Fushun, China. I had the same experience as Takahashi. The Fushun experience changed me. With other soldiers, I had taken part in a cruel war and brutally killed, bayoneted, and beheaded people. I raped and abused women,' he said.

Though I tried not to recoil at his first admission of raping and abusing women, I was disgusted. I tried to steel myself to keep going. Kaneko may be used to seeing women react that way. He continued talking about his treatment at Fushun by the Chinese. 'In 1956, there were 310 of us prisoners of war gathered in front of a judge. I thought we were about to be executed because we did so many terrible things during the war. But the judge called each of us by name. We waited for our death sentence or more prison time. Finally, the judge said we were all released from indictment. We were all so astonished. I was so overjoyed. About fifty of us cried on hearing that we had been set free.'

He and the other Japanese doubted the mercy of the Chinese and couldn't comprehend it. Then the staff of the concentration camp of Fushun organized a farewell ceremony, and the manager of the camp presided. It had a transformative effect on him and his fellow soldiers.

'I said to the Chinese staff, "We committed so many cruel crimes. Why do you forgive us?" They responded, "We don't want war anymore. Please go back to Japan and have a good family. Let's become friends." I had doubts and thought these Chinese would ask for compensation money from Japanese soldiers, but our former Prime Minister Kakuei Tanaka met Chinese Premier Zhou Enlai, and we learned that China has never demanded compensation from Japan. This is the very reason why I'm working in Chukiren. I want to bring real peace and friendship with the Chinese people.'

After years of marriage, he opened up to his wife about his past war experiences, and she travelled with him to China. She was touched by the Chinese at Fushun who set her husband free. They eventually donated one million yen to the Fushun camp facility to convert it into a museum so that visitors could go and learn lessons from it. They invited the manager of Fushun, 'Mr K', and his wife to visit Japan with his two sons and kept in close contact with them.

Clearly, he was able to forge long-lasting friendship with the Chinese, and I wanted to know if he had forgiven his captors in Siberia. 'Have you forgiven your captors from the Soviet Union?' I asked after remembering Takahashi's comments about hating the Soviets.

He visibly looked disturbed as he responded, 'No, I cannot forgive them. I did not have enough food to eat. They beat me. I had a really horrible experience in the Siberian concentration camp. I had to dig deep tunnels there, and it was extremely cold. We were treated very inhumanely. The toilet was outside in the freezing weather, which shows that they did not treat us as human beings. It was terrifying to use the washroom at midnight when it was −20°C outside.

'We were constantly looking around for something to eat. I picked up what seemed to be a potato, but it turned out to be frozen horse dung. I was so hungry that it looked like a potato to me. Once I went to the warehouse to pick up cleaning tools. I saw piles and piles of dead naked bodies of Japanese soldiers. It was too cold to dig graves for them. It was a cruel and sad sight. I thought of their mothers or family members seeing their bodies and how unbearable that would be. There was a shortage of food constantly, and we ate the insects we found while cutting trees. We ate stray dogs in the camp.'

The survival instinct was so strong and by the time he returned to Japan after being treated humanely and even warmly in China, he was motivated to form a good family as the Chinese judge ordered him to.

He insisted that he was blind to the suffering of the women in the military brothels set up for the Japanese soldiers, but I doubted that. Surely the women would have been visibly miserable. He said, 'I did not know about the plight of the comfort women at that time. Every time I went to the comfort station, there were about five to six Korean women there. Each time, it cost 1.5 yen. We got paid 8.80 yen a month. I was conscripted on 2 November 1940, and was sent to the Qingdao port to train for three months before going into China.'

'How many comfort stations did you see?' I asked.

'I've been to at least three comfort stations, and there were ten young women at times. Almost all of them were Korean, and one or two were Japanese. The soldiers waited in line, and we had no time to talk with them. Altogether, I've seen thirty women at one location. There were also teenagers and Chinese women.' As he said this, he pointed to his genitals and tapped them. I recoiled, but I was confident that he was a sincere man and didn't intend to be grotesque.

'Many of these women used opium,' he continued. 'The manager of one of the comfort stations, who ran it as a private business, profited from drug dealing, and he allowed the sex slaves to use drugs. Even ten comfort women could not make him much money since they brought in 1.50 yen each. The military comfort women were used to transport opium sometimes. They carried opium in a condom and hid it in their vaginas. The drugs were cultivated in Manchuria.'

'Did you use opium?' I asked.

'No. I tasted opium, but I did not use it,' he said.

'Why did the men use comfort stations? Why did they rape?' I asked.

He paused before giving a raw and honest answer that made me uncomfortable. 'The comfort stations were expensive. It cost 1.50 yen out of our monthly salary of 8.80 yen. Rape is cheap. It is free. At the time, the men did not think it was wrong to use comfort stations because we paid for it. We only had 3.80 yen after 5 yen was deducted for other things. We had to scare and terrorize the locals, so that's another reason why rapes were committed.'

'What if the military comfort women were Japanese?' I asked.

'If we had Japanese military comfort women, it might have demoralized our soldiers because it would be as if their sister or mother were in the comfort station, and that would be so discouraging. To avoid being raped, the Chinese women made their faces really ugly and kept their bodies dirty. The soldiers raped secretly. They knew it was wrong to rape, and they were afraid they'd get in trouble.'

'What do you think now of rape and using the comfort stations?' I asked.

'Of course I feel sorry. But that was during the war, and it was a special circumstance in the battlefield. I did not know when I would die. Every day I faced death, and therefore I wanted to have sex with military comfort women before I died.'

I asked for his insights on why some men and former soldiers refuse or are unable to see these sex slaves as deserving a sincere apology from the Japanese government. He replied, 'At that time, rape was cheaper than paying for the tickets at the comfort station.

The soldiers did not feel bad or guilty because the comfort stations were managed by the military, and we paid for it.'

I was surprised by his answer and then asked, 'Why do they not see the former sex slaves' fight for an apology as a human rights issue?'

'There are two reasons. The military established the comfort stations and managed them. And secondly, they paid money to use the comfort stations, and therefore they don't have feelings of guilt or see their actions as human rights violations. But I agree with the former military comfort women and support their fight for an apology and compensation.'

Because of his own suffering in the Siberian labour camps, Kaneko stands by his beliefs that the elderly women survivors of Japanese wartime sexual servitude deserve a sincere apology and compensation. He feels lucky to have survived and to have been treated with undeserved compassion by the Chinese in Fushun. His is an extraordinary story.

'What do you want people to remember about your story?' I asked.

'Never again should we have war. We need peace. The one thing I want to say is that I can't forgive the high-ranking officials in the Imperial Japanese military,' he said with anger flashing in his eyes.

'What about your captors from the Soviet Union? Can you ever consider forgiving them in the future?' I asked again to see if I'd get a different response.

He was silent for a moment, and then he quietly said, 'It is so painful that I cannot think about forgiving the Russians. Frontline soldiers like me became prisoners of war, but many high-ranking officials and officers did not get jailed. They were not forced to take responsibility. I feel angry about that because they caused the war—they should have taken responsibility for causing the cruel war. I'm a victim in this. The ones responsible evaded responsibility and were set free. I was a scapegoat. Also, the most painful thing about Siberia was the food shortage. Many soldiers died during that time. I was shocked to see the piles of dead bodies. Is there any person who is happy that their son died in war and is honoured in Yasukuni Shrine?'

Kaneko's eyes filled with tears, and he began to cry. His chest heaved as he managed to talk. 'My mother waited for my return. This is a sad memory for me. My mother waited for me for more than ten years. She touched my face and soon after passed away,' he said softly. 'I returned in July of 1956, and she died in October that year. There should be no more wars. That's all I want.'

I mumbled, I'm so sorry. I may have reached out to touch his shoulder briefly but all I remember is feeling his heavy sadness. I wanted to say something to Kaneko about reconciliation and healing. He was the one who needed to hear it most out of the three soldiers I had met on this trip, but instead, I felt the eyes of my translator on me. Regrettably, I only ended up conveying that I admired him for speaking out, and that he should not feel defined by his past.

These former soldiers built hope that reconciliation is possible. Okumura, Takahashi, and Kaneko couldn't be more different from one another in personality and mannerisms, but their catalytic convictions to raise awareness for historical truth and support victims of Japanese war crimes were the same.

Their lifelong sacrificial commitment to bridging and healing relationships with the Chinese restored a new blazing hope in me that we can forgive our enemies and that reconciliation or conciliation between victim-survivors and perpetrators, between people groups and countries was, indeed, possible. These elderly Japanese men were unlikely radical change agents who transformed my mindset. They helped catapult me on a different path of forgiveness and to release the bitterness of the past.

# 8

# Reconciliation

The encounters with Okumura, Takahashi, and Kaneko left a lasting impression on me. They made me feel even more strongly about pursuing justice for the victim-survivors of wartime sex slavery and brought me back to the first time I had heard of attempts to cover up the years-long systematic rapes of girls and women. In 1999, while working as a magazine editor and news reporter, I interviewed the renowned civil rights lawyer Gay McDougall, who had recently authored the second report on Imperial Japanese military sex slavery as the UN special rapporteur. The report was called 'Contemporary forms of slavery: Systematic rape, sexual slavery and slavery-like practices during armed conflict.' She was so formidable that Nelson Mandala sought her counsel on how to eliminate the abhorrent Apartheid system.

McDougall told me that the Japanese government had spent a lot of time and money trying to bury and cover up her report. I asked her for more details about how they tried to do that. She simply said they made every effort and used a tremendous amount of money to try and stop her report from being released to the world. Her forceful words left me speechless and rang alarm bells in my head . . . and they continue to do so as I persevere to uncover the truth about these atrocities.

McDougall has also been a powerful voice in saying that racial discrimination of the Japanese towards the Koreans, Chinese, and other ethnic groups was a driving factor in enslaving girls and women into systematic sexual violence on the frontlines of war. After all these years, she was still advocating for the women at a review of Japan's record conducted by the UN Committee on the Elimination of Racial Discrimination in 2018. The committee urged Japan to focus more on the victims of wartime sexual slavery, and also provide full redress and reparations to the victims. McDougall has succinctly pointed out that Japan should do more for victims of wartime sexual slavery. I teared up and became emotional after learning that she was still fighting for these women since my phone interview with her in 1999. Both of us hadn't given up, despite the many challenges.

I have always thought of McDougall's pointed message with every interview I've had with survivors, former soldiers, and activists. At the time, her words exposed the Japanese government and made me realize that I had stumbled onto a very big story, way beyond my experience as a junior reporter. I couldn't simply forget about it and move on. It was a watershed phone conversation that changed the trajectory of my journalism career to focus more on human rights, rather than on local news coverage like fires and city politics.

Years later, as a fledgling journalist hearing Kim Soon-duk's fateful and horrific testimony of enslavement in Washington, DC, I felt compelled to write an op-ed for one of the newspapers of record in Canada. The op-ed led the Japanese Embassy to investigate who I was—two people working at the local university and a leading journalist were approached. It again left me with a foreboding about the Japanese government, and that I was onto something much bigger and more sinister than I had anticipated.

Over the years, Japanese politicians have repeatedly publicly denied historical facts about the wartime sex slavery system that has outraged the survivors, Japan's neighbours, and activists around the world. Prime Minister Abe has repeatedly visited or sent ritual offerings to the Yasukuni Shrine that honours the Japanese war dead, including fourteen war criminals convicted by the Allied tribunal.

I felt an inexplicable pull to Asia, what I would describe as a sense of exciting adventure, and I moved to Beijing in 2004 to do more research on the issue and stayed there until 2011. I didn't have a job lined up, so it was a risk in relocating there. After a study tour trip across China during the summer that was organized by a Canadian activist group, I met a survivor of Japanese military sex slavery in China and others who survived Japanese war crimes and massacres such as the Rape of Nanking. I simply fell in love with the people.

From my very early days in Beijing, almost on a daily basis, I asked people—young and old, Christians and atheists—what they thought of the Japanese. They all said they hated them. 'Why?' I asked. A typical reply would be, 'Because of what they did in the war against China. The enslavement of comfort women and the Rape of Nanking. The Japanese government hasn't said a proper sorry to us. They need to say sorry!'

In 2004, I visited the Korean Council for Justice and Remembrance for the Issues of Military Sexual Slavery by Japan, which is the most prominent activist organization in Korea that provided care for survivors.

A few of the older women activists said they had read Kim Hak-soon's story in the newspaper, and like me at sixteen in Canada, they were shocked and in disbelief at the Japanese military's recruitment of underage girls. Professor Yun Chung-ok, the impressive pioneer of the activism for wartime sex slaves, remembers hearing of young Korean women who had returned after WWII, obsessively washing themselves over and over again in the countryside. There were whispers that they were mentally disturbed from being systematically raped by the Japanese soldiers.

I often heard of how tired the survivors were and how disappointed they were to not have received an adequate apology from the Japanese state. Feeling resigned that an apology would not be issued anytime soon, the *halmoni* survivors want the fight to continue as a legacy to the younger generation.

Raising awareness of Japanese military sex slaves has helped turn the tide of the public's perception of women's issues in Korea, thanks to the radical courage of women like Kim Hak-soon and others who came forward to talk about their harrowing experiences. Their stories slowly changed mindsets to the extent that today, the younger generation in Korea are fired up and passionate in raising awareness and funding for the cause. In the past, I remember hearing the reaction of my relatives and older people I met in passing who spoke of wartime sex slavery in hushed tones as if it were a shameful thing. But now military 'comfort women' activism has become a larger global movement for women's rights and in the fight against sexual violence against women in war zones.

I had heard from the activists that the saddest part of the Imperial Japanese military sex slavery system was the group of Korean survivors living in China who were said to have suffered worse conditions than any of the survivors in Korea. Because of the short duration since relations had normalized between China and Korea after the war ended, the Korean women could not easily return home. It had been a long process for Korean women in China to regain their Korean citizenship. And, in order for them to receive financial support from the Korean government, they had to become Korean citizens again.

I reflected on these Korean women trapped in China and the terrible ordeal of living in a foreign country at that time. It was particularly poignant to me because I had freely chosen to live in Beijing, and had the freedom and privilege to travel and do whatever I wanted to.

After these conversations with the activists at the Korean Council, I was reeling under their responses as to why the plight of these women was not as well known as Holocaust survivors, and why more wasn't being done to bring justice to them. They blamed the US for failing to conduct a thorough investigation of what happened to these women, even though they knew about it. The Americans were blamed for deliberately burying Japan's role in Korea unlike in the case of Germany, in which there were tribunals and judgements for Nazi war criminals and a lot of information being released about the Holocaust. Then the Korean War erupted with an ensuing economic hardship which prevented a thorough investigation of Japan's colonial rule and war crimes.

Since 2007, in a series of milestones in the international activist movement in support of the 'comfort women', the governments of Canada, the Netherlands, South Korea, and Taiwan, as well as the European Parliament, have all passed resolutions that demand the Japanese government take full moral and legal responsibility for directly planning and implementing the military sex slavery system. The US resolution called it 'one of the largest cases of human trafficking in the twentieth century'. These nations called on the Japanese government to offer an unequivocal sincere apology and compensation to the survivors that would satisfy them.

A controversial Korea–Japan Comfort Women Accord was brokered in December 2015 without consulting the survivors themselves. The deal included an apology from the Japanese prime minister and US$8.5 million in assistance for victims. But this only hurt and provoked the traumatized survivors who felt the apology was not strong enough. It failed to bring healing and closure. The deal also angered and re-traumatized their family members and affected the Korean and Chinese communities and other ethnic groups affected by Japanese war crimes all over the world.

\* \* \*

While I was still living in Beijing, I made a personal trip to Hong Kong in 2008 when a friend told me about a reconciliation team from Japan. They wanted to heal the racial divide between the Japanese and the Chinese. At a meeting in a church, they gave a sincere apology to the Chinese for killing and torturing people during the war, including using women and girls as sex slaves. The Chinese wept, or rather wailed. I sat rigidly and stone-faced as they faced me to apologize. I doubted their apology would have an effect—clearly, no civilian apology could ever replace an official one from the top government leader. Some survivors have also expressed a wish to hear an apology from the Japanese Emperor. I also did not identify with my Korean identity as a Canadian who had grown up in Vancouver since two years of age. I had always thought of myself as a very Westernised Asian person and joked to friends that I was a 'White' person trapped in a Korean body. I felt cynical that their words for Koreans would affect me. I doubted in the power of their apology. But the apology from the Japanese team was given with the sincerest intentions, and, to my surprise, I wept to the point that I had no more tears to shed. A big pool of water by my feet was a testament to the love in their words. Their simple apology triggered a profound release of pain, and what I call generational racial hatred towards the Japanese.

Imagine the depth of impact that an official government apology from the prime minister would have.

This experience with the Japanese reconciliation team marked a crucial turning point in the direction of the Japanese military sex slavery book that I was writing. I would go on to write a different book entirely—no longer the point of view of an angry activist. Instead, I would go on to focus on obtaining justice and a truly sincere apology from the Japanese government for the survivors. I focused more on racial reconciliation and healing of trauma and pain suffered by survivors.

I also came to realize gradually over several years that my work on the wartime sex slavery issue helped me to come to terms with the trauma of what happened in my first marriage. I was processing something so deep and layered within me. In addition to my questions over my Korean identity and belonging, in my fight for an apology from the Japanese government, I was also subconsciously crying out for an apology from my ex-husband.

I had moved to Beijing in 2004 before he did while we were still dating, and we got married in 2006. I was always ambivalent towards him but I admit that I was a needy person and preferred to have companionship than be alone. We met at work when I first worked at a TV station as an intern. The warning signs were clear for all to see. I had postponed our wedding for almost a year and a month before it finally took place. I even confessed to him that I was considering calling things off. He had screamed at me on the phone over something insignificant while he was on a work assignment. The wedding venue was booked, and so were all the vendors such as the florist, the decorations, entertainment and more. Fear ruled me to my utter regret.

After a little more than a year of marriage, during which time he was mostly away working in war zones, he sent me a text message asking for a divorce. A few weeks after that, I learnt of his adultery through a friend who met the other woman and heard her admit to the affair in a church meeting. He denied everything. It was a needle-in-a-haystack kind of miracle to have something so hidden confirmed unmistakably.

He didn't love me, and I didn't love him, and perhaps our brokenness drew us to one another. I never quite knew why we got married when we were not madly in love. But the very act of failing sent me reeling. I had an aversion to it. As a performance-oriented perfectionist, I had never really spectacularly failed at anything. I was always in control.

There were red flags in the early stages of our relationship, but I foolishly ignored them despite warnings from my friends who knew him from years before. When I walked down the aisle at my wedding, I was crying—not tears of joy, but tears of profound sadness.

I learnt during a counselling course that my father and grandfather's lack of enthusiasm and acceptance for me as a baby girl could have led to some of my current-day issues of perfectionism and striving to receive acceptance. On a subconscious level, I was out to prove to my father that I was indeed better than ten sons. My lack of acceptance of myself had its roots in my earlier experiences of gender and racial discrimination.

They say if you don't know your identity, you cannot understand your destiny or purpose in life. If I didn't achieve in something at school or work, it led to a feeling of worthlessness and emptiness. I didn't know my own worth as a woman, and it led to complications in my dating life. Add to this mix an intense cultural pressure to get married, and I truly felt that, at 29, I would not have many other chances to find someone.

After the divorce, I found solace in my work. For the first few months, I lost so much weight that my skinny jeans looked loose. I had to find a new place to live and sold my antique furniture. Friends rallied around me, and I joined a group of friends that met weekly to openly discuss our personal issues. There was unconditional acceptance and love. I felt lighter and happier as a person after the divorce. It was as if an oppressive weight has been taken off of my shoulders.

I also learnt that one way to overcome adversity is to turn your suffering into helping and loving others.

Tomoko Hasegawa, who was there when I interviewed Okumura, the former soldier in Tokyo, had told Cindy about my book. This led to Cindy asking me to produce a documentary with her in 2012 about their healing work to apologize to elderly 'comfort women' survivors and their families in China. They called their group Healing River-Rainbow Bridge.

Because of their own government's lack of a sincere apology, these radical Japanese Christians felt compelled to make a wrong right. I believed it was serendipitous and not a coincidence that we were all connected.

Cindy was looking for a producer who would have the same vision for reconciliation between the Japanese and Chinese and Koreans.

The timing was uncanny because I had completed the first draft of my book before she asked me to meet for coffee. She happened to be visiting relatives in Vancouver. We resonated on our mutual dream of seeing the survivors of wartime sex slavery find healing and closure. She relayed touching stories of helping several elderly survivors in China who desperately needed medical and financial support, and I ended up adding a chapter on Cindy's pioneering work in my book *Silenced No More: Voices of Comfort Women*. Over the years, Cindy has been extraordinary in her unwavering commitment and vision. This film, *Healing River* that would air on a popular Internet channel in China would be one of the major milestones in my life and a vital part of our campaign to raise awareness and action for justice for survivors of Japanese military sex slavery.

Tomoko, Cindy and their friends wanted to bring God's love and healing to wartime sexual servitude survivors. They prepared fan dances and poetry with calligraphy, as well as beautiful gifts wrapped in Japanese-style paper for the survivors. During trips to China, which they paid for themselves, these humble Japanese bowed on the ground to apologize as one of them held up a poster with a poem written in Chinese calligraphy expressing how deeply sorry they were for the suffering brought on by Japanese military war crimes.

Their humility and love transformed lives. Wherever they went in China, people wept after reading their signs with their sincere apology. Their sincerity touched ancient pain.

Sadly, these Japanese involved in grassroots reconciliation faced intense persecution and rejection from fellow Japanese and family members. They said that most Japanese had not learnt about the 'comfort women' issue or other crimes against humanity committed by the Japanese military in their history books, so they did not understand how it impacted other Asians. One forty-year-old woman in Tokyo, a newly-wed, was ordered by her husband to never participate in the reconciliation work again, and she asked us to blur her face in the documentary.

My husband Matt and I, and a small group of committed people launched the 852 Freedom Campaign, a Hong Kong-based movement of 'passionate compassion' against human trafficking and modern slavery. We mobilized more than 120 churches, NGOs, and organizations and later expanded to other nations such as Malaysia, China, Canada, South Africa, and the US. With the help of more than fifty-five slavery awareness and fund-raising events including a Battle of the Bands, a music CD production, art exhibits, sweatshop simulations, and jewellery-making for fundraising, our team reached more than 25,000 people in eighteen months in universities, schools, and major corporations like Goldman Sachs.

Through this campaign, we have screened *Healing River* in churches, schools, and universities in China, Hong Kong, Canada, and the US in what has also unexpectedly become a campaign to release generational racial hatred towards the Japanese. After the film ended, I usually spotted a few people crying, sometimes more. I asked them why the film moved them. One student said she was touched that there were Japanese willing to say sorry, and she didn't know there were good people in Japan. Others said their grandparents or parents were affected by the Japanese invasion of China, and they still hated the Japanese. At the end, I asked people to raise their hands if they had ever felt generational racial hatred that was passed down from their grandparents or parents. I then asked them if they felt open to releasing this hatred. Most nodded yes. I concluded by leading them in words or a prayer of forgiveness towards the Japanese.

It was meaningful for me to be able to bring change as a bridge between people groups and catalyse healing of generational pain and racist attitudes towards the Japanese, especially among young people.

While writing my book *Silenced No More: Voices of Comfort Women*, I was mesmerized by the iconic image of German Chancellor Willy Brandt on his knees, giving an apology to the Holocaust survivors and their children in 1970, which was splashed across the media worldwide. His sincere gesture helped some survivors forgive and feel their suffering was properly acknowledged.

I wrote my book with a new vision for healing and racial reconciliation and a last push for a sincere apology and acknowledgement from the Japanese government that would bring closure to these war wounds, once and for all.

The issue of wartime sex slavery was surprisingly a lightning rod, and it took a long time for me to accept that it was part of the pioneering journey to foster conciliation. I once experienced an angry reaction from a Japanese missionary at a Christian conference luncheon, who said he knew a Japanese academic who knew 'better than you' even though he hadn't read my book.

An American angrily confronted me at a Christian conference and asked why the Korean soldiers weren't being confronted for raping Vietnamese women during the Vietnam War. I had compassion for these Vietnamese women and hoped they would get closure too. But I told this American, who had lived in Japan for many years, that he was repeating the Japanese Right-wing 'comfort women denier' arguments word for word. He had no idea.

More recently, my friend OKow hosted a dinner for two singers from a city close to Tokyo and two Japanese friends including a pastor of a Japanese church based in Hong Kong. All of a sudden, the Chinese owner of the restaurant felt uncomfortable in interacting with the Japanese guests. It was as if generational racial hatred was triggered. She had read an article in the Chinese media about my book and the call to racial healing, and she came up to me and shared her story. Her grandparents were very wealthy but lost everything when the Japanese military stole it from them. They were left destitute. She said she felt a hatred for the Japanese that was passed down from her grandparents. I urged her to forgive as an act of her will to release herself from the prison of bitterness so that she could experience freedom. She let go of her hatred after a struggle, and said she felt different afterwards.

I didn't expect to become involved in an anti-racism and racial reconciliation campaign. We must truly heal the wounds from the war and from racial hatred and injustice that sprang from the perceived racial superiority of the Japanese military and government. In his published sermon, my friend award-winning author Ken Shigematsu said part of the reason why many Japanese people subjugated other Asians to cruelty, slavery and even murder in the years leading up to and during WWII was that they viewed themselves as descendants of the gods and therefore superior to other people. He cited the example of what happened to the First Nations people in Canada: 'Part of the reason that colonists from Europe stole the land of indigenous peoples [steal seems to be the plainest word as the First Nations people in some cases were physically forced off the land and never compensated], broke treaties, enslaved, raped and murdered many native peoples was because they saw the indigenous people as being savages, as being less than human.'

Shigematsu was influenced by Miroslav Volf, a theologian at Yale who grew up in Croatia, a nation long torn by ethnic conflict and war. Volf believes that ethnic cleansing is the result of a false sense of purity of our own race or bloodline.

Even today, many Japanese view Koreans, Chinese and other minorities as second-class citizens. A Taiwanese–Japanese woman I met told me that some apartment advertisements in Tokyo stipulated 'No Koreans, No Chinese, No dogs.'

I spoke about this issue at a Rotary Club event in Macon in the US state of Georgia. I described the racial hatred and the violent riots that happened in Beijing and other cities in China after the prime minister of Japan visited the Yasukuni Shrine. Some protesters set themselves on fire in South Korea in response to the Japanese government's approval of whitewashed history textbooks that downplayed 'comfort women' sexual slavery and other wartime atrocities like the Rape of Nanking, where more than 300,000 men, women and children in the Chinese city of Nanjing were tortured and massacred. Both Black and White audience members came up to me afterwards and said I spoke a parable of race relations in America.

For anyone to speak on this issue of Japanese military sex slavery and call for racial healing in Japan would be like an African American going into the heart of the segregated South to speak about lynching and racism. Online attacks and harassment from the Right-wingers or ultranationalists are regular occurrences for Japanese involved in raising awareness of forced prostitution by the military and other war crimes.

Takashi Uemura was one of the first Japanese journalists to write about wartime sex slavery. His interview with Kim Hak-soon in 1991 for *Asahi Shimbun*, an open-minded and liberal Japanese newspaper, made him the target of Right-wingers who felt his reporting was false and humiliating, and that it stained their reputation as Japanese nationals. They maintain that 'comfort women' were opportunistic paid prostitutes who enriched themselves during the war. In 2014, a magazine article accused Uemura of making up stories on wartime 'comfort women' sex slaves, and this triggered an avalanche of intimidating letters being sent to him, as well as menacing threats to a university in Kobe that ultimately cost him a job there. Perhaps, the most difficult part of the harassment were the online messages urging his teenage daughter to kill herself.

I hid my identity for a year after my book was published and wrote under a pen name to protect myself from harassment. However, over the years and through my encounters with many advocates and activists including the former Japanese soldiers, I'm willing to go to Japan after my book is published in Japanese. Especially, if it means I can help shed light on the truth and these harrowing narratives to raise an urgent need for racial healing and reconciliation between the Japanese and Koreans, Chinese, and all people groups affected by Japanese war crimes.

It saddens me to hear that a group of Japanese Canadians opposed the 'comfort women' statue in Burnaby, where I grew up, with one representative saying the issue has no relevance to Canadians. The same happened in Atlanta, Georgia in the US and in other cities around the world. The statue and the work towards raising awareness are not intended to point fingers at the Japanese community. The purpose is to take a stand; remember what happened to these enslaved women and girls, and say 'never again'.

In 2018, the city of Osaka cut off its sixty-year 'sister city' relationship with San Francisco in protest at the statues that honoured the victims of sexual enslavement by the Imperial Japanese military. The previous year, a museum in Atlanta, Georgia cancelled plans to install a memorial to 'comfort women', and there were suggestions that the decision had been prompted by pressure from the Japanese Consulate and businesses.

UN experts, including Gay McDougall, urged the government of Japan to do more for victims of wartime sexual slavery and offer full redress and reparations during a two-day review of Japan's record before the UN Committee on the Elimination of Racial Discrimination. McDougall, one of eighteen UN committee members, said, 'I think it is a wound that has been festering for far too long.'

I attended the opening ceremony of the new 'comfort women' museum in Nanjing in December 2015 alongside officials, the children of the survivors, and special invited guests, including activists from Korea.

As I took in the different exhibits that featured the testimony of 'comfort women' and walked through the different floors of the haunting exhibit, I was struck by the faces and stories of the victims and the indescribable suffering they endured. I had interviewed survivors for my book over a ten-year period, but to be in the actual building where women and girls were raped by thirty to sixty Japanese soldiers a day was haunting. I renewed my commitment to helping bring justice and peace to this human rights issue in Asia that has not yet been resolved and that still affects Asian race relations today.

At the museum's opening lunch reception, I sat next to a museum official and across the adopted children of wartime sex slave survivors. Throughout this time, tears rolled down my face non-stop.

'I was born in Korea, and I am now free to leave this city. I have choices and many options. But the wartime sex slaves were trapped and couldn't leave. They suffered beyond what any of us can imagine,' I said. It was a bonding moment with the people at the table.

* * *

The wounds of war have never healed. Even seventy-six years after the end of WWII, I share my arduous journey of raising awareness of this crime against humanity—the wartime Imperial Japanese military sex slavery issue. My journey is also an attempt to reiterate that we also need to heal the divisions within the Asian communities in the twenty-first century. For inspiration, one can consider Canada's Truth and Reconciliation Commission, which called on the government and churches to acknowledge, address, and educate people about atrocities committed against indigenous people throughout history.

There are less than thirty-five confirmed 'comfort women' survivors of Japanese military sex slavery around the world today. In Korea, as of July 2021, there are only fourteen survivors who have reported to the government. More survivors have been coming forward in China in recent years.

Kim Hak-soon bore witness to an atrocity in her life and in history that has left a gaping wound in Asia that still festers many generations later. Her haunting eyes and her visage of mournfulness has become the symbol and rallying cry of the growing women's movement in Korea and now internationally through 'comfort women' statues in Toronto and other cities in North America, Australia and Europe.

As I remember the wrinkled faces of Kim and the other survivors, I am astounded by their resilience. I mourn for their lost youth and innocence. Yet, their powerful testimonies are a source of incredible hope. These are women who have broken every barrier—cultural taboos, personal shame, rejection, oppression, trauma, and fear—to speak out against human rights violations. They have found their voices and raised awareness of sexual violence and enslavement during armed conflict around the world.

Reporting on the victims of historical sex slavery has changed my life. It was a painful personal transformative journey as I worked through my own issues and my own efforts at reconciliation. It helped launch and influence my activism. The bitter memories of my first marriage lifted completely and faded into oblivion with this paradigm shift, this new focus on what truly mattered. I felt freed from the past and had found a new purpose for living. Meeting these women, who suffered so much during the war, inspired me to continue reporting and raising awareness on the issue of human trafficking and human rights violations. They helped me accept and process my generational pain and racial hatred as a Korean woman and through this wrestling, I welcomed my Korean identity. My experience in understanding what happened to the women and girls forced into Japanese military sex slavery in the 1930s and 1940s allowed me to see that history is repeating itself. I was fired up and determined to find more ways to make a lasting difference.

# Part III

# The Cycle of Slavery Continues

# 9

# North Korean Refugees[*]

The open wounds of Japanese Imperial military sex slavery still weep across the Asia Pacific as modern-day sexual servitude and exploitation continues unchecked. I was especially saddened to learn that it wasn't an isolated incident in our history books and that the cycle is repeating in China—the very nation where more than a thousand rape camps were established by the Japanese—in the form of sex trafficking of North Korean women and girls.

According to frontline workers in China, most North Korean refugees who have entered China in recent years are female. Many of them resort to desperate measures to establish a better future for their children.

North Korean women escaping into China are especially vulnerable. Today, as many as eighty per cent of all North Korean refugee women are tricked into sexual slavery or sold as brides into violent marriages to Chinese men. Many of them are drugged and

---

[*] This chapter is partly based on my articles titled 'From seeking refuge to slavery: How North Koreans become victims of human trafficking', published in *South China Morning Post* on 2 July 2017, and 'Trafficked North Korean "bride" reveals her desperate flight from China', published in *South China Morning Post* on 9 September 2017.

raped by traffickers when they arrive in China in search of food or
medical help. These vulnerable people leave their country because
they are desperate to feed their families.

For about $50, a trafficker will pose as a businessman and
enter North Korea on behalf of a Chinese farmer who is unable to
attract a desirable bride due to his impoverished circumstances. The
North Korean women are then enticed with promises of an arranged
marriage and a better life. Seeing no other options, many agree to the
arrangement.

Often, these arranged marriages to impoverished, physically
disabled or alcoholic men result in these women being raped,
physically abused, forced into prostitution or labour, re-sold to
other rural men and ultimately abandoned. Because they are illegal
economic migrants and have no legal rights, they have to endure all
this merely to survive.

According to the Korean–American frontline workers I have
spoken with over the years, many of these North Korean women are
sold into online pornography consumed by South Korean men.

One of the most common ways that refugees get into China is
to wade across the narrow Tumen river, or walk across it during the
winter months. I visited the border area in 2007 with a few brave
South Korean volunteers who were involved in helping North Korean
refugees get to safety in Thailand, Laos or another country before
being flown to Seoul. As I was driven along a dirt road on the Chinese
side of the Tumen river, I could see guard towers, police barracks, and
little houses for border guards on the other side. Skinny North Korean
armed guards stood on the riverbank with binoculars, and we used our
own to watch them. I turned my head to look at the rest of the North
Korean banks and was surprised to see so many guards peppered across
the grassy area by the river. Some North Korean people were working
in the fields, but it wasn't clear what they were planting.

We rented a boat and got as close to the North Korean side as
we could. Our guide threw a small package with American money,

but the guard who caught it set it alight with a cigarette lighter and then gave us an angry look. I was taken aback by the severity of his facial expression and wondered about the effects of brainwashing. I shuddered to think of the unimaginable suffering and collective trauma of the North Korean people. It is, indeed, staggering.

When Kim Il-sung founded North Korea in 1948, he cut off contact with the rest of the world. He controlled the country through a cult of personality, demanding absolute loyalty through the control of food and his nationalistic 'Juche' ideology. The regime has been led by three generations of dictators, with Kim Il-sung being succeeded by his son, Kim Jong-il, and then his grandson, Kim Jong-un.

About ten per cent of North Korea's population starved to death in the country's great famine of the 1990s. Starvation, crushing poverty and the need for medical attention have caused tens of thousands of North Koreans to seek refuge in Mainland China, while the dictatorship continues to siphon off foreign aid donations and most of the country's food supply to the disproportionately large military and the capital's elite. Micro-famines over the years have led to reports of cannibalism. In that 2007 trip, I had an unforgettable encounter with a gutsy North Korean woman, a tiny refugee with short permed hair named Hee-young. She was the first North Korean person I had ever met. I had long imagined what North Koreans would be like and what would their pronunciation be like. I could barely comprehend her circa 1950 Korean vocabulary. To my utter shock, she casually admitted to eating a stew made by a neighbour who later told her it was made of human body parts! She had no other food sources and would have starved to death if she hadn't eaten it. I could sense her feelings of overwhelming shame and a steely resilience within. She could be ruthless, I sensed. My heart broke to know of the possible cannibalism in the country, and the knowledge that thousands would have done the same out of a sheer will to survive. I reached out to hug her but she shrank back. I realized that she was not used to hugs. Would I have done the same had I been born in North Korea and I was starving in that famine? I couldn't be sure. She told me of how she rode on top of a fast-moving train in North Korea to get to the Chinese border to cross the river. I was astonished by her courage.

Despite calls from international human rights organizations and governments for more humane treatment of North Korean refugees, including a halt to forced repatriation, the Chinese government has not given them refugee status, viewing them instead as illegal economic migrants to be sent back. When these North Korean migrants are forcibly repatriated, they either face beatings, torture, sexual violence, and endless toil at the Hermit Kingdom's infamous labour camps or public executions.

As a young girl, I watched highly emotional reunions between family members from North and South Korea on TV—weeping brothers and sisters, parents and their children, who had been living on different sides of the border. I never forgot this TV programme that had left me in tears. I could feel something generational stirring within, and it left a lasting impression about the lack of closure after the Korean War. Learning more about North Korea gave me a deeper connection with my roots, my parents' motherland and the painful history of my birthplace. My basic grasp of the Korean language was limiting, but I overcame that barrier with help from translators and a determination to understand more about the sexual slavery of women from the Korean peninsula.

\* \* \*

In 2007, to secure interviews with some of these refugees, I made contact with a group of courageous volunteer smugglers who were part of the Underground Railroad. This network stretched more than 3,000 miles across China and was made up of daring people, many of them missionaries with family ties in North Korea. This group of people rescued refugees and helped get them safely to a third country like South Korea or the US. They offered secret safe homes, as well as medical and spiritual support, on a journey that was fraught with peril because the secret police and citizen spies were everywhere.

I connected with those involved in the Underground Railroad through a friend of a friend of a friend who had some contacts within the network. It is virtually next to impossible to meet these people because they rarely trust outsiders let alone journalists. I met with these contacts at a Chinese café and explained that I wanted to interview some North Korean refugee women who had been sold into sex slavery or forced marriages. I told them that this was so I could help raise awareness of their plight to donors and people all over the world.

The main guy asked me two dozen questions and then concluded cryptically by saying that I'd get a call. I wasn't confident that this trip would move forward because I knew how secretive they were.

Months later, another journalist and I made arrangements to meet 'Johnny' at a location in a northern Chinese city. I had no idea what to expect. An American friend who had made a similar journey told me that he had to switch cars and was blindfolded at one point before meeting some refugees at a remote park. I balked at this initially, but thought of the wartime sex slaves and how I wanted to interview the North Korean women as part of my argument that the cycle of forced prostitution was continuing.

I packed my notebook before going to meet Johnny, a gutsy middle-aged Chinese man. Could I trust this stranger with my life? I doubted it yet it was too late to back out. We were at risk of being found out.

We got acquainted quickly and hopped in a car. On a country road, Johnny and the driver made small talk with us. They shared some recent stories of women refugees who had escaped into China, only to be caught and raped by traffickers and sold as brides or sex slaves. Fear washed over me and I hoped I wouldn't be caught.

During our journey to a safe house, we had to switch cars at least a dozen times. I tried to mentally prepare myself for the possibility that we would be discovered by either the police or traffickers. Both parties would be unhappy about our goal of getting the stories of these refugees out to the world. Christian missionaries, aid workers, and locals who provide assistance to refugees are routinely jailed.

I set my gaze anxiously out of the window and tried to guess how far we were from our hotel. I saw farmland with rows of green stalks and golden halos. Mountains covered with hundreds of tiny green shrubs stood protectively along the edges of the land. Bright blue trucks, red taxis, and large tourist buses raced down the narrow roads. Farmers with brown leathery faces wizened by the sun in dirty clothes worked the fields, some of them holding sickles. It was as if this part of the world was frozen in time. I thought the calm and charming idyllic countryside was a stark contrast to the fear and anxiety the refugees must have felt as they hid in these parts. I could identify with their terror now.

After three hours of driving, we arrived at a house where I met a North Korean refugee who was a victim of bride trafficking. Her name was Su-jin. Her skin had a dull yellow pallor, and she had her unwashed hair in an updo. Her handler told us that she had jaundice. She looked frightened and traumatized. I was surprised by her ragged appearance, and she reminded me a little of wartime sex slavery survivor Kim Soon-duk's nervous energy. I hugged her, and she seemed taken aback by this. In Korean culture, bowing is the norm, but I felt compelled out of compassion to show some affection.

I found her North Korean dialect hard to follow. I was convinced that some of her words were circa 1940s pre-Korean War diction. A volunteer helped interpret.

Su-jin told me with no emotion that she was sold for 1,000 RMB to a Chinese man in Heilongjiang province, northeast China for the first time. She lived in a smelly, dank cave with her 'husband', and it was a terribly traumatic experience for her. The traffickers had lured her from North Korea with the promise of a job, knowing she desperately wanted to send money back to her impoverished parents.

I felt her deep sadness when she spoke of her children whom she had left behind in the cave. That's when she began to cry. She didn't mention them by name and glossed over this part of her story, but I could sense there was unspeakable anguish. It was *han*.

Su-jin was sold a second time as a bride for a poor Chinese farmer. I was outraged for her. She eventually escaped and found refuge with an ethnic Korean man who forced her to work in a dance bar, pouring beer for local Chinese businessmen. She told me she was scared to dance and pour drinks, and she began to find solace in alcohol to escape from her problems. She became an alcoholic, and her unhealthy toxic lifestyle caught up with her when she was diagnosed with liver cancer. A few Christians reached out to her during visits to the bar, and after initially resisting, she experienced a dramatic conversion. I was blown away by her faith conversion.

After years of abuse and uncertainty, Su-jin found peace in her newfound faith in God. She was able to sit quietly to pray and read the Bible regularly. She sang hymns during the day when she was feeling sad or afraid. 'I wish I didn't have to leave my country,' she said with a small voice. One day, she discovered the symptoms of her cancer were gone, and a doctor confirmed that she was indeed cancer-free. Su-jin believed she was miraculously healed by God.

With some prodding from the volunteer, she told me that her newfound peace had led her to think of those in her homeland who were more in need of physical and spiritual nourishment than her. She was even considering returning to North Korea to share her faith, knowing that this would most likely result in imprisonment or execution.

Our hosts interrupted our conversation and said we had to leave. I wanted to spend the entire day listening to Su-jin's stories of her life in North Korea, of her dreams and longings. I wanted to do more to help her. But it wasn't safe to stay because our presence could arouse suspicion from neighbours. After taking some photos of the back of her head, since it would have been unsafe to capture her face on camera, I hugged Su-jin and squeezed her hands. I promised to help her and other North Korean women refugees like her by telling their stories.

She thanked me and looked down at the ground. Her shoulders drooped as if a heavy weight had just landed on them. Then, she turned to walk to her room.

At another safe home far away, there was a Bible study group. Most of the women there had been coerced into prostitution or forced to marry men they didn't desire. Sadly, their stories were all too similar. They had to flee again and again for mere survival. Some had to leave children behind in North Korea for one reason or another, but then found it was too dangerous for their children to come to China. They were praying for protection. I tried to underplay myself because I didn't want them to feel intimidated by a Westerner like me who didn't speak fluent Korean even though I looked like them.

After this trip, one safe home volunteer working with North Koreans in China told me, 'When we find North Korean women refugees, we find that they're living in harsh, terrible circumstances. It's so awful! They often live in a one-room apartments, some of them live with their husband and children. They say, "I didn't come here for these kinds of desperate living conditions. I came here to support my parents."'

One local non-profit group in Yanbian prefecture, Jilin province told me that in just one year they had assisted dozens of North Korean women refugees who had abandoned their abusive Chinese husbands and children.

There are thousands of children of North Korean mothers and Chinese fathers. Hundreds, if not thousands, of these children are abandoned by their mothers if they escape to a third country like South Korea or if they are sold again to another 'husband'. These children are stateless and have no access to education or medical support. They are trapped and imprisoned in their homes out of fear of being caught. I was in despair over their complex situation with no help or solution in sight.

Ju-hee's family was starving, and the desperate hunt for food drove her to cross the Tumen river in 1998 after a stranger offered her a regular job. As she crossed the river, holding onto the hands of two men, she recalled, 'I was scared out of my mind in the water. As I walked, I thought I'm going to a better place. I kept repeating to myself—I'm going to a better place.' She was told she could make 10 RMB a day in China, and she planned to travel back and forth from North Korea to bring money to her mother and two daughters. But unfortunately, she fell into the hands of traffickers and was sold twice to local Chinese farmers. The first man, a disabled farmer, had paid 2,500 RMB for her. 'I'd rather die than live with this man,' she said. Ju-hee managed to run away by hopping on a bus, and she eventually found initial help from some Korean–Chinese.

Ju-hee used to live in fear every day thinking that the Chinese authorities would deport her. In order to stop living a life of constant fear and for some semblance of security, she decided to marry her second Chinese 'husband' in a desperate attempt for security and peace of mind. When I met her, she had a nine-year-old son with this man. Although she was more relaxed, she suffered the pain of being separated from her two daughters, then aged twenty-one and sixteen. She said with deep sobs, 'It's impossible for my two daughters to come over . . . sometimes I regret ever coming here.' She hadn't been able to see them or speak with them, nor did she have a lot of money to send back to them. I cried with her and felt helpless. I was frustrated and wished I could do more beyond writing the stories of voiceless women like her.

Some refugees who make it to China try to get to South Korea or another country by sneaking into embassies in Beijing. In 2005, forty-four refugees managed to enter the Canadian embassy in the Chinese capital by posing as workers and climbing a ladder.

Chinese authorities caught one elderly man and sent him back to North Korea. It's believed he was executed. Another woman made it safely to China, but she fainted when she heard her daughter had been caught at the embassy and sent back.

Hae-ri couldn't stop thinking about her mother and younger brother, who had paid a heavy price for her safety in China. She had vacant dark brown eyes, shoulder-length stringy hair and fine features on her oval face. There was a shroud of sorrow all around her. My protective instincts were out in full force when we were together. In 2002, she paid some profiteers 100 RMB to help her cross the Tumen river. She was starving in North Korea and so decided to risk her life to cross the border. 'Life was so hard in North Korea. That's why I came,' she said. 'If you ate one meal a day for thirty days, that was considered a good thing.'

Hae-ri was promised a job and said that she could make money and return home. This is how she described her unbelievable journey from North Korea to Chinese soil: 'I came in September because the river is not too deep at that time. But I couldn't cross because parts of the river were too strong, so I climbed onto something wooden that floats, and a man pushed me across. It took forty minutes to cross. Once I was in China, I met someone from my neighbourhood. He was the first one to tell me about coming to China. I thought I'd make money here and go back. I stayed at that neighbour's house at night. I arrived in my drenched clothes, stayed there for three days and then found work. I found work building homes, digging ditches and doing odd labour jobs. Then, after a month, I met my husband through work. I want to see my mother. My father died, and I wish my mother and younger brother can come before the river freezes in November. Please pray that my mother is safe.'

Hae-ri did not want to discuss the abuse she had experienced, but our host told us that she had had a very difficult time. I was pained to see that she was living with a great deal of unending pain. But Hae-ri said she was not sold to her husband. I did not want to press her on this, and I just listened quietly and held her hand. She said that after working odd jobs that paid poorly, she met a Chinese rickshaw driver and married him. They had a five-year-old daughter and lived in a crude one-room apartment where the bathroom was an outhouse and a hot shower was a luxury.

When the North Korean government found out that Hae-ri had escaped, the police immediately sent her mother and brother to a prison labour camp. The government said her mother had failed to 'raise her daughter correctly'.

'My mother was taken, and she wasn't told where she was going,' she said. 'Because we supported her a little financially, they accused her of living well. In the night, they took my mother and my twenty-four-year-old younger brother. So far, they cannot escape . . . If they try to escape, they'll be killed.'

Her youngest brother and sister were living by themselves, and they had no way to support themselves other than to live on the funds that Hae-ri sent them. She had to stop talking and simply cried softly for a while. It was unbearable to see her like this. 'When I think of my family and the hardships in my homeland, I can't sleep,' she said before wiping away her tears. Hae-ri said that she was able to speak with her other brother and sister once or twice a month by phone. I asked her if she could ever go back to find her family. She responded without hesitation. 'I would never go back. But I wish I could see my mother again.'

North Korean refugees live in fear of getting caught by the local police and sent back. When I asked if she was living with fear and how she was coping, she said, 'I'm not afraid of the police. It's okay. Living in China is hard, but after believing in God, I have found peace and I feel better.' Her faith was inspiring and put mine to shame. I was so grateful that she still had a glimmer of hope in these darkest of circumstances.

So-young was fifteen years old when she crossed the river to enter China with a friend. Chinese men were waiting for them on the other side and promised them jobs fetching $30 a month. They agreed, thinking they were too young to be sold as wives or slaves. The next day, So-young's friend was sold, and So-young was forced to work. Her traffickers were waiting for her to grow taller before they could sell her as a bride to a forty-year-old Chinese man. After four months, the man came to get his new bride. So-young said she was 'so disgusted' when she saw him. But because of her sheer stubbornness, her captors couldn't sell her. After several months, she alerted a sympathetic local Chinese man, and together they planned her escape. She ran away the next morning and lived in fear of being sent back to North Korea by the Chinese police.

Her fears were realized. After living in China for three years as a refugee, So-young was discovered and forcibly sent back to North Korea. She was imprisoned for six months and then fled again to China, where she was caught by traffickers and raped. After that, she was sold to a Chinese man who raped her multiple times. She eventually escaped to a safe house in China. Her perseverance and strength was staggering and as she told me her story, I was gripped with secondary fear and trauma. I wanted to feel what they felt so that their experiences could flow through my fingers onto the pages for maximum impact; I wanted my words to motivate people to action.

So-young faced the constant risk of being captured and sent back to North Korea, where she would be faced with imprisonment and death. 'There are many people coming out of North Korea,' she said. 'But they don't have anywhere to go and no other choice but to go down that route.'

Countless North Korean women and girls like Su-jin, Ju-hee, Hae-ri, and So-young are in hiding or living with abusive husbands as trafficked brides in China. They are in dire need for help, yet few people want to risk their lives by getting involved because they will be hunted down by the police and citizen spies. I could think of no easy answers to help them, and it was indescribably heartrending for me to leave them behind.

These risks were laid bare to me when I learnt that one of the smugglers who helped the other journalist and I to connect with these trafficked women had been arrested and tortured in North Korea. He was released back to Seoul and then hospitalized for months in a psychiatric unit. I was told that other journalist's video footage of the interviews had somehow been broadcast with his face on camera. I will never know for sure if this was the cause of the man's arrest but the episode haunts me to this day. This incident further strengthened my resolve to continue putting a spotlight on trafficked women so their stories could reach people across the world and hopefully lead to positive action.

* * *

Several years later after my seminal trip to meet North Korean women in 2007, I met David Kang, an older Korean–American man in his sixties. We had an easy rapport, and he poured out his testimony to me. For most of his adult life, Kang had been a successful businessman, but in 1999 his company went bust because of what he described as his own 'greediness'. His change of circumstances prompted him to take stock of his life, and he began to earnestly attend church activities, support disabled communities, and donate scholarships. This came as no surprise because, as I mentioned before, for many Koreans living overseas, church is the centre of their community life. A profound seminar about forgiving one's own father and healing a sense of an orphan spirit transformed Kang's outlook on life. He resolved his issues with his philandering father who had deeply disappointed him and his mother.

When I asked Kang about refugees, he told me how he first began to help them. This was when he was living in Guangdong, China. His pastor in New York asked him to host an undocumented North Korean refugee named Taenam at his home. Taenam was the first North Korean refugee that Kang had met. He was thirty years old and had defected to China after being discharged from the North Korean Army. Kang helped him find a job and a place to live while he was looking for a safe way to get to South Korea. Seven more refugees then came to Kang, and he gave them jobs at his factory. They all wanted to go to South Korea too.

Before he knew it, helping refugees had consumed Kang's life. He likened his new calling of providing jobs to North Korean refugees to the Oscar-winning Holocaust movie *Schindler's List*. He seemed to enjoy telling me of the James Bond-like elements of the Underground Railroad, making clandestine calls and meetings, and arranging logistics to elude the Chinese police. He said that helping deeply traumatized North Korean refugees required a high level of commitment and perseverance amid extreme uncertainty and danger. I wholeheartedly agreed with him, and said it was very dangerous. I related my experiences in meeting the women.

Kang said his most significant meetings were with two North Korean women who had been sold into forced marriage. Their names were Mee-hua and Young-sook. I was particularly interested in their stories.

In 1999, Young-sook crossed the Tumen river with her eight-year-old son on her back. She arrived at a village where she met the Hwangs, a couple who were ethnic Korean raised in China. They promised her a job in another province and took her to another town to wait for four days. 'They were professional human traffickers,' said David Kang. An old man covered with dust showed up, and the Hwangs told Young-sook that he would take care of her. The couple spoke to the man in Chinese, which Young-sook couldn't understand. She refused to go with this man. The Hwangs told her they would collect more money from people and then return to pick her up. She waited for two weeks and then realized that she had seen them collecting money for selling people on their last trip. She never saw the Hwangs again.

Kang's eyes were teary as he shared the story. He said that Young-sook and her son stayed with this man for one year and seven months. She hated him so much that she couldn't bear to even recall his name. She went on a hunger strike and demanded to be returned to North Korea. One time, she escaped, but after only getting half a mile away, the village people took her back to the man's house.

Young-sook had no other choice but to enrol her son in school. One day, some villagers turned her in to the police as an illegal alien from North Korea. Her 'husband' could have paid 3,000 RMB for her release but he never came for her, and she was repatriated to North Korea with her son. There, she was tied with ropes with nine other women and three men in one line and taken to the police station where they were stripped naked, interrogated, and beaten. After drinking some water from a fountain, she became seriously ill with a high fever. The authorities called her sister to pick her up, and she was released with her son to die outside.

Still desperate, she crossed into China again to look for a job at a restaurant. Their desperation to survive and find a better life was heartbreaking. Kang said her son joined her after a while, and she found a Korean–Chinese man to live with whose wife was away in South Korea for long-term business. Through the Underground Railroad network, Young-sook found Kang's shelter, and he was able to help her.

Mee-hua, the other refugee that Kang spoke of, was sold into forced marriage twice when she was twenty years old. She fled to China in 1998 because of starvation. Three days after she crossed the border, she was sold. She lived for four months with the first man. Then, he sold her to another man. She became pregnant and gave birth to a girl. Mee-hua finally sought out a way to Seoul and met Kang through the network who helped her get a flight.

This was the turning point for Kang as he began to look into how to send his North Korean friends to Seoul safely. Some operators charged more than $4,000 per person, but faith-based operators charged around \$450–600. If there were more than four people, the cost was \$450 per person including accommodation in Vietnam. Kang said he travelled on his own initiative to Vietnam to find and meet operators who could house the North Korean refugees in his care. 'All of these people in my shelter had the same story,' said Kang. 'They knew that if they went to South Korea, they would automatically become Korean citizens. So, their daily prayer was to go to South Korea. They had enough afflictions and troubles. They deserved to live the life that everyone else had in Korea.'

Kang arranged the train tickets and a guide to take the refugees across to Vietnam. Once they arrived, they would be taken to Seoul via one more neighbouring country. In 2002, he sent thirty refugees. Eventually, more than a hundred refugees went through his shelter.

One day in 2004, the police came and arrested Kang, and he was interrogated for several months. A few South Korean and Korean–American pastors were in the same cell block as him. All were charged by the Chinese police for helping North Korean refugees, but they had not been sentenced yet. Kang said there had been a steady succession of pastors and missionaries from South Korea and North America going through that very detention centre. I was shocked by this and said this was not in the international newspapers.

With his business skills and can-do spirit, Kang organized an underground church in the prison. They met mostly in the toilet and shower areas to sing quietly and study the Bible with at least two other North Korean inmates attending each gathering. The North Koreans began to confide in Kang and saw him as their father figure. I said I couldn't imagine his hardship in prison, and that he didn't look like he had gone through such an ordeal. He had found meaning in his sacrificial life, which made him happier than when he was a just a businessman.

After four years, Kang was released from prison. He reunited with his wife and three children, and he spoke about his experiences across the US. He then started a US-based non-profit organization to rescue North Korean refugees and support the underground church inside North Korea. I asked him about the churches there, and he described them as literal holes in the ground where Christians met. The hole had to be covered up with tree branches and leaves! I was stunned and inspired by their willingness to risk death to gather for church.

Since 2008, Kang has helped rescue dozens of trafficked North Korean women, many of whom were sold to work for Internet pornography websites targeted at men in South Korea. One woman he helped was sold six times. 'One man bought her for 600 RMB and slept with her for three or four months,' he said. 'Then, he sold her to another man for profit for 1,000 RMB. Several months later, she was sold again. She was crying, weeping as she told us. She had become a commodity. It's terrible.'

Besides supporting North Korean women in forced marriages, Kang also gives funding to church programmes for ninety North Korean women refugees and their stateless children. In 2015, he sent 580 gift packages to North Korean homes for orphans and the elderly. One year, his organization sent 1,500 tonnes of corn to North Korea. He is looking for more women to come forward so he can provide assistance. 'Most of them are still living under fear and live desperate lives. We want to find them and help them to come out in the light like the other church members,' he said.

I asked whether he was afraid of getting arrested again in China. 'Never,' he responded firmly. 'If I get arrested again, I know what's inside there; God has prepared someone whom I should meet in prison. So, nothing to be afraid of. I don't blame China either.'

\* \* \*

Another prominent member of the Underground Railroad I interviewed was Tim Peters, a Seoul-based American humanitarian and Nobel Peace Prize nominee. He founded Helping Hands Korea in 1996 with the aim of assisting North Korean refugees, bride trafficking victims, and the vulnerable children of North Korean women in forced marriages in China.

He was very cautious and requested that we conduct our interview by email so he could write out every word to prevent miscommunication. I was bracing myself for another emotionally charged story about the agonizingly painful situations that North Korean refugees face. They were willing to sacrifice everything and take extreme risks to meet their basic living needs and help their families rise above impoverished circumstances. 'Based on our experience, the situation is particularly harrowing now,' said Peters. 'The tolerance level of the Chinese authorities for North Korean escapees living in China seems to be dropping very noticeably. There seems to be a shift from rewarding Chinese citizens for turning in the North Koreans to authorities to actually punishing citizens who are employing or harbouring the refugees in some way. Add to that the type of treachery that faces the refugees in the form of Chinese human traffickers teaming up with North Koreans to victimize women especially.'

Mi-young was one of the refugees whom Peters helped rescue. Like so many North Koreans who choose to escape the totalitarian dictatorship, Mi-young too fled to China to find work to support her desperate family. Her father had been arrested by North Korean authorities. Mi-young suspected he was involved in illegal trade in China, just across the Yalu River from her city Hyesan, where many North Koreans cross over near the popular tourist attraction Mount Paektu or known as Changbai Mountain on the Chinese side. Hyesan is just opposite the small Chinese border city of Changbai, which has a sizeable Korean–Chinese ethnic minority population. Mi-young's father had provided a comfortable living for her family, but after he was sent to a labour camp, she had to quit her college to start a hair salon business in her home. 'It was difficult. Suddenly, I had to fend for myself. Our family's destiny in North Korea seemed very dismal,' she said. I had heard the same from all of the North Korean women I had interviewed over the years.

What she shared next reminded me of the deceptive recruitment of wartime sex slaves. Mi-young was promised a waitressing job in a restaurant by a Chinese trafficker posing as a peddler in Hyesan. He said she would be able to send enough money back to her family. Out of desperation, she agreed to cross over illegally into China with the peddler's instruction and help. If the North Korean border guards had caught her, it would have meant immediate imprisonment in a labour camp or even death. If she was caught on the Chinese side, she would be sent back. 'Many of the refugees carry razor blades to slit their wrists or arsenic to commit suicide in case they are forcibly repatriated,' said Peters.

After Mi-young arrived in China, the trafficker passed her off to another Chinese broker and his North Korean wife who locked her in their home until she agreed to live with her new Chinese 'husband'. Mi-young said the couple used psychological coercion to force her to marry a Chinese man. 'They did everything to convince me to live with a Chinese man as my best choice to help my family back in North Korea,' she said. 'They took me to multiple households of various disabled men of different ages in China for me to choose who I wanted to live with. I wept bitterly at my situation. I knew the punishment that awaited me in North Korea would be severe since I'd left without permission.'

She was 'sold' for 50,000 RMB to the mother of a divorced man who Mi-young described as being very passive and having a mental or emotional disorder that seemed to prevent him from communicating. 'He would stare at the wall and be silent a great deal. This, in turn, was very depressing for me,' she said. The man's mother lived in a nearby village and kept a close eye on her, which added great stress to an already traumatic living situation. To avoid getting pregnant, Mi-young pretended to be sick. In time, she was allowed by her mother-in-law to run errands in the town. She was able to escape during one of these excursions through a network of volunteers on the Underground Railroad. This organization actively searched for North Korean refugee women in villages across China so they could be helped or supported in case they wanted to defect to a third country.

After a long and harrowing journey, Mi-young and her friend snuck across the border from China into Laos and then travelled to Thailand. They surrendered themselves to the Thai authorities and were sent to the immigration detention centre before being released to the South Korean embassy in line with an unspoken agreement between Thailand and South Korea. At the time of my interview with her, she was waiting for the South Korean embassy to complete the paperwork that would allow her to 'defect' and re-settle in Seoul. I was so thrilled for her and her new beginnings.

'One of the biggest challenges facing the Underground Railroad workers is that due to overwhelming media focus, the world's attention is increasingly riveted on DPRK's ICBM missile launches and nuclear tests while concentrating less and less on the human rights catastrophe, including the refugees in China,' said Peters.

* * *

Jihyun Park is a North Korean refugee who now lives in the UK. I reached out to her on LinkedIn after reading her harrowing tale in the news. Somehow, she had read of my articles on wartime sex slaves, and she resonated with their struggle for justice and closure. She was more comfortable responding to my questions through email, and she told me that she first escaped North Korea with her brother in 1998. They travelled into China where they were preyed on by human traffickers who separated them and sold her into a forced marriage to a Chinese farmer for 5,000 RMB. She had a child who was deemed stateless by the Chinese government. I remembered learning of the tragedy of the stateless children of North Korean mothers and Chinese fathers back in 2007. They were trapped in their homes with the blinds shut with no access to a normal life, to education and regular medical services.

In 2004, local villagers reported her to the authorities. She was repatriated to North Korea and endured horrific conditions in a labour camp. She developed gangrene, and the guards threw her out of the prison as they believed she was close to death. A kind stranger nursed her and helped her to escape for the final time and reunite with her son. She settled in the UK in 2008.

One of the most distressing things Park said was that from the moment she woke up until sunset, her Chinese 'husband' forced her to work in the fields. But, instead of giving her proper shoes, she was given slippers to prevent her from running away. She knew other North Korean women had the same experiences.

Today, it is inspiring to see Park rise up as an important voice for North Korean trafficked women. She has raised vital awareness as a survivor. As some of the outspoken elderly survivors of Japanese military sex slavery have done, I hope more North Korean women and women from Door of Hope can find their voice and share their authentic and powerful testimonies of finding redemption despite their experiences of basic human rights violations. The transformed lives of the humble and repentant ex-Japanese soldiers and Tomoko and her reconciliation group—unlikely advocates and healing agents for sex slavery victims—helps me believe that the impossible is possible.

# 10

# Hong Kong's Flesh Trade*

After I finished the first draft of my book on wartime sexual servitude, I marked a new beginning in my life by moving to Hong Kong in the winter of 2011. The previous year, I had spent a gruelling five months writing in my parents' basement in Canada to escape the distractions of friends and work in Beijing. For nearly three of those intense months, I woke up daily and robotically walked six feet from my bed to the desk, and my mother lovingly brought me breakfast, lunch and dinner on a tray every single day. She believed in my dreams and wanted to help me finish my book that documented an important historical war crime. If it weren't for her, I am doubtful I would have been able to complete the book. It seemed fitting and a full circle return to my Westcoast Canadian roots to birth a marathon project that began when I was fifteen and helped me process and accept my identity, refine my core beliefs, and solidify a human rights calling in the media.

After nearly seven years of living in Beijing, I was finally ready to leave the old ghosts of that season behind and to settle in to a full-time

---

* This chapter is partly based on my article titled 'I was forced to sell my body in a Hong Kong bar: a Filipino's experience of trafficking, prostitution', published in *South China Morning Post* on 19 February 2017.

job. I had taken a sabbatical of a few years with the aim of focusing on writing and gathering information, using part of my savings and taking on consulting jobs in philanthropy advising for ultra high net worth family offices to cover flights to different cities to interview people. My sabbatical funding sources were low, and I took a risk in relocating. I learned quickly in the early days of exploring Hong Kong and networking that the people here were not interested in human rights. The seductive love of mammon and power prevailed in this glittering international finance centre. I struggled with doubts over choosing Hong Kong as my new home as it seemed at odds with my values, and what I wanted to accomplish in amplifying the voices of the voiceless.

I was offered a job at a TV station as a producer of current affairs documentaries, and I had a goal to produce films on modern-day human trafficking, though I didn't know what the first step would be. Human trafficking was not a term known to professionals in Hong Kong at this time, and I would have to break new ground and look for victims of modern slavery myself. A few months into the producer role I found myself at the American Chamber of Commerce filming a guest speaker for a documentary series I pitched on modern slavery.

His passionate speech blew me away and relit the fire in my belly for the fight against slavery. His compassionate stories of survivors resonated with my experiences and the women I had met. I knew immediately that I wanted to support his mission. His name was Matt Friedman.

He said that only five per cent of people who have been forced into slavery are kidnapped because it's a difficult crime to commit and gets a lot of media attention. He explained that most people are trafficked through deception; they're in dire poverty and dream of a better life so they'll accept any job offer, despite their reservations because they have no other choices.

He spoke of an eleven-year-old girl who had begged him to save her; he went back with the police to get her but she was gone.

He spoke of his work for the UN, assisting Lao, Cambodian, Burmese and Indonesian people who were in forced labour on fishing boats in Thailand. He spoke of a trafficked woman in Nepal who was angry with him rather than the traffickers; she blamed the good people—society as a whole—for not standing up to stop slavery.

He said that traffickers are motivated by greed, and they have no respect for human life.

He said that if we lined up all the slaves in the world, they would be shoulder to shoulder from Beijing to Cape Town. He challenged us by saying that if one million people each gave one hour of their time, then slavery could be reduced.

He told us that there was no human trafficking law in Hong Kong, and that this needed to change if we are to have any hope of fighting slavery in the city. He said the corporate sector holds the key to eliminating slavery, not only in Hong Kong but also in Mainland China and all over the world.

His expertise, his first-hand experiences, and his passion as a storyteller inspired us all. I was there with a few friends and we were all deeply wowed. He was the catalyst for our involvement in the abolition movement, and several of us went on to initiate city-wide events to mobilize people to take action. Without his speech on this day, we would not have stepped out; it felt like a divine intervention for me in this cold money-oriented city. He helped steel my resolve further to continue the fight against modern slavery and to surrender to this new sense of calling I had in Hong Kong to raise important awareness. Little did I know on that day that he was my future husband!

Matt was launching the Mekong Club, a non-profit organization that aimed to mobilize the private sector to take the lead in the fight against modern slavery. From its humble beginnings in Hong Kong, the Mekong Club has since become the leading catalyst in the global anti-slavery movement among corporations, and Friedman is still its

CEO to this day. I had planned to interview him after the event, but he was sick with a cold and forced to postpone. I brought him some medicine in the hope of speeding up his recovery and sealing the deal on the interview. He later told me that he was touched by the gesture. We became fast friends and emailed several times a day. Corporations and banks were not responding to his cold emails so I helped him knock on, or rather kick down their doors through the journalism contacts I had. I was persistent in my networking mission and pursued every connection. The executives I reached out to probably wanted the media coverage and responded quickly to my emails connecting them with Matt and urging them to host him for a talk on modern-day slavery. The tiny trickle of water became a mighty rushing river, one speech after another. The response from each audience was similar to what I had felt that first day hearing Matt talk at the American Chamber of Commerce about suffering men, women, and children.

Our pioneering partnership was very fruitful and from those early years when no one knew about human trafficking and outright denied that it was happening in this day and age to now where leading global banks and top brands are seeking to work with Matt to help eliminate modern slavery and anti-money laundering from trafficker's criminal profits.

Matt said that debt bondage was often used to keep women in forced prostitution. 'There are all types of threats that can be used,' he said. 'The debt may be HK$15,000 but it may take two years to pay it off. And the amount that she earns as a result of selling herself could be as much as HK$155,000. These women get trapped in a circle of debt where they're actually forced to work for somebody else. They lose control of their lives. We're talking about human slavery.' A pivotal piece of information was offered when he said the domestic workers from South East Asia in Hong Kong are deceived into debt bondage through exorbitant agency fees, including some illegal ones. With his counsel, I exposed for the first time in Hong

Kong through a documentary called *Helpers' Hell*, the slavery-like debt bondage that domestic workers are subjected to.

\* \* \*

As part of my documentary series on human trafficking in Thailand, Mainland China, and in Hong Kong, I was in search of sex trafficking victims to interview in my city. There were no victims or survivors of modern slavery according to local NGOs. Matt suggested that they may not know how to look for them.

It was an unattainable kind of assignment but I was extremely determined. I was convinced there were slaves hidden all over Hong Kong. For nine months during my research, I scoured the red-light districts in the streets of Jordan and surrounding areas and the notorious Wanchai bar strip with the help of some missionaries and frontline workers to identify victims. After producing two documentaries on sex trafficking and finishing a book on historical Japanese military sex slavery, I felt confident as I walked through the seedy neighbourhoods. Some of the smaller side streets in Jordan and Tsim Sha Tsui were downright dark and scary, and I edged closer to my companions in those places. I would have probably grabbed their hand if that were acceptable for an investigative journalist like me!

One night, we met several women from Africa and Mainland China who told us that they had been trafficked into Hong Kong and forced into prostitution. Most were afraid to speak on camera but said they wanted help. We met Abby on the street and approached her as if we were tiptoeing near a frightened deer. I zoned in on her because she was receptive to my greeting, and I sensed a tiny crack of an opening in her heart towards us. I held my breath as we said hello and asked her a non-threatening question about the time. I desperately wished with all my soul for this to be the right connection, and I thought I might faint from inner exertion. I could feel my neck veins bulging from the stress. I really wanted to get a victim's story on videotape, even if it was taped on my iPhone.

Abby was initially reluctant to admit that she was forced into prostitution, but she eventually opened up after a few meetings with us on the streets. She said that in January 2012 she was flown on a tourist visa to Shenzhen from East Africa. I asked her to interview on camera. She agreed as long as we didn't film her face.

Every night, Abby walked the streets of Wan Chai, Hong Kong's infamous red-light district. She was forced to find clients for sex. 'I know some men. Even ladies. They bring girls from Africa, like a business. Many girls. They are like sex slaves,' she said.

She told me that she was lured by the promise of earning more money to pay for her twelve-year-old daughter's education. The African traffickers paid for her air tickets and expenses. When she arrived in Shenzhen, she was forced to have sex with several men every day. Her earnings for the first three months went towards paying off her 'debt' of HK$31,000. 'Yes, you are a slave. We hold your passport until you have paid up. You have to do whatever you have to do in order to get that money,' said Abby, recalling what the traffickers had told her that she owed them for flights and room and board. 'It's very hard. You have to do it.'

Abby was later brought to Hong Kong to sell her body from Shenzhen. Her traffickers had menacingly told her that they knew where her daughter lived. It was enough to keep her in line even though she walked freely on the streets. I told her I was sad to hear of the threats against her daughter. She shrugged and seemed resigned to her fate.

When I asked her if any man had hit her, she sighed deeply and looked to the ground. 'Prostitution is a dangerous thing,' she said, with a deadness in her eyes. I imagined she used to be a sassy, joyful woman full of life before she was deceived and lured into a heartless trafficking ring. She was now a hollow version of that person.

Through a friend, I met Karen, the founder of a non-profit organization that reaches women working in the sex trade in Wan Chai and the New Territories. She also asked Matt for advice from time to time. Matt knew just about everyone in Asia working in the fight to abolish human trafficking. Karen said that she had met at least a hundred victims who were brought into Hong Kong on tourist visas or smuggled in. 'I've met women from the Philippines, Thailand, African nations, India, Nepal, Colombia,' she said. 'All these women believed that if they didn't pay back the money, there's a real chance of physical harm. These women were scared and hopeless. They might end up in jail but they would still feel unsafe with the police.'

We brought Abby to a church service one Sunday. We were hoping to speak with her about finding her a different means of livelihood to support herself and her family. We wished to explore whether it was possible for her to escape her traffickers. We were in unchartered waters and felt apprehensive about speaking with her; we were afraid that she may have no escape options. After the service, Matt, Karen and I asked Abby to join us for dinner at a nearby Pizza Hut. Abby was seated diagonally from Matt. She looked terrified and couldn't look him in the eyes. To help Abby feel more comfortable, Matt focused on finishing his dinner while Karen and I did all the talking. We surmised that Abby was traumatized by what she was forced to do with the johns. It was something we had not anticipated, but it was obvious in hindsight. It was another confirmation of the personal cost of sexual enslavement that robs a person of normalcy and healthy relationships.

We went to see Abby again in the hopes of helping her escape her slavers. She was staying at Chungking Mansions, a notorious building known for cheap accommodations that drew backpackers. It housed many hostels and small businesses as well as hole-in-the-wall restaurants that catered to the African and Indian communities. Perhaps her traffickers had seen us. After this visit, her mobile was disconnected and I could not track her down ever again. I thought of her often and her daughter, hoping they were safe, as I continued to reach out to terrified looking women in the red-light districts. On several occasions, I thought I spotted Abby on the streets and called her name. Each time, I was met with silence.

After we met Abby, at one of the bars on Lockhart Road, Karen and I met Maria, a pretty woman with long, straight black hair and eyes that radiated intelligence. I had a small camera on me, and I filmed the bar inside to capture the grotesque way these women were reduced to sexual objects. One man draped his arms around Maria after buying a drink. I was shocked to learn that she had a college degree and was a mother of two children. She had left them behind in a small town outside of Manila. With her pimp standing nearby and keeping a close eye on her, Maria said that she had been deceived into sex work. She looked terrified as she asked us to quickly order a drink, which we did in order to continue speaking with her. I felt I couldn't breathe in the bar and everything within me wanted to run out; it was oppressive and full of a demonic lustful energy.

I felt so much compassion for Maria who was forced to work in this dank atmosphere. I steeled myself to keep going and I boldly asked if she wanted to get out of this work. She said, 'Of course. But I have no other job options.' I felt a lump in the pit of my stomach as we walked away and saw her quickly force a smile and begin a conversation with a foreign man. I was free to walk away, while selling her body against her will was her regular routine.

Could we do something to get her out safely? No one had any easy answers and there was no way to stay in touch with Maria. Her traffickers would have total control over any phone that she would use. I hoped she was safe but it is very likely that she would be vulnerable to sexual violence and unspeakable abuse. Her fate is still unknown to me.

On another evening out in Jordan district, Karen and her team met and prayed with several women controlled by their pimp traffickers. In a McDonald's window, I spotted Suzanne, who was from Africa, wearing a tight-fitting canary yellow shirt. She looked anxious and something about her demeanour caught my eye. My radar sensed she was someone to speak with and I rushed inside with Karen following.

We approached her gently and showed care. She seemed relieved by our compassionate gesture. After some initial small talk, she opened up to us. We found out that she was a single mother of two boys. She had been flown to Hong Kong by her traffickers, leaving her sons with their grandmother.

'Someone convinced me about a job in China,' she said with fear in her voice, and her eyes scanning the place to ensure she wasn't being monitored. 'They said it was work at a hotel and with a better salary. But there was no job. It was prostitution. My visa soon expired. I was trapped. I had no other place to go, no money. My family is poor. I had to pay HK$31,000.' As she said this, Suzanne was looking around again, in paranoia, to see if anyone was watching her. She was terrified. She said the HK$31,000 was to cover the cost of her plane ticket, but she was forced to keep working even after she had repaid the debt. She estimated she had made at least HK$310,000 for her pimps in her four months in Hong Kong. Karen and I felt unspeakably sad to leave Suzanne behind. I had no means to find her or call her. Meeting Suzanne and Abby left me reeling with guilt and frustration over our inability to rescue them. At this point in Hong Kong, no group or NGO was able to do that. I thought of the Door of Hope team's ability to offer practical help to women in forced prostitution, through means of jobs and healing care. Incidentally, Amy reached out to me by email to ask about the red-light districts in the city.

She had planned to launch Door of Hope in Hong Kong soon, and she wanted to scope out the territory. I took her to the Temple Street neighbourhood in Kowloon. We walked into a decrepit building known for its one-room brothels. A man in his thirties wearing a baseball cap walked by to intimidate us. He was likely a triad member. Amy told him that we were missionaries. He walked out into the stairwell without saying a word, but I sensed we were still under surveillance by one of the many cameras above us. We continued to knock on some doors, and a Mainland Chinese woman in her thirties invited us into her place. She looked like a sales lady at a make-up counter at a mall in her black miniskirt, white blazer, heavy eyeshadow and lips painted bright rouge. She was more open and vulnerable than we had expected since all the other doors we had knocked on, we were met by frightened young women who said, 'No I can't speak with you.' The woman told us that she commuted from Shenzhen every week and would sometimes go back on the same day because of visa restrictions. As a single mother of a young son, she struggled to pay the bills. A friend introduced her to prostitution work in Hong Kong. She wanted to desperately escape her life of pain and hardship.

Amy and I met several other women on the streets the next day. She wrote a report detailing our experiences meeting the trafficked women and sent it to the Head of the Department of Justice and others including Matt.

Debbie, a former outreach worker at Operation Mobilisation, an international non-profit organization, said these trafficked mainlanders were forced to work in one-person, single-room brothels that were controlled by triads. 'There are human trafficking victims in the sex industry,' she said. 'They are even more hidden than the prostitutes. We need to search carefully to find them. I've met a few girls who are underage, under sixteen years old.'

'We've got a number of cases where the hallmarks of trafficking appear,' said Kevin Zervos, a former Director of Public Prosecution at the Justice Department in an interview. 'Every year, there are about four thousand women getting arrested in relation to vice activities. And they're seriously exploited.'

Liz was falsely promised a job as a waitress in a restaurant. She was flown to Hong Kong with her trafficker and two men from the

Philippines to make sure she didn't cause trouble after she found out that the restaurant job didn't exist. She came on a tourist visa and had to shuttle back and forth every fortnight between Hong Kong and China to avoid overstaying. The agency created false hotel reservations for her and other trafficked victims to show the customs officers. Liz had to pay the agency for the hotel accommodations, even though she didn't stay there.

Kat, a twenty-three-year-old single mother, was recruited in the Philippines and deceived into forced prostitution at a bar in Hong Kong in December 2016. She was paying back a crushing debt for the next three to four months. 'I'm traumatized. There are three other women at my bar who feel the same. I always feel like I am in danger. I take a risk every time I go out with a male customer. But I have no other choice,' she said as she wept. Kat said she was forced to participate in 'wild parties' where hard drugs were used. The mama-sans allowed her to keep the commission made from drinks bought by johns in the bar. Most bars charge HK$100 per drink, and the mama-sans keep HK$50 and give HK$50 to the bar girl. While the bar girl sits with the client, he can touch her in any way he wants. Kat managed to send a monthly commission of around HK$5,000 back to the Philippines to support her young daughter and ill mother.

When I first met Kat, she was bright-eyed and cried easily at the thought of entertaining men. A few months later, she was emaciated, her skin had turned sallow, her long jet-black hair was limp and greasy, and her eyes had the wide-eyed bloodshot look of a regular drug user. She used hard drugs to numb herself; it was the only way she could get through the night.

Almost every day, Jean, a small twenty-five-year-old Filipina with long curly hair and a girlish face, worked long hours into the night to sell her body to multiple johns in a bar on Hong Kong island. Jean said a criminal network of pimps and enforcers with tentacles in other countries also made her take hard drugs with these johns in order to make more money for them. 'Life was hell—I was just surviving,' she said. 'Clients ask you to buy drugs like cocaine, ice, marijuana—anything the clients want. They make you take it with them. We can earn a lot of money from using drugs with clients.'

In 2014, a recruiter came to her town in Pampanga in the Philippines and promised her a good life and a pleasant job in Hong Kong. Jean, a single mother of a four-year-old girl with no family support network, took the job out of desperation.

Marcela Santos, a frontline worker, was a feisty short woman in her late fifties and a raucous laugh that could shatter glass. I met her through a friend, and she wanted to raise awareness of women forced into prostitution in the Wanchai bars. She told me that Pampanga was also where many survivors of sexual servitude for the Japanese military in the Philippines were from. It made me think of the generational cycle, much like opium addiction that flourished across generations leading to the current-day drug addiction problems in the region.

Jean was brought to Hong Kong by this criminal network for two months on a tourist visa. Upon arrival, the recruiters told her she owed a heavy debt for the cost of air travel, visa, and living expenses. She was immediately put to work and forced to take as many as three johns a night to pay off her debt bondage to her agent, the pimp trafficker. 'Of course, it's torture to pay back the debt,' she said. 'The agent doesn't care. They don't know how badly clients treat you. I worked three times each night to pay back my debt faster.'

Subsequently, the recruiters arranged a two-year domestic worker visa for Jean as part of the arrangement with a bar on Hong Kong Island. Jean said there were twelve other women from different countries who had been forced into prostitution at the bar, just like her. 'There were Colombian women, Filipina, Indonesian, Thai women,' she said. 'It was shocking to know these victims were right under our nose. I had walked by these bars often in search of sex slavery victims, and here they were, right in the open.'

Jean was rescued and repatriated back to the Philippines, thanks to the help of an NGO and Santos. Jean who was now speaking from Manila, said, 'I was deceived. These girls are deceived . . . then forced because their passports are taken.' Jean said no one told her exactly how much debt she owed, but she estimated she'd paid more than HK$380,000.

The mama-sans charge the clients at least HK$5,000 and keep HK$4,000 out of the total for themselves. The remaining HK$1,000 goes to pay the prostitute's debt. The victims are not aware of the total debt amount, and it is common for pimps to change the total of the debt on a whim.

Physical force was regularly used to keep women like Jean in line. 'I was beaten up by the mama-sans,' she said. 'They slammed me against the wall. Mama-sans have a big control over us. It was very traumatic. I can hardly talk about it.'

Jean said the bar she worked in was co-owned by a Hong Kong police officer before it was closed down. In an unrelated case that same year, the Independent Commission Against Corruption reported that twelve people, including three police officers, had been arrested for alleged corruption in relation to enforcement action against two nightclubs. It was claimed that the arrested police officers might have accepted a 'substantial amount of bribes in cash and other forms of advantages from the operators of the nightclubs' in exchange for tipping them off on police action against the nightclubs.

I wondered about the cycle of sex trafficking repeating with no end in sight, as a steady stream of Filipina women and women from other nations, forced against their will, filled the bars in Hong Kong's infamous red-light district. Beneath a façade of forced smiles and heavy make-up, they all had heartrending stories bearing down and almost suffocating them.

Nurul Qoiriah, the former head of the Sub-Office IOM Hong Kong, a Geneva-based international-governmental agency that assists foreign migrants, said, 'These victims of sex trafficking are often found in the streets or working in particular establishments that facilitate commercial sex acts such as strip clubs, brothels, pornography production houses, night clubs, bars, spas, etc. Sex trafficking in Hong Kong SAR is usually an underground crime, where it's often challenging for law enforcement personnel and service providers to identify potential victims. In most situations, victims cannot escape from the traffickers. Traffickers may also threaten to turn victims without valid visas or proper work permits into the authorities, and may tell victims that police will harm them if they seek help.'

Qoiriah said that identifying victims of trafficking is also hampered by their dependency on their abusers. Many are afraid of deportation or imprisonment, unaware of their rights and the concept of human trafficking and have feelings of guilt and shame about their exploitation.

'It's very hard for people to understand unless you've gone through trauma. It numbs you,' said Santos. 'It's a Stockholm Syndrome situation for these ladies. They hope [the mama-san will] be nice to them. She is like their mother. She kind of pits the other women against each other and controls them.'

Santos helped Jean escape by buying her a plane ticket back to the Philippines. She had met eight women from the Philippines who were forced into prostitution through different trafficking rings. Most of these women were issued domestic worker visas. 'Jean was completely clueless of what the agency was doing because the mama-sans were taking care of the visa process. It's their way to control, making sure the women don't know any of the processes. Also, they don't have the skills to ask questions or they don't think they can find a way out of their bad situation,' she said.

Santos believes police and immigration officers should be trained more rigorously to identify victims of human trafficking. 'I know of this lady who was trafficked here in Hong Kong and she told me that the immigration officer knew she was trafficked and knew she would be forced into prostitution, and yet she stamped her passport and let her through. So even with detection, this immigration officer still let her into Hong Kong when all this victim wanted was to go back to her home country. I feel a heaviness in my heart every time I think of the women who work at the bars. I think of the darkness, loneliness, and pain that goes beyond the physical abuse they receive from clients, mama-sans, and bar owners. I think about one lady who told me about the ugliness and disgust she feels every night and how she tries to erase that when she says her prayers. How could I not want to get her out of that?'

In 2021, the US State Department's *Trafficking in Persons Report* ranked Hong Kong as a 'Tier 2 Watchlist' territory, just one rank above worst offending nations like North Korea. The annual report stated that Hong Kong's government was not meeting the minimum standards required for the elimination of trafficking, and that local authorities had failed to investigate, prosecute or convict in trafficking cases. It also criticized Hong Kong for lacking a comprehensive law in line with the internationally recognized UN Palermo Protocol on Human Trafficking.

Hong Kong's Security Bureau, which oversees law and order as well as immigration, said that existing laws that deal with criminal activities relating to human trafficking, with penalties ranging from ten-years to life imprisonment, are sufficient.

Sandy Wong, a formidable advocate, was chair of the Anti-Human Trafficking Committee of the Hong Kong Federation of Women Lawyers. She said, 'We do have laws to tackle sex trafficking but not in the sense of how the international community understands the issue. We also do not have specific labour trafficking laws. So, on that front, there can be a lot of improvement. But it is not only the government, the community also has to rise up to tighten our laws.' Sandy was also there when Matt spoke at his first event in Hong Kong at the American Chamber of Commerce. Our paths had crossed several times over the years, and I admired her huge compassion for women and for supporting NGOs including organizations that were combating sex trafficking.

Sweden's prostitution laws criminalize the buying of sex and put the criminal focus on the johns rather than the prostitutes. Swedish laws also offer support for women who want to leave prostitution. 'We also need to go to the source of demand and supply,' said Wong. 'Despite the police's efforts in combating vice establishments, many operate in broad daylight. If we don't stop the source of demand, there will always be someone who will provide the supply—by hook or by crook. Punishing the johns in Sweden proves to be an effective measure and should be a model to adopt.'

When I spoke with Jean, she was going through a rehabilitation and healing process in Manila and recovering from drug addiction. Santos has visited her in Manila to help her find job opportunities.

'My daughter keeps me going,' said Jean. 'I'm studying to finish my high school education. I don't know what kind of job I'll get. I want to go back to a normal life . . . I want dignity.'

Jean reminded me of the North Korean women I met on the Underground Railroad and their anguished desperation to provide a better life for their families back home, which in turn tragically led to their systematic sexual exploitation and worse. The noble people rescuing these women were far too few in number and the challenges they faced to do the impossible work of wrenching the victims from their traffickers was a David and Goliath scenario. It seemed like a losing fight. I came to believe that raising awareness about these untold stories could help mobilize more ordinary people like Karen and Marcela to take action out of love and step out of their comfort zone. I resolved to do more to tell the world about these victims through films and to raise funding to help them. I am convinced that even one small act could help rescue at least one human being out of the living hell that is modern-day slavery.

# 11

# A Mama-san and a Pimp*

In my research into modern-day slavery over the years, I have learnt that it was incredibly rare to find former traffickers, pimps, and mama-sans who were rehabilitated and regretful of their past actions. A friend said she knew a former mama-san, Mary Zardilla, who was a sincere Christian with a powerful testimony and she was willing to talk with me. Immediately, Guo the former pimp trafficker in China came to mind. I asked for a meeting to be set up and we met at a church. When I interviewed her, she was sixty-three years old and petite, with a pretty wrinkle-free face. She looked a few decades younger than her actual age. She was very charming and sincere, and from the start we embraced each other and there was a warmth as we spoke. She had an innate ability to connect with people and earn their trust.

Through the gift of her intuition and humorous storytelling, she had acquired a reputation for luring and captivating wealthy johns by quickly understanding their tastes in women and matching them up accordingly with the hostesses under her control. I could clearly

---

* This chapter is partly based on my article titled 'I trafficked women at a famous Hong Kong nightclub', published in *South China Morning Post* on 11 June 2017.

206

see why she was successful. A skilled mama-san bringing in a lot of money for a nightclub was arguably the most prized part of this entertainment business for the triads who were rumoured to be in control of the operations.

For that reason, Mary had the confidence to be unusually bold and ask to leave for another establishment. 'Some mama-sans got beaten and hospitalized as a warning to others who might want to leave. But I said, "Please don't hurt me. I served my contract. I have to support my poor family in the Philippines."'

Mary looked proud to tell me that she had two bodyguards with guns protecting her for several months after she left one nightclub to work for the grandest of them all, Club Bboss, in 1986. The 1980s marked the peak of hedonism for colossal Japanese clubs with lavish décor in the Tsim Sha Tsui district of Hong Kong before businesses and the escort industry migrated to Mainland China. Luxury cars were once parked outside of Club Bboss, a 70,000 sq. ft amusement park catering to men and staffed with more than a thousand perfectly coiffed hostesses. Golden mini-golf carts designed to look like Rolls Royces would transport the clients around.

I couldn't imagine the decadence. It's not common in Hong Kong today. She continued to describe the clientele as a veritable who's who of Hong Kong society, including celebrities, politicians, and businessmen. Mary learned to speak fluent Japanese so that she could serve her many Japanese clients. I shivered as I thought of the wartime sex slaves suffering as they served long lines of Japanese soldiers on the frontlines of war. I thought of the repeating cycle of history, yet again.

There were about a hundred mama-sans at Club Bboss from Australia, Japan, China, and Korea. Other clubs had mama-sans from Malaysia, Indonesia, and Singapore. For seventeen years, Mary managed about a hundred girls like herself, girls who began working voluntarily at the nightclub because unemployment and impoverished family backgrounds had driven them to it. 'We were trapped with no other options,' she said. It made me think of the fate of the many exploited women I had met on the streets of Hong Kong and in other countries.

As a glamourous mama-san, Mary mentored her girls in everything from etiquette to elegant styling. Every night, she introduced her girls to johns who were charged hefty fees by fifteen-minute increments. These fees were paid directly to the nightclub and amounted to anything between HK$1,900 to HK$3,500, sometimes even more, per encounter.

To get around the laws on prostitution, the girls' salaries were paid by the nightclub accountants, and they were taxed as hostesses since it was considered legal work. To keep their mama-san happy, the girls gave Mary money or gifts as a 'favour'. The girls needed this favour to get an edge over their competition for the highest paying, most attractive johns. Mama-sans like Mary were in command of their own schedules as contractors, and they were at the top of the food chain. She only answered directly to the nightclub owner.

I asked whether Mary recruited and trafficked girls into the club from other countries but she replied that the girls were already there—some from Japan, the US, the UK, Latin America, the Philippines, and Mainland China, alongside local women. I doubted this and felt they were likely brought in by those who ran the club.

One of the most sorrowful stories Mary shared with me was that many of these women were hoping to meet men who would sweep them off their feet and take care of them, just like the saccharine ending of *Pretty Woman*. They must have been destroyed by the vicious reality. Many of the women came in with a tourist visa and then voluntarily applied for work at one of the ten most successful clubs at the time. 'The girls can make more money in clubs than at brothels,' said Mary. 'Brothels are faster movement, but they are more controlled. Nightclubs give more freedom and pay more.'

Mary admitted that some of the girls were underage. 'Even then, I saw the girls were young, like 16 years,' she said quietly. I didn't want to imagine what had happened to them; their futures were undoubtedly cut short. At other nightclubs, Mary knew of girls who had been specially recruited from abroad and could not leave at any time. This was trafficking I pointed out each time she shared a hallmark of modern slavery. The club and agents had paid for their plane tickets and expenses and wanted to control their 'property'.

'Some girls wanted to find a decent job, but unfortunately they didn't finish school or have skills,' said Mary. 'Freelancers could leave anytime they wanted . . . but they didn't have other options and ended up trapped.'

One of Mary's girls, named Isabelle, was trafficked from Manila into Hong Kong by a gang more than thirty years ago. Isabelle was deceived and trafficked into prostitution in a private home. She had twenty to thirty clients a night, and the triads charged HK$50 per john. A man guarded her all the time to prevent her from escaping. One day, her bodyguard decided to buy her out from her owner after they formed a bond, and they eventually got married. She then joined Mary's group of hostesses and worked at the nightclub with more freedom and more pay.

Mary's descent into pimping women happened slowly. She dropped out of school and started working at sixteen at a factory to support her parents and seven brothers and sisters in Manila. Her father died three years later, leaving her mother, a laundrywoman, devastated. Mary stepped up as the oldest daughter to support the family.

She left the factory job to join a cultural dance troupe and performed in the evenings. The troupe travelled to Hong Kong in 1972. A few months later, President Ferdinand Marcos declared martial law in the Philippines, so Mary and the other dance troupe members decided to stay on in Hong Kong to find more permanent work.

That year, she dated a Filipino man who was working in the entertainment industry, and a few years later they were married. He cheated on her with a revolving door of women. Pained, she focused on making money to send back to her family in Manila. 'I longed for love. I didn't have love. I became a slave to money!' she said. I suspected she felt worthless like the women victims of trafficking who had shattered self-esteem.

She applied for what she thought was a receptionist role at a nightclub in Tsim Sha Tsui, but it turned out to be a hostess job. 'I was innocent. So deceived. Many are deceived into working as prostitutes,' she said. Mary refused to sleep with the johns and because she was older and resolute, they eventually left her alone. She also had a strong will.

She was then groomed to be a mama-san by one boss, and this might have saved her from being forced into prostitution. Unacquainted with this underworld, she initially had no idea about what mama-sans actually did or the big money they made. She learnt on the job. 'I was entertaining customers like a public relations person. I studied Japanese and became good at my job. I asked them what kind of girls they preferred . . . then I brought out the girls who were at the back. I also learnt that Japanese businessmen like young girls,' she said with a grimace.

The money hardened her. She discovered that other mama-sans were paid HK$30,000 a month and that when they signed a contract, they were given a one-time *lai see* payment or bonus of about HK$20,000. So, Mary asked for a raise. Her starting salary was about HK$20,000 a month plus commission and HK$15,000 in *lai see*. She worked at other leading nightclubs before being recruited by the largest club, Bboss, where she made more than HK$500,000 a year plus HK$80,000 *lai see*. She was in charge of seventy to hundred girls. 'We charged HK$1,000 for sex in the 1980s,' she said.

The clients gave her girls jewellery or money to buy land, houses, and apartments back in their home countries. Sometimes, Mary was given a blank cheque by the clients. She had several wealthy boyfriends on the side. Some of the girls became savvy at buying and selling real estate and left the club with a small fortune. They were regularly paid to attend parties and dinners with high-profile Hong Kong businessmen. 'They were high-end call girls, dressed so elegantly,' she said, with a wistfulness of the glamour in this season of her life.

But deep inside, Mary said she and the women were suffering and lost, some with drug addictions and alcoholism. I was drawn to her honesty and leaned in. 'While working in the club, we didn't have a life. It's so temporal . . . nice restaurants, fancy clothes, all temporary happiness. Any prostitute who says they're happy is in denial. You're forced to make love with a man you don't like. Your soul and emotions have to be numb. Only drugs numb.'

Then there was the abuse. She said it happened all the time. 'Lots of sexual abuse and exploitation . . . one man strangled a girl. The girls go back and cry even if they've made 10,000 US dollars that night . . . with a man from the Middle East.'

Sometimes clubs were tipped off about police raids in advance. Sometimes, the police caught girls without proper visas. 'Corruption is everywhere,' she said.

Campaigners say that even today, someone provides a tip-off, and all the bars know a week in advance that the US Marines are coming, even though this information is not made public.

The mama-sans and women were fearful of the police. Mary said that some lives could have been saved if there had been more police trained to identify women victims in prostitution. 'The police must have a deeper understanding that these women are trapped and, in their heart of hearts, these women hate it. No one wants to be a prostitute,' she said.

A police spokesperson said that in Hong Kong, they've found victims of trafficking among prostitutes from Mainland China, Southeast Asia, Europe, and South America who were recruited and trafficked from their homeland. However, according to the police, these women are reluctant to speak out or assist police investigations.

While some nightclubs and operators from Tsim Sha Tsui have migrated to the Wan Chai bar street, the days of the luxurious nightclub scene are over. Estimates for the number of people working in prostitution in Hong Kong range from 20,000 to 500,000. A spokesperson for Zi Teng, a support group for women in prostitution, said that around 1 in 50 are under eighteen.

One NGO frontline worker, who asked to remain anonymous to protect their staff, told me during a meeting that there are a number of underage Chinese girls in forced prostitution through debt bondage in smaller nightclubs in the Kowloon area. She said these vulnerable girls were born and raised in Hong Kong and come from broken families. They were lured by Chinese mama-sans who engaged them on the streets by asking if they wanted 'easy money' or 'pocket money'. Some of these girls get into a debt bondage situation where they owe the mama-san thousands of dollars for living expenses or to finance their drug habits.

Sandy Wong said that more rehabilitation and resources are needed to help women and girls coming out of prostitution. 'Structured and caring counselling paves the path of healing. Job training provides skills and alternatives so that [trafficking survivors] do not fall prey to economic pressures. But more importantly, it helps rebuild their values and identities,' she said.

\* \* \*

Every night, Mary and her girls drank to ease the pain. Their daily routine before their evening shift began was lunch together then a beauty parlour session. In 1991, her friend Grace, who was from Cebu in the Philippines and owned a beauty clinic, visited her in Hong Kong. Grace wanted to launch another beauty clinic in Hong Kong and asked for Mary's help. Mary admitted that she was a mama-san and that her girls sold their bodies to wealthy johns. Instead of making judgements, this friend stated that the Bible says Jesus came to save the sinners, tax collectors and prostitutes, and she offered to do a Bible study together. 'All of a sudden something pinched my heart. But I was a millionaire. I was afraid to say no. I was afraid of getting cursed by God and that I'd lose my money!' Mary said.

As she prayed, she felt cleansed for the first time, but she struggled with guilt and shame. What sealed the deal for her was seeing her young nephew who was dying of cancer in a hospital in Manila instantly healed after Grace's friend Rita prayed for him. Mary felt there must be a God or higher power. To this day, Rita and her church pray regularly for her nephew who is now a healthy young man. I expressed amazement at her miracles. Mary said there was more and excitedly kept talking.

Mary said she invited Rita to return with her to Hong Kong to speak with her girls, hoping there would be more supernatural signs and wonders. For the next month and a half, they conducted Bible studies every day. Mary said that around ten of the girls experienced a new hope and the power of God, and they were healed from emotional pain, anger, depression, drug addictions and alcoholism. 'All of a sudden, their countenance changed, their attitude and character changed. They had so much hunger to learn about the Christian faith,' said Mary.

Mary didn't resign from her job straight away, but she did use a karaoke bar she owned as a place of gathering to learn about their new faith during the day; it continued to function as a bar for prostitution at night.

Once by one, the girls stopped working, she said. Mary's boss was angry with her for thinking of leaving the business and demanded that she pay HK$1 million. Mary gave her HK$200,000 back and resigned in November 1992. 'I knew it was time to quit because of my conviction, and I felt so bad and could not set foot into the club. I didn't care if I didn't have money or a job.' I wondered what took her so long. Money was a factor, she admitted.

The next year, she sold her bar and moved back to the Philippines for good. Club Bboss closed down permanently in 2012.

In the Philippines, Mary's marriage was revived, and she formed a strong relationship with her husband. He passed away in recent years and Mary feels devastated by the loss. Over the years, she's mentored many women, especially those who are hurting, to help them overcome their challenges. She is also taking on more public speaking opportunities.

Annabel, an outreach worker at a church, said that Mary's testimony moved her entire congregation of domestic workers to tears when she spoke one afternoon and encouraged them. 'She has had a miraculous journey from a mama-san to being set free. She is a transformed life,' said Annabel.

Mary wants to tell as many mama-sans and bar girls as she can that there's hope. 'I want to tell them they're not stuck,' she said with tears in her eyes. She got emotional when she thought about what could have been. What if no one had come to reach out to her about a new hope. 'I don't know where I'd be . . . You can bring the human traffickers to jail, but the only thing that made me change is my faith in Jesus because I had a change of heart.'

She was still in regular contact with six of her girls who left the world of prostitution around the same time. Some of them were working as dishwashers or cleaners, while one was a restaurant floor manager.

'We may not have luxury but we have peace and joy,' said Mary. 'There's no oppression. Our identity is restored . . . money cannot buy that.' I sat up when she mentioned identity restoration. I could deeply relate to having one's identity restored and healed. Through the process of writing the stories of hurting women and girls over many years, I have gone through a metamorphosis myself and eventually accepted who I am. If there is anyone who has the charisma and the credibility to help enslaved women leave their traffickers, it is Mary.

\* \* \*

Around the same time that I spoke with Mary Zardilla, I met up with Kaushic Biswas who has since become a good friend. A friend had put us in touch and said that Kaushic had a lot of knowledge about human trafficking because he was a former trafficker. I jumped at the chance to have a dialogue with him. He was very charming and gentle and connected deeply with the people around him. I noticed that he probably had a luring spirit that the traffickers Guo and Wu had; however, now he channelled it into doing good.

In a twist, during our first conversation, he wanted to get to know me first and asked me several questions. I was not prepared for the tables turned on me and I panicked initially because I thought he wasn't going to give me an interview, but I answered as comprehensively as I could. He was keen on knowing why I was interested in this topic. I described the Japanese wartime sex slavery victims I had written about in my book and the North Korean trafficked victims, the Chinese women at the Door of Hope, the victims I had met and interviewed on the streets of Hong Kong. I said we need to raise awareness to touch hearts and mindsets of people to inspire them to help abolish modern slavery. That seemed to satisfy him and he voluntarily shared about his life from the beginning, the very roots of how he began to pimp out women in the most notorious red-light district in Mumbai.

He had grown up in Kolkata. His parents split up when he was a teenager. 'In Bengali society, it is really looked down upon, so many of my friends and family rejected me,' he said. 'It went to a point where my younger sister committed suicide, so I stopped believing in God.'

After completing a cookery course, Kaushic began a career as a chef in Mumbai but soon slipped into bad company. 'I got involved with a group of people who were running a flesh industry. My job involved walking into five-star hotels, mainly to the coffee shops because they are usually open twenty-four hours, and just find a man who looks lonely and interested in women, and hook him up. I used to get a big cut out of it.'

He said that many of the women he pimped came from normal families. 'When they were ill-treated by clients or johns, of course there is a lot of pain because they were not doing it willingly.'

Kaushic said that some of the johns were 'inhuman, like animals' and that when the women had finished with them, they would sometimes confide in him. 'They used to pour out their hearts, sometimes cry, sometimes scream and throw things. It was extreme emotions,' he said. 'Most of the time, we would end up crying together.'

The women couldn't escape because of threats to their families back home, but they encouraged Kaushic to leave because he was not constrained in that way. So he ran away and ended up in Hong Kong.

'While I was working here one Sunday, I remember I was pretty lonely and saw a beautiful church, St Andrew's Church. Watching Bollywood movies, I felt like church was the place to go for solitude. And I was right. When I walked into the church it was really a quiet place. Suddenly, I heard music, and after that the pastor came. He gave a message on friendship and then he talked about Jesus Christ. He said that Jesus is not only going to be your friend on Earth but also after you die. So, that made me think about life, and I thought I would like to have Jesus as my Lord and Saviour, and I accepted him.'

A year later, in 1996, Kaushic began working at a new drop-in centre in the notorious Chungking mansions in Tsim Sha Tsui, which was known for its rampant drug trade and sex trafficking. Jan Ganny, a British woman from the church, saw the potential in Kaushic to reach other South Asians and helped Biswas start this outreach. 'I've met Nepalese women forced into slavery – more than 200 women,' he said.

For the next seven years, he offered cooking skills training to hundreds of trafficking victims, drug addicts, prostitutes, drug dealers, and asylum seekers. 'With my chef background, I thought how wonderful it would be if I could give them a skills training, and with those skills they could have hope and a new beginning,' he said.

In Kaushic's case, he was a person who had a fundamentally good foundation and found himself in this type of work,' said Matt Friedman. 'He struggled with it from the beginning. He felt like it was something that went against the grain in his life, and eventually got to the point when he recognized that he had to get out. The number of people who have that transition is not very high. And it's partly because once you get into that world, it's difficult to get out of it. The money is there and you've established relationships. And sometimes you just can't leave, because if you try to leave, the institution will try to hold you in place . . . He, unlike many other people, has the skills and abilities to reach pimps to understand the errors of their way and help them get out of it. And that's why he's so important. It's really rare to have somebody like Kaushic who was in a situation where he was part of a very dark world doing not-so-good things to go from that to actually rehabilitating himself, and then using the experience to be able to reach other people in trafficking situations. It's a remarkable situation and it puts him into the one percentile of individuals who are really able to reach people because they understand. Because they've walked the walk themselves.'

A few years after he became a Christian, Kaushic reconciled with his mother. Now, together with his wife, Dang, he is serving in the Philippines as a missionary, and he plans to launch a social enterprise to provide vulnerable people with jobs.

'It's my dream to see, like God has changed me, that same power change another pimp or prostitute and help them out of the trap. To come out. I'm open to be used to reach out to them,' he said.

He would prove to be an insightful guide on my investigations into different manifestations of modern slavery, and he had a deep understanding of traffickers and victims alike. Most of all, he had a passion and a tender heart to help the victims of all forms of human slavery.

He already knew about and could confirm the sad phenomenon that I had exposed in a news article called 'Slave Grooms' or 'Slave Husbands' where South Asian men, mostly from India and Pakistan, are tricked into arranged marriages and trafficked to Hong Kong to work as bonded labourers or indentured servants. He introduced me to undocumented migrants who were exploited working as cheap labour for companies that distributed food. I interviewed Kaushic for my 'Slave Grooms' documentary, and I produced a short film on his testimony to tell the world about his remarkable transformation. I also produced a music video that showed the horrors of sex trafficking and a film on the suffering of Indonesian children deceived into domestic work. When I embarked on these short films with Kaushic and then produced music videos and other films, I wanted to try something radical—something I hope that I can continue to do in future film work—and I hired individuals from marginalized groups and victim-survivors. We had several Indonesian women who were former child domestic workers, a sex trafficking survivor as well as a recovering drug addict helping us out with these films. Despite the challenges, it was exhilarating to give them an opportunity that excited them, gave meaning and a chance to help others and tell their own stories through the films. I ensured that we did not put them in exploitative situations that would trigger and harm them. But unfortunately, in one film, one actor slid his hand on the protagonist's bottom. He was a stranger and I hadn't checked his references as I should have. We were livid. I humbly learned that we will have to vet the actors and all involved even more.

Through Kaushic, I was also able to meet his friend Jowel who was a former child slave smuggled into Hong Kong as he laid flat in a small boat. Jowel was working for a pittance in construction companies at great personal risk because he was forced to do dangerous tasks. Indeed, as a former trafficker pimp he does have an encyclopaedic knowledge of the underworld and the underbelly of Hong Kong. He knew the players in Chungking Mansions and once pointed out a South Asian victim of sex trafficking out of the corner of his eye. I found his street smarts fascinating and his sincere Christian faith and transformed life made him an extremely savvy outreach worker. He was a most effective change agent for traffickers and victims alike.

# 12

# Compensated Dating[*]

The concept of compensated dating (CD) originated in Japan in the early 1990s, where older men would offer luxury gifts and or money to mostly schoolgirls for sexual favours or companionship. This then spread to Taiwan, Korea, Malaysia, Macau, and Mainland China. It took root in Hong Kong in the early 2000s and has since become popular with underage girls and boys who are in need of money.

The main channel for young people to advertise themselves is social media, where they can reach a wide audience of potential clients. This private world, hidden from parents and police, allows the vice to flourish and increases the vulnerability of children and teenagers. The young people offering CD are often described as part-time girlfriends (PTGF) and part-time boyfriends (PTBF).

Encounters like this are becoming commonplace in today's dating scene because of the advent of digital and social media. I had been looking for a survivor of CD for years to understand this lesser-

---

[*] This chapter is partly based on my articles titled 'Last Christmas, I gave you my body: Hong Kong's professional boyfriends and girlfriends' and 'Child sex abuse, compensated dating: Christmas trends Hong Kong would rather ignore' (the latter co-authored with Andrew Raine), both published in *South China Morning Post* on 23 December 2018.

known form of sex trafficking and prostitution that was rampant among underage girls and boys.

I met Esther at my first church in Hong Kong in 2011 and from the moment I heard of her story from a mutual friend, I asked her for a media interview. Six years later, she agreed though she was still very hesitant and distrustful. One of the first things she divulged was that she knew many other women at her church, my first church, who used to be in prostitution through CD like her, but are too ashamed to come forward. The taboo and shame was so strong that even their spouses did not know.

She was a petite, pretty Chinese woman with a sleek style of dress. You could tell that she had spent a lot of time applying precise make-up. She had a controlled hairstyle and beautiful flattering clothes. I was careful to earn her trust and spent a long time talking about my first marriage and painful divorce and the powerful meetings I've had with historical wartime sex slavery victims and modern day ones. She was hanging onto every word and empathized. She seemed to know a lot about their plight already. She warmed up and spilled out her story, even the parts that were really personal.

Esther went on a dinner date with a man in his forties in Hong Kong. They had dinner after a movie and enjoyed small talk with a lot of easy laughter. Esther's date lavished her with gifts. She had met this man online using a simple description of herself as 24 years old, 5 feet 2 inches, and working as an 'office lady'. After spending the night together, Esther asked for a payment of HK$1,500 for intercourse. She later discovered the man was married with children. He was one of many men that Esther dated in exchange for money and gifts through an internet forum for CD where she went by her handle 'Helena'.

Men, most of them in their forties, contacted Esther and asked to see intimate photos of her and her price list for the cost of a date or something more. Feeling unloved by her father, neglected by her mother and often suicidal, Esther filled the emptiness inside by engaging with these men. She lived under a cloak of shame and was afraid to tell the truth to family and friends that she sold her body. But that isolation put her life at risk. 'I felt in danger because I was exposed to different guys,' she said. Esther faced unexpected consequences that almost got her killed by violent clients. She contracted STDs twice and had an abortion. I expressed my sincere sympathies for what she had gone through and encouraged her by saying she was remarkable for overcoming adversity.

I sought out experts and frontline workers to further understand the world of CD that Esther was involved in. All unanimously said that it was a type of escort service, albeit with a deceptively innocent name. Cassini Sai Kwan Chu, an honorary lecturer at Hong Kong University and author of *Compensated Dating: Buying and Selling Sex in Cyberspace*, said, 'If some people regard CD as a euphemism of teenage prostitution, then PTGF is another euphemism of CD. Some girls simply provide two types of services: one with sex, one without, for the clients to choose from.'

T.Y. Lee, an associate professor at City University, has found through his research that it's a precursor or significant gateway to long-term prostitution. He said, 'For those underage teens engaging in sexual trade, it's better to describe it as "juvenile prostitution", which can be labelled as a form of child sex slavery.'

Jacky Cheung, also an associate professor at City University, believes that CD and its second-generation version, PTGF/PTBF, is a chronic problem among Hong Kong's youth that brings health and psychological risks. He said the practitioners are 'more distrusting of other people and thus antisocial', which can lead to problems with 'social integration and harmony.'

I tracked down some frontline workers to learn of how they were helping victims of CD. Staff from one NGO that asked to remain anonymous remarked that they don't have enough government support or resources to help young girls and boys involved in CD. I was frustrated to hear this. Linda Chan, a veteran social worker who has done outreach to girls, told me her NGO had not received government funding and that their former private donors had long moved on. 'For Hong Kong people, our culture is so fast,' she said. 'Trends are fast. They think CD girls is outdated and not a hot topic. It was a trendy and serious topic a few years ago. It used to be easy to get funding. Now it's difficult to get funding. It is evil! It involves children. In Japan, it's even worse. Many girls go into porn. If these girls were in Japan, it would be a one-way road to pornography.'

The risks of CD came shockingly to the fore with the high-profile murder of a sixteen-year-old girl by one of her clients in the Sham Shui Po district of Hong Kong in 2008. Another fifteen-year-old girl, believed to be killed by her CD client, was found dead and half-naked in 2014. The risks also extend to being publicly exposed. In 2018, more than a thousand photos of PTGFs were published on the popular online forum LIHKG. This website is described as Hong Kong's version of Reddit, in which different topics are discussed by members who can reply and vote for the best answers.

I learnt that many of the girls and boys in CD are understandably ashamed and hide what they do from friends and family, thereby putting themselves in greater danger. 'One of my respondents always wears a face mask when she is out because she is afraid that she will bump into her clients,' said Chu. 'Their CD history also presents some difficulty for some girls to find a "regular" job. Some girls are reluctant to take a job that requires them to interact with different people every day because again they fear that they might bump into their clients.'

The trend has shifted from CD to Japanese-style nightclubs where teenage girls sell their bodies under the control of gangsters. It is hard to believe that CD is even more dangerous as compared to being forced to sell your body under the watch of Triad members in a nightclub. But Chan argues that girls in CD and PTGF are isolated and on their own. They're also much younger than the girls working in nightclubs, and they don't have Triad protection or back up when they're in crisis.

I asked Esther what made her so vulnerable to be engaging in CD that brought so much hurt. She explained with an ease that suggested she had processed and healed from her wounds. She grew up with great instability in her young life. She remembers her father raging with anger and his periods of manipulation. Her parents divorced when she was just four years old. She recalls that her father had some kind of trauma from abuse by his parents and also from his childhood experiences during the Cultural Revolution in China before he moved to Hong Kong. After her parents split, her mother had to work double shifts to make ends meet and eventually placed her and her younger sister in the care of an aunt. This temporary housing situation led to her being raped by an older male cousin for a year. This cousin was addicted to Japanese manga pornography.

She said, with tears, that she felt such feelings of despair from the abuse that it led to attempted suicide with pills and slashing of her wrists. She almost died. I cried with her and held her hand. We stayed silent for several minutes. She was re-traumatized by re-telling one of the darkest times of her life.

While in high school, Esther often skipped classes. Her grades plummeted and she became rebellious. She sought attention from boys and began dating at thirteen years of age. 'I began to indulge myself—crazy shopping, drinking, music, smoking marijuana, one-night stands,' she said. 'I began to believe men just want my body, and only money is my sense of security. You have a wrong concept . . . You have no value about your self-esteem and physical body. One man or two dozen men is all the same. If you can exchange for money, even better.'

Esther said there was no one she could turn to for help from the time she was abused to when she became rebellious. There was no help available at her school. 'The root cause why I turned to CD is that I was sexually abused and raped. Makes me feel I hate myself. You can't trust anyone. You feel like you caused it. I felt criminal.'

Chan gave further insight into Esther's story and explained that more than sixty per cent of girls in CD had been victims of sexual violence and child sex abuse. She saw a link between the two because it affected their self-image and made them more vulnerable to further abuse. Before the funding dried up, Chan offered counselling and health outreach to girls involved in CD. Her team began providing care online after they discovered these girls had little knowledge about sexual health and that put them at risk for STDs. The girls refused to see the social workers in person but were receptive to health information online.

'Most of the girls at that stage are still young and green in this industry,' said Chan. 'They don't know what sexuality is and how to protect themselves from STDs. We used a public health angle to engage them. We say we won't stop you from doing this, but you need to be aware of the risk of getting STDs or we'll provide free medical consultation. All of the girls were under twenty. A few cases were thirteen or fourteen years. We searched for the girls on Facebook or online forums. We inbox them to try to offer them care service initially. What we understand from these girls is that they come from complicated families with no love from their parents. It makes sense that they seek love and care from outside. They don't get it from home.'

After gaining their trust, Chan's organization offered more counselling and therapy group support and mentoring programmes. They helped connect the girls with a healthier social network with mentors and friends from university or church.

One girl Chan reached out to said she felt safe and in control when she was selling her time and sexual favours on dates through CD. She didn't expect to sell intercourse and did not realize that CD was a type of prostitution. 'Some girls do this, but don't consider themselves as PTGF,' said Chan. 'They don't see it as wrong. We worry that some girls are very young . . . and they are very weak in rejecting people. Their naiveté is being exploited.'

An NGO worker Melissa Wu said, 'Some teens do CD as a part-time job. Some of them regret it, some don't. The majority of them are not controlled. Some have a history of child sex abuse. They don't want their body controlled as a result. Their body or self-value is distorted.'

In his interviews with thirty young people, T.Y. Lee found a wide variety of reasons for selling 'dates' and their bodies; these included idling away one's time in pleasure-seeking, being disappointed in a love affair, poverty, family members in debt, no proper job, being victimised or extorted, authoritarian parenting, parents who emphasize material wealth, and child abuse. Even girls and boys from so-called good families and wealthy families were found to have participated in it.

Most of the girls Chan came across were looking for 'easy money'. They said they could be paid HK$1,000 to go to a movie with a guy. The entry point of this industry is attractive, but it could entrap the girls. Chan said the girls with stronger self-esteem can say no to unacceptable requests, but most of them are from difficult dysfunctional family backgrounds, and it's hard for them to reject a client. Chan added, 'These girls have a difficult time trusting others. We have often heard the line: "I've been dirty once, it doesn't matter if I'm dirty ten times." For young victims of sex abuse, how they see their body is critical. When they feel it's dirty, it becomes a tool for men.'

I had seen the same pattern in the victims of sex trafficking I had interviewed. Trauma is the common thread and yet trauma healing resources are rare to find.

At the age of twenty-four, when Esther was working as a CD girl, there were new girls every month on the online forum she used. She saw at least a hundred active girls every month, and they were all competing for clients. It was a highly secretive, isolating kind of job as she hardly interacted with the other girls in person. 'You'll see ads for secondary students,' she said. 'Some johns told me [some girls] were really sixteen but would claim they are eighteen. Johns avoid illegal things. If they go to a hotel, police sometimes check. I got enquiries. They contacted me on MSN messenger . . . The clients asked you for naked photos . . . they wanted to check the product.'

Esther explained how she was exposed to danger. I could barely believe that she would put herself in that kind of high risk circumstance. 'You don't know who you'll meet. You could meet very violent clients. When you get into a room, you don't have power. I didn't want to do it . . . After the first client, I took a shower . . . I never felt clean again . . . I washed my body really hard . . . The scent from the man seemed to linger. Some want to take photos to spread on the website. That's happened to other CD girls.' She reminded me of the women in the countryside in Korea, suspected of being victims of wartime sex slavery, who obsessively washed themselves after they returned home.

Despite the drawbacks, the allure was the luxury handbags that she got as gifts and a source of income higher than she could have earned in a regular job. 'The average age of my clients was forty years. They were lonely . . . or did not have a good sexual relationship with their wives or girlfriends. They didn't want prostitutes but normal women and girls. They thought CD girls were more clean. It was more like an affair . . . a fantasy relationship.'

Esther said that CD girls post on WeChat or other social media platforms nowadays. 'It's more hidden,' she said, adding that she was very concerned for the young women involved.

One fifteen-year-old girl named 'Momo' promoted her non-sexual CD services on social media using a photo of a group of young girls with the caption 'SOO YOUNG'. She said her main motivation was money. She said she was feeling down and was in debt from shopping, so she needed money desperately when she first started. She had rules for her clients: she only went on dates in Mongkok or

Yau Ma Tei during the day to avoid being seen by friends and family. 'I'm scared people will discover what I am doing,' she admitted. For an hourly shopping date, she charged HK$350 an hour. For holding hands or a hug, it was HK$50 extra. She attended high school full-time and learned about CD on the Internet.

Another Hong Kong girl, aged eighteen, was working as a full-time secretary in an office but sold sexual favours through an Instagram account on 'private mode'. She learned how to work as a PTGF through an article on Facebook. She was seventeen when she started, and money was her main incentive. 'So far, the experience is very pleasant and good,' she said, adding that she didn't offer sex but still earned around HK$2,000 to HK$3,000 a day. Many clients were nice to her.

Much of CD takes place online, and that's concerning to police and frontline workers because of the rise of Internet pornography and paedophilia. The issue is serious enough to take up a significant amount of police resources, including an entire police unit from Crime Kowloon West Headquarters that is dedicated to the crackdown on illegal activities related to CD.

After a seven-month undercover sting, the police busted a CD ring that ran its operation through a website called 'hklovely' in March 2018. The ring started in 2012, grew to 100,000 members and made more than HK$20 million off women and underage girls through CD. Police arrested nineteen men and eleven women aged 17–67 for 'living on earnings of prostitution of others', 'dealing with property known or believed to represent proceeds of indictable', and 'soliciting for immoral purposes'. The founder of the website, a thirty-three-year-old IT technician, had been charged in 2015 for living off prostitution earnings from a CD website with 90,000 members called 'hkbigman'.

One of the higher-profile cases of CD involved Henry Chui Che-hung, a sixty-year-old man who was married with children and had close ties with Hong Kong tycoons. In 2009, he was convicted of seven charges including 'unlawful intercourse with a girl under sixteen and buggery of three young girls'. Two of these victims were fourteen and the third girl was fifteen. The court documents state that one of the fourteen-year-old victims was 'demonstrably immature and vulnerable' and participated in CD to replace her lost mobile phone. Chui was described as an 'Internet predator' by the judge. He lured and manipulated the girls by messaging them and deceptively offering HK$300 for simply meeting and sharing a meal with him. He was sentenced to four years and eight months in prison.

Hong Kong police have said that CD girls are at risk of being sexually abused, videotaped secretly, and contracting STDs. A police website section called 'What Youngsters Should Remember When Social Networking Online' contains the following warning:

> Recently, some teenage girls have been tempted into compensated dating as a means to make money. They reach out for potential customers, often through internet blogs and instant messaging. This situation has brought many social problems, but more importantly these teenagers are gambling their personal safety with complete strangers who may be actively targeting lone and vulnerable girls or seeking to lure girls into prostitution. Many times such risky encounters have resulted in criminal intimidation, physical and sexual assault, rape, robbery and in one unfortunate case murder of the girl concerned.

Some girls deliberately advertise themselves as 'young' to entice clients in order to make more money. Having sex with a child who is under sixteen could result in a five-year prison sentence. If the child is under thirteen, the guilty party could face life imprisonment.

Sandy Wong said, 'For men who pay for CD girls, the mindset is probably no different than paying a prostitute. Underage sex is unlawful. Whether this law will be invoked depends on whether anyone complains about it. Usually, it is the parents that go to the police to complain about underage sex or if the girls run away from schools or become pregnant, then schools or social workers would get involved and complain to the police to arrest the men.'

Melissa Wu spoke of a girl who was raped by her father at eight years of age and forced to get an abortion at ten. Wu said the girl's father kept telling her, 'When you grow up you need to be a prostitute and give me money.' At sixteen, she reported him to the police and the case took about three years to go through the courts. During this time, she coped by finding johns through CD. Wu said she tried her best to help this traumatized young woman but admitted that she didn't get the trauma care she needed to prevent her from engaging in at-risk behaviour such as prostitution. 'Victims are not offered enough services for intensive counselling and support,' she said.

I was shocked to hear of the lack of help and resources in a wealthy city like Hong Kong. I could understand why NGO workers were frustrated. They were in touch with the victims, yet they had nothing to offer to them as they slipped away on a path to destruction.

Public sentiment towards CD is complex in Hong Kong. When child pornography cases are featured in the news, the blame is placed squarely on the mostly male perpetrators. But the public sentiment towards young people in CD is often condemning and judgemental. The girls are often perceived as greedy gold-diggers.

'It is a really serious issue in Hong Kong . . . everyone is blaming the girls,' said Linda Chan. 'But it's a societal problem. They think it's an individual problem, but their family failed them. Society and culture failed them. It's cultural thinking to individualize the problem and blame the girl and the behaviour. It's a Chinese morals concept of blaming the girl because culturally girls should be good girls.'

Esther said, 'In Hong Kong, it seems people turn a blind eye to those in CD. It's too shameful. People are clueless.'

Melissa Wu, through her NGO, was looking after a young girl who simply wanted to buy luxury goods. 'Her case was related to attachment issues because she doesn't have love from her family,' said Wu. 'She felt empty and lacked self-esteem, and she was trying to fill her emptiness. What they need is a very stable secure community . . . to grow gradually. It's not easy to deal with these cases.'

While the victims of the other forms of sexual exploitation detailed in this book are overwhelmingly women and girls, I was surprised to find out that CD is something that also affects young men and boys to a significant degree, with both men and women providing the demand.

A friend helped me reach out to a nineteen-year-old man named James Zhu on Instagram where he talked about his line of work as a PTBF. Zhu was very skittish and did not trust me at all. I spent time sharing about my past work with trafficking victims and my personal journey. He slowly told me about the venues he found himself in.

Before he became a PTBF for hire, he began working as a 'massage boy' catering to gay men between thirty and sixty years old in disreputable parlours found in motels and old residential buildings in Causeway Bay, Mongkok, and Tsim Sha Tsui. He said the parlours were run by men involved in illegal gambling including betting on football. It was certainly not the kind of place you would expect to find a young man like Zhu, a university student majoring in engineering—unfailingly polite and neatly dressed in preppy shorts and a T-shirt and carrying a backpack.

'Old guys and fat men tried to force sex while I massaged them,' he said, adding that he was paid HK$300 to HK$600 for intercourse only and wouldn't be paid for the massage. He said there were a few boys under seventeen in these parlours. I felt sad that he was engaging in this kind of work and thought of his mother.

The dangers of the work and inflexible working hours in the massage parlour caused him to turn to being a PTBF where he had control over choosing clients and could manage a more 'emotional connection' with them. But the biggest incentive for him was money.

He said he could make at least HK$10,000 a month which is more than what a summer engineering internship would pay.

Zhu explained matter-of-factly that he was open to both male and female clients, usually between fifteen to thirty years old, and he found them on various dating apps like Tinder. He preferred boys because girls paid less for hanging out and watching a movie.

'I don't have to pay for meals and entertainment,' he said. 'This career is really special. But I saw the dark side of being a PTBF. No one taught me about the dangers. I lost innocence.' He said there's a group on Instagram called Moonlight Blue that offers legal support and a hotline for PTGFs and PTBFs who are arrested by the undercover police.

If you discuss prices for intercourse in public, the police can arrest you, but Zhu said he hadn't heard of any PTBFs being arrested. He believed that was because the police do not know how to handle investigating boys. 'It could be homophobia,' he said.

To know what motivated the johns, I reached out to a twenty-three-year-old young man named Jason. He was unemployed and seemed to be an average young man. He still managed to hire four different PTGFs through Instagram over the previous four weeks, and planned to continue paying for dates with teenage girls even without a steady income. It seemed like an addiction. 'I haven't had a girlfriend before. I want to know what dating feels like,' he said. 'Secondly, I want to find younger girls, aged around sixteen to eighteen. Hiring a PTGF allows me a bigger chance to approach girls in this age range.'

He said he had paid between HK$300 and HK$500 for a few hours with a PTGF and claimed there was no awkwardness. The dates were casual and the girls he hired didn't even ask for his real name. They called him 'older brother'. 'I feel so good when I have a girl to hold hands with. We will normally chit chat, have meals together, and talk about our own background, for instance things that have happened at work or school. If I can get along with a particular girl well, I will hire her a few more times,' he said.

Jason dated girls who were as young as sixteen, but he didn't think it was illegal because he didn't buy sex from them. 'Girls who are at the age of sixteen to eighteen are more innocent and pure, less money-minded,' he said. 'There is no girl in my social circle . . . girls who are in their twenties, they value money so much. For instance, to them, your ambition and aggressiveness are equal to your ability in earning money.'

Jason told his friends about paying for dates, but would never divulge it to his family. I found it sad that he had to buy dates. However, he didn't consider it as prostitution. 'I don't find it awkward; it's just a trade. One who sells, one who buys. PTGF is a trend, just like those young CD girls in Japan. In this materialistic society, many girls just use this way to earn quick money. They don't necessarily need to sell their bodies—just holding hands and hugging.'

Cassini Sai Kwan Chu believes CD will become more normalized in the days to come as relationships are becoming more transactional. 'The line between CD and non-commercial relationships is getting blurred,' she said. 'I believe the trend of CD will continue due to the changing sexual attitudes and values among Hong Kong youth. Age of the first sexual intercourse is getting younger.'

Some adolescents believe that CD is simply a new form of social networking and a platform to earn quick and easy money. 'One female respondent told me that she had had casual sex numerous times before entering into CD. She felt that CD is a wiser and better choice because she could earn money from CD but nothing from one-night-stands,' said Chu.

William Sin, an assistant professor at the Education University of Hong Kong, told me over a telephonic conversation that if more support is not offered for youth engaging in CD then the issue could go even further underground with the rise of more private and encrypted apps like Telegram, Line, and WhatsApp. 'These tools and operations are perplexing and difficult to manage from the viewpoint of traditional educators and social workers,' said Sin. 'They just have no idea what kind of life young people may be living in the world of social media. The phenomenon of CD or PTGF is to be learned; it indicates something that the existing authority has missed and lagged behind for a long time.'

A spokesperson for Hong Kong's Education Bureau said that since 2011 they have offered teaching about the dangers of CD and 'Internet indulgence', and strengthened sex education at the primary school level. The Moral and Civic Education curriculum of junior secondary schools addresses 'love, sex and marriage' and 'aims and principles of setting limits of intimacy'. However, the Education Bureau does not have a formal policy on preventing teenagers from falling into prostitution through CD.

Some campaigners say that improving sex education is not enough and that schools need to raise more serious awareness of the risks associated with CD using real-life case studies appropriate for each age group. T.Y. Lee said, 'For teachers and educators, only those who violate the law and school regulations are likely to be identified as potential risks. But if they do not violate any regulations, or if they deny any involvement, then the school could only refer such cases to seek school social work services . . . Some of them may be helped to leave such risky activities . . . some may just carry on until identified by the police.'

Chan says there is a need for overall education training and a self-esteem programme, especially targeting those who have been exposed to materialistic culture and have difficult family backgrounds. 'There must be an open discussion and platform for girls to talk about this freely. We need to educate them of its high risks and issues of public health,' she said.

The men who buy sex must also be treated, but social stigma prevents them from getting the help that they may need. 'They run the risk of disclosure and thus live in a closet alone or with other men who are also clients and risk breaking up their marriages,' said Travis S.K. Kong, associate dean at Hong Kong University.

Sweden's model of punishing the buyers of sex and protecting the women in prostitution has been examined in Hong Kong. 'The Sweden Model is by far the best way forward, but arresting all these men or putting them in jail will not solve these complex issues,' said Sandy Wong. 'It would only be successful if the surrounding areas also adopt the model.' Wong also argued that advertising and media portraying girls as sex objects are part of the problem. 'There has to be a better mechanism to complain and take down objectifying women advertisements,' she said. 'For instance, why is a naked body selling perfume? Or why is a thirteen-year-old in suggestive motion or posture being used to sell clothes?'

In a vulnerable moment, Esther said one day she looked in the mirror and couldn't even recognize herself. She had lost herself in the lies she had told her clients and to herself. She felt trapped.

At twenty-six, she began dating a man and stopped her CD work after two years. They fell in love and got engaged. But his friend discovered her photo on a CD forum. 'He said how could I do CD? He asked for more details. It was really hurtful,' she said. 'He wanted me to disclose all details. I didn't want to. After he knew, he used it against me. He looked down on me.'

Her fiancé broke off the engagement, and she spent days in her room crying. Feeling suicidal, she began to pray as she remembered learning about God in primary school. One day, a strange peace flooded over her; it was a kind of a spiritual encounter of love and total acceptance, despite the shame of her past. She felt clean for the first time in years. Eventually, with the support of her church community, she became an image consultant and fashion designer. Her monthly salary doubled compared to her CD work. Her mission was to help women feel beautiful from the inside out—something that she struggled with and subsequently led to her selling her body. It's a mission that's so needed.

Esther's message to others in CD is this: 'You don't want to be a compensated girl. It's more like a drug. It numbs. Later on, you'll be killed by it . . . You're not alone . . . If I can get saved, you can too.'

After meeting Esther, I asked an NGO to consider launching a campaign in schools to raise vital awareness about the dangers of this subtle form of sexual exploitation of minors, albeit with a glossy new name. They were open to doing so and speaking on raising the self-esteem of young girls. I volunteered to help drive the project as an advisor. However, due to a lack of funding, this potential new campaign that could have saved many young girls and boys from a slippery slope to sexual abuse and worse, floundered and died an early death. To do something to counter my discouragement over the lack of help for these young people in CD, PTGF, and PTBF, I produced a music video that depicted the dangers of CD for Cybil Chan's beautiful and haunting song in Mandarin called 'Where were you?' A lawyer by trade, Cybil had written this song herself and entered our Battle of the Bands contest, and this song was included in our music CD for the 852 Freedom Campaign.

I couldn't help but feel like I was fighting a losing battle. With no resources and very few highly trained social workers with the compassion and understanding to help rescue traumatized girls and boys out of CD, PTGF, and PTBF, I was afraid that more young people would self-deceive and consequently, be brutally exploited. For generations to come, a multitude of young people will dreadfully lose their innocence in ugly ways and miss out on the normal path that leads down to a loving family and healthy connections. I shuddered to think of what society would look like then.

# 13

# Domestic Workers' Hell*

Vulnerable girls and women are at risk of another distressing and prominent form of modern slavery and human trafficking in the form of domestic work. For years, underage girls from South East Asia and other parts of Asia have been trafficked as child labour under the guise of domestic work by predatory agencies in Hong Kong and Singapore. I was determined to find a victim of child labour and through a friend I was able to meet Lia.

When I first met her, she initially avoided my gaze. Her boyish crew cut hairstyle framed her plain features, tan skin and the metal-framed glasses perched on her nose. Lia was quiet during our interview, which took place at a restaurant in Tsim Sha Shui, close to the Chungking Mansions building. She had an athletic build and wore black track pants and a grey sweatshirt with a hoodie that emphasized her broad shoulders. A stern look seemed frozen on her face. I described my personal journey of meeting survivors of modern

---

* This chapter is partly based on my article titled 'The Indonesian child maids of Hong Kong, Singapore: why they're suffering in silence', published in *South China Morning Post* on 25 March 2017.

slavery and talked about my brokenness from a divorce. She seemed more willing to open up after that.

She said that she ran away from home more than a decade ago. She escaped a daily barrage of physical and emotional abuse from three older brothers, the sons of her father's first wife. Her mother was an oppressed second wife in an extremely fractured family. As a way of escaping her painful family circumstances, Lia's friend gave her the address of an employment agency in Surabaya, Indonesia that sent domestic workers abroad. Staff at that company told her, 'A bigger agency can give you a fake passport to change your age.' She was so desperate to get away from her family that she was willing to try anything, even if it was illegal.

Lia went to a bigger employment agency in Jakarta that helped Indonesian women migrate for work as domestic workers. The women were charged fees for flights, health checks, application processing fees, and training sessions. They were also expected to pay this back once they began working as maids in other countries.

This agency forged Lia's date of birth on her passport to make her appear older. She then flew to Macau fraudulently on a tourist visa to reach her new employer. According to an Indonesian law that was passed in 2004, women working abroad as foreign domestic workers must be at least twenty-one years old. Lia was fourteen. 'I was a big kid,' she said as she explained how she passed through Macau customs with her fake passport.

It was plausible to me that she could pass for twenty-one. She was broad-shouldered and manly and walked with confident wide strides. Wasn't she afraid, I asked? She said, 'I was in a broken family. That's why I left home. I wasn't scared of anything because of the trauma I faced at home.'

'Really?' I countered and didn't fully believe her. At 14, I didn't have a will of steel to go through customs with fake papers!

Lia said what came next was even more diabolic than her family. As soon as she arrived at her new workplace, a three-storey salon and a home, Lia was forced to work every day from dawn until late at night. Her responsibilities included cleaning, cooking, laundry, and massaging her female employer. Lia said the work was exhausting but the abuse was the worst part of working as a maid. 'I didn't understand the language, and the employer was always screaming at me,' she said with a soft voice and eyes downcast. 'The wife would verbally abuse me. They kept my passport.' Lia was trapped.

After four months with that employer, Lia was locked up in a bathroom overnight when she failed to feed their five dogs fast enough. She was broken by what her employer said to her. 'She poked my head with her finger and made fun of me. She ordered me to eat the bowl of dog food. I didn't eat it. I cried. I couldn't handle it.' I was in disbelief that she was told to eat dog food. How utterly dehumanizing and as a child, she wouldn't have known how to process that kind of abuse.

I wasn't surprised to hear that Lia ran away that night and found herself walking the streets. She reached out to her agency, but they were unwilling to help. 'The agency said my passport belonged to them because I didn't finish my contract,' she said.

On the street, she met a sympathetic Indonesian woman, an illegal migrant, who recruited her to work as a dishwasher in a restaurant. When the place was raided by the police, she ran again and found another restaurant to work in. About two years, her luck ran out and she was imprisoned at the age of sixteen for not possessing the correct travel documents or visa. She didn't tell the authorities her real age out of fear.

I later learnt that had there been a comprehensive anti-child trafficking law in Macau, Lia would have been protected from imprisonment because it was the agency that had illegally altered her passport and sent her to work as a child through fraudulent means.

Lia was soon deported to Indonesia. I was shocked to hear that she signed up with another employer because she couldn't bear to return to her family. The agency asked her to work for them while waiting for eight months to receive her new passport. Her new job was to process travel documents. 'I had to add fake signatures on different documents,' she said. 'I know more than two hundred who were underage in Hong Kong. I meet other domestic workers here, and I ask them how long they've been here. You can tell they're young.'

Lia was only seventeen when she arrived in Hong Kong to work for her new employers. 'We get in trouble . . . we are still young. We cannot fend for ourselves or deal with problems. I feel pain. Pain from everyone. Scared. Scared of getting beaten,' she said. She reminded me of so many of the traumatized young women I met in China who went from one terrible frying pan of trauma to another. They were caught in a vicious cycle of pain and abuse.

Lia had to pay HK$22,000 to the agency as recruitment and migration fees, which was well above the ten per cent legal limit in Hong Kong. She had anger in her voice as she described these fees. These often fraudulent and illegal fees place undue hardship on migrants like Lia, and they are considered by the United Nations and NGOs to be debt bondage. These women usually do not understand agency fees and accrued interest rates and often agree to exploitative contracts unknowingly.

Now twenty-six, Lia feels heavy and tears up easily whenever she reflects upon her life. 'I never thought I would become a domestic worker. What I really wanted to do was study. I would like to work at a bank. For anyone from a broken family, it's better to protect them from going to work in another country. I don't want children to work as domestic workers in other countries.'

Since 1974, Hong Kong has allowed foreign migrant domestic live-in workers to work full-time for families, freeing up many Chinese women with children to work outside the home. These women, mostly from the Philippines, were replacing Chinese maids in Hong Kong. As per rules, employers must provide monthly wages of at least HK$4,630 along with food and board, travel costs, and one day off a week. To me, it was indescribably wrong to know that the monthly wage for these women working at least 12 hour days, 6 days a week, is the cost of an iPhone. It is for this reason that I have not hired a live-in domestic worker. I just cannot bring myself to do so. But I don't want to judge others if they do because I cannot control what others decide.

About one in eight households employs a maid, and that figure rises to one in three for families with children. There are more than 340,000 foreign domestic workers in Hong Kong, mostly from poorer Asian nations such as the Philippines, Indonesia, Thailand, Sri Lanka, Nepal, Bangladesh, and Myanmar. In addition to Hong Kong, these women also migrate to Singapore, Taiwan, and Malaysia and the Middle East to work as domestic workers and support their families back at home. Indonesian domestic workers began working in Hong Kong in the early 1980s.

Campaigners have told me that there are hundreds of girls under eighteen like Lia who are trafficked into child labour work as domestic workers in Hong Kong and other parts of Asia through predatory agencies that forge their passports to make them appear older.

I met Eni Lestari, Chair of International Migrants Alliance, during the production of my previous documentary, *Helper's Hell*, on the abuse of domestic workers and another documentary on the infamous Eriwana Sulistyaningsih case that made headlines globally. Eriwana was an Indonesian woman who was beaten to a pulp by her employer in Hong Kong. Through numerous media interviews about Eriwana's case, Lestari became more known internationally.

I asked Lestari why she didn't raise the issue of child domestic workers with me when I was producing other films. A local NGO had even produced a report on the prevalence of human trafficking and forced labour among domestic workers that took a year to research and yet there was no mention of child labourers. Lestari explained the women themselves were afraid to go forward about it. She said, 'This is a crime that agencies in Indonesia have committed for years. Child trafficking of migrants should be criminalized. Agencies falsifying to send underage girls as domestic workers to other countries should be punished, and also government officials who help commit these crimes. It should be investigated. This is very common.'

According to Lestari, child migrants with forged passports from Indonesia have been sent out since the 1980s and the numbers peaked during the Asian financial crisis. 'No one is giving attention to this. No NGO yet is doing an in-depth study on underage women among overseas migrants,' she said.

Through a friend I met Maylin Hartwick, an outreach worker from Harmony Baptist Church in Hong Kong who has helped Lia. Hartwick is a passionate and very hospitable and generous Filipina woman. We had a common empathy for trafficked women and wartime sex slaves for the Japanese military. During my interview with her about child slaves in domestic work, she said, 'Lia was a child and more vulnerable to abuse because she didn't have critical thinking skills. Instead of preventing a child to go into work, the employment agency encouraged her. Anyone under eighteen is still a child, so it is child labour trafficking, especially since she was transported to another country.'

According to the UN Convention on the Rights of the Child, which was adopted in 1989, 'a child means every human being below the age of 18 years'. In a 2013 report, the International Labour Organization (ILO) said that at least 15.5 million children aged five to seventeen years were engaged in domestic work globally, with almost half of them being under fourteen. The ILO says when the movement of the child is done with the purpose of labour exploitation, this is child trafficking, and migration-related child labour is considered 'a worst form of child labour'. Worst forms include work which, by its nature or the circumstances in which it is carried out, is likely to harm the health, safety, or morals of the child.

Hong Kong's Labour Department says children under thirteen are prohibited from working at all, and children under fifteen cannot work in production, factories, or heavy industries.

In a rare documented case of child slavery in domestic work, the *Hong Kong Medical Journal* reported a tragic case from April 2005 when an eleven-year-old girl from Guangdong, China was admitted to a hospital in Tun Muen with multiple injuries. She had been working as a domestic worker for her aunt for one year. The aunt paid her parents HK$1,000, and the girl, who was ten at the time, had to repay this money in the form of labour. She was tortured physically with pliers by the aunt and taunted by her children if she made mistakes during her long hours of work. The authorities said this was a child abuse case, and the girl suffered in slavery-like circumstances like a *mui tsai* from the nineteenth century.

In the nineteenth century and the first half of the twentieth century, there was a system of child slavery whereby young girls were kept as *mui tsai* or domestic servants. Girls were sold by their impoverished parents to wealthier families, and there was an unspoken agreement that they would be free to leave at eighteen, a marriageable age, but many were re-sold into prostitution. Wan Ai Hua, the first Chinese woman to testify that she was forced into wartime sex slavery by the Japanese military, was also a *mui tsai* who was sold into slavery to work as a child maid. She bounced from one form of enslavement to another.

The Hong Kong government banned the sale of *mui tsai* from around 1930 after the UK became one of the signatories to the International Slavery Convention. The rise of communism also led to the abolition of this system.

Cynthia Abdon-Tellez, general manager of the Mission for Migrant Workers, said there were many underage Filipino domestic workers in Hong Kong during the 1980s and 1990s. I had worked with Abdon-Tellez on other documentaries on the subject of abuse of domestic workers and felt fortunate to be able to ask for her insights on this issue of child labourers. She was wise, fiery, and an incredibly selfless person. I admired her solid down-to-earth character. She wasn't flighty like several other NGO workers I had met.

She alerted me to how in 2006, the Philippine government changed the legal age for women working abroad from twenty-one to twenty-five to further protect workers abroad. 'I would say there are hundreds of domestic workers who are underage. We have a few Filipinos. It is child trafficking. It is evil. It damages the child. It's still the responsibility of the home country government,' she said.

Abdon-Tellez explained how employment agencies in Indonesia expedite the process for migrant women to start working right away. 'The agencies change the name and birth date. Most Indonesians don't have surnames . . . These forged documents are also connected to government departments that are responsible for this practice. There's a whole lot of corruption going on.'

I felt especially grateful to expose the suffering of child labourers because the NGOs and the victims themselves have been aware of the problem of forged passports of underage girls as domestic labour for years; yet they kept silent. They were mostly Indonesians. Many women have been too afraid to speak out for fear of imprisonment. 'The problem is they didn't realize that Hong Kong is very strict in terms of information like that on passports. If there's wrong info, you can get jailed,' Abdon-Tellez said. 'We knew fourteen Indonesian people jailed for that—ten of them fought it. At least ten of our clients were able to avoid arrest.'

A spokesperson for Hong Kong's Immigration Department said it is an offence to use forged travel documents and make a false representation about one's identity to an immigration officer. Both offences, upon conviction, can lead to imprisonment of up to fourteen years or a maximum fine of HK$150,000. Aiders and abettors, or those who make the forged documents, are liable to the same prosecution and penalty. The department regularly meets with local consulates to discuss issues related to illegal migration. Last year, the department found 461 forged travel documents, mostly used by illegal workers. They were so poorly made that anyone could discern they were forged.

Sandy Wong said, 'This is certainly a crime on the part of the agents taking advantage of the workers. It also contains elements of human trafficking as listed in Hong Kong's prosecution code, as long as they are credible. As far as the law is concerned, forgery is a punishable crime. The difficulty is on prosecuting these agencies from the exporting countries. Local agencies facilitating submission of documents should be prosecuted if they are aware of such forgery. The question is whether or not they know and how to establish that. Unfortunately, the workers' criminality, as they are the holders of such forged documents—and as long as they possess them or use them—is hard to deny.'

Hong Kong's Immigration Department does not specify a legal age requirement in its guidelines for foreign domestic workers, but every candidate must have at least two years of related experience in order to get a work visa. The application must be supported by a reference letter.

Lestari said that ages on passports are changed to fit the demand of the market in receiving countries, with most employers asking for maids aged between 21 and 35. 'This is not only applied to underage people. Even for older people, they change their age to fit the market,' she said. Lestari also said that there are more underage maids in Singapore than there are in Hong Kong.

A managing director of an employment agency for domestic workers in Hong Kong refuted Lestari's comments and said, 'We don't have any underage here. Most of our applicants have experience and have worked in Singapore, Malaysia or the Middle East. They are not very young. I've also heard that many workers in Singapore are underage.'

I wanted to find out for myself if Singapore had child maids. Through my network, I was connected with Jolovan Wham, former acting executive director of The Humanitarian Organization for Migration Economics (HOME), which supports migrant workers in Singapore. He said by phone that cases of underage maids have increased in recent years. HOME assisted ten underage workers with forged documents from Myanmar, Indonesia, and India. He said, 'They are immature and not prepared for life as a live-in domestic worker, which can be very stressful. They are also vulnerable to sexual abuse.' These girls reached out in desperation to HOME for help because of physical, verbal, and sexual abuse, and some were exhausted from long working hours. I thought of the North Korean refugees and the other victims I've met who had no NGO to reach out to readily. 'The agents are falsifying their passports. These women are unwilling to disclose their age out of fear of being penalized. They could be prosecuted. Singapore doesn't have any laws. The government looks at each case based on the circumstances,' said Wham.

A chair of a group of agencies said she had received only a few complaints about underage domestic workers in Hong Kong, and that they were more than a decade ago. 'You cannot ask a child to look after your child. She is herself a child too. She needs someone to look after her too,' she said, somewhat sympathetically. I was sceptical of her concern.

Zee was the legal age of twenty-one years when she moved to Hong Kong for work. She decided to work abroad as a maid to support her parents financially and to save up money for post-secondary school. Her willingness to sacrifice for her family at a young age was astounding. She attended domestic worker training for several months in Jakarta alongside a thousand other young women and girls. 'I couldn't even count the girls under eighteen. Eighty per cent of the girls were underage,' she said.

Zee said her date of birth was changed by a few months on her passport, and she didn't know why. 'In my experience, the changing of age has nothing to do with the Hong Kong agency, but the Indonesian agency,' she said. 'They're the ones to process passports.

The passport department knows the real age. From my experience, the Indonesian agency will let you know they're changing your real age, your data and then, the Hong Kong agency just knows everything is done and they don't ask questions.'

Zee worked in Hong Kong for four years, and for two of those years she worked at an agency. 'I was working illegally part-time, helping the agency as a recruiter to find new people through Facebook in Indonesia to work in Hong Kong. I have lost count of the number of women with forged passports,' she said.

Abdon-Tellez said thousands of women have returned to Indonesia in recent years to avoid imprisonment in Hong Kong. Campaigners say that Hong Kong needs a comprehensive anti-trafficking law to prevent Indonesian women from going to jail because agencies have illegally changed their personal information on travel documents.

Wong said, 'Having one law to deal with all forms of human trafficking, like Singapore, Taiwan or Macau did, is probably the way to go as it is more organized and target-oriented, as opposed to what we have currently—different sections in different legislations not catching all aspects of human trafficking as the international communities are working on.' Wong adds that a comprehensive law on human trafficking is no substitute for proper allocation of resources, continuous education and community resolve in eradicating all forms of human trafficking.

Campaigners have asked the Indonesian Consulate to raise awareness among domestic workers to ensure they correct the information on their travel documents. 'Many countries believe Indonesian women are criminals and cheaters. But they have to see it from an angle of human trafficking and cheating. The government is most responsible for allowing this system to exist through corruption,' Lestari said.

The Indonesian Consulate has reportedly spoken to the Hong Kong authorities to work out this situation and avoid prosecuting in cases where there is wrong information on passports. But I am not optimistic that the women will be able to easily avoid prison if caught with a forged passport.

Wong recommends that information about falsified passports be included in the leaflet on human trafficking that is distributed by the Immigration and Labour Departments upon first entering Hong Kong. 'Explain to them the law on forgery and allow them to return to their countries immediately if they tell the immigration officer the truth. Such repatriation costs should be paid by the consulates of the exporting countries,' she said.

Former Indonesian Consul General Tri Tharyat said that since January 2015, the Indonesian Consulate in Hong Kong has been correcting data from manually processed passports which have now been transferred to the new biometric system which reads fingerprints. He said the Consulate found thirty falsified passports out of 154,073 Indonesians working as domestic workers in Hong Kong. He blamed the employment agencies in Indonesia. 'It's about agencies making fast money,' he said. 'On the other hand, the women don't have a choice. Some of them were given a passport on the day of departure. The government has no ability to control what happens on the ground.'

Tharyat was a sincere man. I had no reason to not believe him. He said he was monitoring forty-two cases involving information on passports, of which four were sentenced to jail, two were released from jail and deported, twenty-three were given new visas, and thirteen were waiting to hear whether they would be jailed or deported. 'They had different names or different dates of birth, or a combination of both. Sometimes made older or younger,' he said. He believed the women had 'no wrong intentions'.

\* \* \*

While I was looking for more child maids from Indonesia to interview, I came into contact with Pastor Selamet Yap of the

Indonesian church of Solomon's Porch in Hong Kong. He was wrapping up his doctorate on domestic workers suffering in modern slavery and solutions to help them. I asked him if he knew of any women brought to Hong Kong as children on a forged passport. He had helped several of them. He was the quintessential pioneer: strong, immovable, and visionary. I visited his church and was encouraged to see a full congregation of smiling and beautiful Indonesian women who clearly respected and appreciated him and his wife.

His joyful approach to life and ministry helped balance the sometimes extreme brokenness he saw in many of the members of his church. Their sacrificial spirit was very moving to me. I could understand why Yap had dedicated the focus of his doctoral research to trafficked and exploited Indonesian migrant workers and the abuse they struggle with in Hong Kong.

'This desire emerged when I started to serve them and dove deeply into their lives and began to see more problems,' said Yap. 'The Bible instructs us to care for aliens or those who moved from one country to another , , , to speak the truth and our role is to help them and speak for them.'

Yap was particularly affected by meeting and helping several child victims of trafficking in Hong Kong who were tricked by unscrupulous maid employment agencies in Indonesia. He helped one young Indonesian woman named Tuti. She was recruited at the age of seventeen and promised a job with a good salary in Malaysia. Tuti said her agency bribed an immigration officer and forged her passport to raise her age on paper. Her family was in a desperate situation; her father had suffered a stroke and her grandmother was depending on her to send money back home.

For two years, Tuti worked every day with no holiday. Sometimes, she worked until two in the morning. She had three houses to clean and around ten people to feed and do laundry for. 'I was in shock because of overwork. I felt like a slave. I was lied to,' she said with tears rolling down her face. It was hard to believe that a strong young woman like Tuti could be exploited this way.

Yap supported Tuti for two years with free English classes and cooking lessons when she later worked in Hong Kong.

Many more domestic workers whom Yap has met are suffering because of excessive agent recruitment fees or abusive treatment by employers. Yap believes that more education and pastoral care in Indonesia is urgently needed to prevent more vulnerable people like Tuti from being exploited. He travels back to Indonesia to host prevention awareness conferences for pastors, especially in areas where many women migrate for work. He also dreams of establishing a centre offering human trafficking awareness, legal rights, and foreign-language classes in every city in Indonesia.

After my story on child maids was published in the newspaper, I met Vica at an event run by advocates for Indonesian domestic workers. Pastor Yap was in attendance too. Vica came up to me and we struck up a conversation. I told her that I was a journalist and had researched underage domestic workers. She wanted to tell her story and I was glad to listen. Vica was short with a vivacious, large personality. Her most striking feature were her large brown eyes.

Vica was fifteen when she migrated to Singapore in 2000 to work as a maid. Her employment agency forged her birthdate to raise her age to twenty-three. She was not able to finish high school as she had to support her farmer father and her mother who was often in hospital for diabetes. 'I had no choice. My parents are so sick. I'm very poor. My house is so run down. I have nothing. It was so difficult. I couldn't pay to finish school. I registered with the agency. This small girl had to be strong,' she said. I noted yet again the all too common thread of sick family members and grinding poverty that led to girls leaving school and eventually landing in exploitative situations of enslavement without a path to escape.

After working for six years, Vica returned home. She applied for a visa to Singapore to work for her previous employer, but her agency kept her forged passport. All she had was her birth certificate with the real birthdate. She said the Immigration Department in Indonesia issued her a passport with her real birthdate, but the Singaporean Immigration Department rejected her visa application because she had two different dates of birth.

Vica went to a different agency to apply for work in Hong Kong. This agency used the information on her first forged passport. In 2015, her passport expired and she applied for a new one. The Indonesian Consulate's new system now had two different records of her date of birth. 'When I tried to change my Hong Kong identity card, it was crazy because the Hong Kong government says it's criminal to have different identities,' she said animatedly and looking stressed. She was arrested by the Immigration Department and investigated for five hours at one sitting. It was traumatizing.

In total, it took her ten months to fight for her new visa and identity card, and she had to pay HK$1,000 in fees that brought hardship on her parents. It was upsetting to hear her say that her family could barely afford to cover the small expense that typically represents a dinner tab for most professionals. The disparity between the haves and have-nots never fails to shock me. 'I had to go to Kowloon immigration. It was a criminal case. They investigated me. They recorded me. I felt like I was a terrorist . . . I told them it was not my fault. They asked how come you didn't report it earlier. I said I don't know. They would determine whether I go to jail and this case would go to court. I was sad. But I only think about my parents who are so old. If I go to jail, who will take care of my parents? That made me strong.'

I had to laugh because she was the least likely looking criminal, ever! But she was feisty and had a mettle inside of her that no doubt gave her the ability to fight against being unjustly imprisoned.

As the first person to successfully argue with the Immigration Department and avoid jail time, Vica now advises other Indonesian women on how to deal with forged passports. In fact, she has even been asked to share her case with the Consulate.

'Around fourteen or more girls went to jail because of the same problem I had. They don't know how to answer the officer. There will be more problems. The Indonesian Consulate didn't know how to help me solve this problem,' she said.

Adrian Siu, an agency manager who has worked in the industry for twenty years, said, 'It's a rotten story. It is child trafficking and child labour. First of all, Hong Kong people and Hong Kong agencies do not handle passports. As an agency in Hong Kong, we trust the document that is issued by the Government of Indonesia. We cannot doubt or query the Indonesian government.'

Siu said that local agencies in Indonesia hire brokers, sometimes called sponsors, who recruit women from the villages. They may also lure teenagers to make fast money. 'I believe there may be tricky or deceptive things that could happen with the middlemen. Maybe there is some arrangement there. I cannot verify or clarify. I believe if the date of birth on the passport has been tampered with, the responsibility probably lies with the middleman.'

He said that several years ago, the Indonesian government was concerned about underage domestic workers. 'They received a lot of pressure from the public. This is a kind of child trafficking. In the last few years, they have stepped up security measures for identification.'

The staff at his agency tried to screen out underage girls by interviewing the young women in person. 'As experienced agency staff, they will discern the age of the workers . . . but we're not a hundred per cent sure because we have to trust the passport. We don't have any other way to verify.'

After I interviewed Lia, I turned to her friend Siti to ask for her story. They were in sync in their mannerisms and acted like sisters. Siti was an attractive young woman with smooth olive skin and large cat-like upturned eyes. Her short hairstyle had razor straight ends and combined with her fitted black leather jacket, she looked altogether futuristic. She was whip smart and confident, and we hit it off as friends immediately. To this day we stay in touch.

The two young women became acquainted in Hong Kong yet their experiences of slavery-like treatment ran eerily parallel. Around the same time that Lia was in Macau, fourteen-year-old Siti was sent by a different employment agency from Indonesia to Singapore with a forged date of birth on her passport that made her eight years older. 'They plucked my eyebrows and shaped them to made me look older,' she said. 'I was skinny and looked small. They changed my passport photo and used a random woman's photo. It doesn't look like me. The agent promised me I'll have a big salary, I'll have a good life, and I can help my parents with a house.' She said her parents wholly believed in the agent and ironically, they didn't even know where Singapore was. Yet, they were willing to sacrifice their daughter to go there for work.

Siti signed a contract in English that the agency presented to her, but she had no idea what she was agreeing to. She said it's a common practice and that it's wrong. She was also sent to a training camp for weeks. 'I didn't understand and . . . I didn't ask. They helped me get a passport and changed my birthdate to 1983 from 1991. They trained me to lie about my age and to keep repeating, "I am 23, I am 23." I was scared . . . we are all scared. That's why no one talks about changing our age. I'm scared whenever we deal with the government,' she said.

Siti worked for a Swiss family for fourteen months. The employer's mother gave her one cup of noodles a day. She had to ask for a glass of water each time. 'The grandma thought I was dirty and full of germs,' she said. 'She controlled me. She told me to mop, clean the floor. I couldn't touch the soap, the dishes, or clean the kitchen. I couldn't talk with anyone or smile to others. I cried every day. I was hungry and wanted to eat.' She paused as she shared this haunting memory. There was unhealed trauma here, and I wished I could help. I hoped that sharing her story would heal some of the unspoken wounds of neglect, abuse, and gross injustice.

'One of the things these children will experience is separation from the family, parents,' said Abdon-Tellez. 'Second, they're in situations they have no idea about. They're kept in camps for training for about three months. They're told to follow whatever the employer says. I wonder if they explain to them what a contract is or what it says. Already they're vulnerable.'

Siti said that for her hard work over fourteen months, the agency gave her only a pittance of S$20. She ran away, and then the agency sent her to work for another family. 'I didn't get any pay. I wanted to go home but I felt shame. I had no money,' she said. Shame keeps the abuse and enslavement hidden. For more than two years, she worked like a slave for another family. Her responsibilities included cooking for seventeen people every night. One day, she broke her hand but her employer did not want to pay for her medical bills. Soon after, she decided to go back home to Indonesia in January 2011.

'There was no one to help her when something terrible happened. Her childhood was taken from her,' said Hartwick. 'Her trust was destroyed. This leads to distrust of people who want to help. When one hires a domestic worker, they should find out and care about them as a human being . . . All they want is to be paid living wages and to have a job that will bring dignity to their family and for themselves.' I resonated with Hartwick and wondered if there will ever be a solution to end the abuse and exploitation that women could face in domestic work, or was it an inescapable part of this line of employment.

Several months later, Siti decided to work again and bravely flew to Hong Kong to work for her new employer. She was only seventeen. Her agency unscrupulously charged her HK$3,000 every month for seven months. She was fired after fourteen months. Siti was then placed with another family, a former actress in her fifties living in the Mid-Levels on Hong Kong Island. 'She didn't give me food. She called me "stupid woman" or "crazy woman" every day, all the time,' said Siti, adding that she couldn't stop crying at times.

Siti ran away and filed a complaint with the Labour Department and the Indonesian Consulate against her employers. Thankfully, the Consulate has blacklisted them.

Siti now has generous employers who pay her HK$5,000 a month, well above the minimum wage. 'It has been hard,' she said. 'I've been abused by others. I've been working under pressure. I lost my childhood. I lost everything. I have no experience being a child. I only knew hard work. It's my parents' fault too for trusting the agency. We came from a poor family. It doesn't happen to other children . . . It will affect you until now.'

Tharyat said his government is taking a hardline stance on illegal schemes run by employment agencies. Despite my doubts, I kept an open mind and hoped for systemic change. 'There will be more crackdown on agencies in Indonesia, in coordination with police, mainly to look for bad agencies that change passports of prospective workers,' he said. 'Our obligation is to protect these young women . . . We are parties to the Convention against Child Labour.'

In one year, the Indonesian government suspended 190 employment agencies for illegal procedures related to sending workers overseas, including sectors other than domestic work. The government's new policy of exempting migrant workers from crushing agency placement fees that traps them in debt for months has been postponed. Hong Kong agencies have protested and argued that this new rule would cause hiring Indonesian women as domestic workers to be too expensive.

But these new measures have come too late for Lia and Siti and the other women who have been in debt bondage and were sent as child labour to Hong Kong and Singapore with forged passports. These young women have lost their childhood and innocence. The subtle ways in which agencies exploit women by charging crippling placement fees is eye-opening. For years, domestic workers in world cities like Hong Kong have been victimized, right before our eyes, as modern-day slaves; they were embedded in families across our city.

Compared to most others, I was fairly exposed to human trafficking and slave labour victims, yet I was not aware of their hardship and exploitation until a seasoned expert like Matt pointed out the method of debt bondage used by agencies. Then I could not help but feel disturbed by it. I began to see these women in a new light. I began to feel unsettled that they didn't have their own community centre and had to resort to sitting on blankets on the floor of our concrete jungle.

Still, I could not care until I was fully aware of their suffering. My own paradigm shift has helped me see the greater urgent need to keep raising awareness about the experiences of these women. We must try to change mindsets and open the eyes of their employers and of those who have the power to effect transformation and bring justice and recompense for them. If all employers spoke out against agency fees and cut out the broker, then we will successfully eliminate this type of modern slavery from society.

# 14

# Exploitation in Southeast Asia

Exploitation and various forms of modern-day slavery are especially rampant in impoverished communities in Southeast Asia. To produce a documentary for my human trafficking series, I had an opportunity to witness and expose the underbelly of the notorious city of Pattaya. It is one of Thailand's most popular resort cities, thanks to its pretty beaches and vibrant nightlife. At the same time, it has also been dubbed the world capital of child sex tourism. Children as young as eight years old walk up to strangers on the streets of Pattaya to beg for money. Most of them are from neighbouring Cambodia. I was afraid of my own reaction to what I would find there.

A friend had met Agnes Harper on a trip to Thailand and introduced me to her. At that time, Harper was in her thirties and was the outreach worker and director of the Thailand office of an international NGO with a Christian media network. As soon as we met in Bangkok, we got acquainted in our rented van and began to film her interview. I could imagine her feeling at home in a tough city like New York city. She was extremely tough and street smart and yet she possessed a softness for victims. I wouldn't want to cross her and immediately understood that I would have to follow her rules on this trip. I was relieved to have an experienced guide to lead me.

I admired her for absorbing the secondary pain and trauma of witnessing sexually exploited children. There was a personal cost, though I couldn't put my finger on it then. It's no surprise that NGO workers often have to take breaks from harrowing stories of suffering. I also had to distance myself from the wartime sex slavery issue for a few years. I could not bear to read another headline or watch a documentary on the women because it was unbearably depressing to know that the Japanese government had not yet given a healing sincere apology to victims or offered a genuine victim-centred solution to bring closure.

'There's a lot of trafficked little girls and boys,' Harper explained with a mix of tenderness and firmness, 'They're sent here to sell gum and also used by sex tourists. They have cigarette burns, which is a form of punishment. If they don't bring a certain amount of money home they're beaten. So, they'll do anything for that money. Life is cheap in Cambodia. Cambodia has suffered through a huge war. Because of the poverty, people have learned to exploit that. They come in with a house parent or the person who's selling them. And the person usually stays back in the alleys.'

I couldn't begin to imagine children being used by sex tourists. It was the most distressing piece of information I had heard about a manifestation of modern slavery. I had a hard time processing it.

Harper brought me and the cameraman who spoke little English to the town of Poipet, a popular destination for gamblers on the Cambodian side of the border. She brought a volunteer with her named Arielle, a kind Singaporean young woman in her twenties. We had to line up at customs. While the cameraman, Arielle, and I sailed through, Harper faced questioning both ways. Perhaps, she was known to the officials as an NGO worker and was subject to extra scrutiny.

Hundreds of Thais, Cambodians, and tourists pass through this narrow Thai–Cambodian border each day. This rural no-man's land is a five-hour drive from Pattaya, and trafficking of Cambodian children into Thailand takes place rampantly through both legal and illegal routes in the area. To cross this area like tourists was unsettling and filled me with a passion to expose the trafficking of children that often took place in broad daylight.

I filmed Harper as she visited her outreach programme in Poipet. 'You'll find a lot of single moms with four or five children, with no healthcare and no jobs,' she said in a fiery tone. 'The trafficker will say, "Hey, can I have your child? I'll find the child a good job in the city." But a lot of the moms just don't know the beatings, the rapes, the sexual abuse.'

I had to brace myself every time she spoke of what happened to the kids. My body had a physical reaction, and sometimes I would hunch over and gasp. I was too sensitive for this issue, I said to myself. I prayed for protection over my heart, but it seemed trite compared to what these children suffered.

Harper told me that foreigners look for children to prey on in the Circle Square area close to the Poipet border. 'A lot of the older kids are sent to sleep with foreigners for money,' she said, looking visibly disturbed.

We met a dishevelled nine-year-old boy named Bourey who told us, 'I saw two foreigners rape one little girl in the Circle. I saw a foreigner come in a white van, eight of them, and sell one little girl, take one girl and four boys and take them out of the country and sell them to Thailand.' Bourey was wearing tattered clothes, and I looked at him from a distance, playing with other children in the very grounds where evil took place. I have not experienced that level of helplessness since then. The sincerity and purity of his testimony touched me deeply.

'All these kids are afraid of the vans and the people who sell them,' Harper told me on camera.

While foreigners used vans, the local traffickers smuggled children in carts across the border to Thailand. Andrea, an outreach worker for an NGO in Cambodia, said, 'Eighty-five per cent of children that are trafficked come through this border site from Cambodia, Laos, and Vietnam. You'll see the actual trafficking and selling on the Thai side in Pattaya.'

Harper introduced me to an eleven-year-old girl named Maley who was begging on the streets for twelve hours a day. Her shoulder length hair was tangled and messy. She had a wild-eyed look and clung to Harper. She was a safe person, and I could see that her hugs were healing for Maley. 'My family is poor. My house gets flooded. Often there're a lot of snakes and centipedes that come in. I have seven siblings,' she said.

'Her mom beats her if she doesn't bring 30,000 riel ($7.50) every day,' explained Harper, with a pained voice. She was trying to get Maley off the streets. 'She's even beaten her in front of us.'

Maley said in a soft voice, 'I am afraid of getting beaten. I knew a girl in my village. A foreigner gave her a snack and asked her to come with him to get more snacks at another place. A few days later, I saw the dead girl. The foreigner raped her. I'm very afraid.' To avoid trouble, Maley would stop begging before nightfall. I'll never forget meeting these children in Poipet. It was incredibly difficult to walk away from them, back in the direction of the border. We had to return to Bangkok to continue filming. Our schedule was packed. I looked back often and waved with a breaking heart. Arielle and I bonded over the shock of seeing sexually exploited children for the first time. I was glad that she joined us on the trip as a silent supporter.

I made a decision to air their interviews because of their unusually desperate circumstances. I wanted to tell the world what these children were suffering, and I hoped people would respond and help rescue them as well as offer education and a better future. Some other NGOs vociferously attacked Harper for allowing the children to be interviewed and accused her of raising funds in an unethical way. I wondered if these naysayers were, in fact, jealous of the powerful reaction these children elicited in Hong Kong and the global Chinese world. The documentary aired on YouTube and our website platform for a time. Funds were raised in a short period, a testament to the power of media's vast and lightning speed reach.

We followed and filmed Harper in Pattaya's infamous red-light district, known as Walking Street, as she actively searched for trafficked victims with the help of Pon, a Cambodian translator. Music pulsated grotesquely and neon lights and women in skimpy clothing assaulted the senses. It seemed like a den of unbridled wickedness and if there ever was a hell on earth, this would be the second location after Poipet.

She expertly spotted a Caucasian man with two Thai or Cambodian girls who were under five years old. I hadn't noticed them but Harper's trained eyes concluded the girls had been trafficked. I thought of Maley back in Poipet. 'Trafficked children are brought here, locked here. Often, a relative or the mom needs money for drugs. These children become currency. It usually starts with the dancing and hula hoops,' she said.

We saw two young girls under seven with full make-up, playing hula hoop with a bowl in front of them for donations. I was in disbelief at how they were out in the open for all to see, yet no one was helping them. 'Those two little girls are there to make extra money. Usually, in Pattaya, that means sexual favours. Because Pattaya is filled with paedophiles,' Harper said. She was in a zone of her own and very focused on the girls. I could hardly ask her any questions because she was concentrating on the trafficked children at risk. I didn't know what to expect next, and we pretended to be tourists and just filmed everything we could see.

The police seemed to turn a blind eye. When asked what the police were doing to help children who were being used for sex by foreigners, Jaw Boonlert, a Royal Thai Police Officer said, 'I've been in Pattaya for two years, but I've never seen children offer or be forced to have sex.' Boonlert said that if adults were caught having sex with a child, they would be arrested and sent to jail for 'a long time'.

However, sometimes, the police do crack down. At one end of Walking Street, we saw the police had rounded up a begging ring made up of several Cambodian children.

In one of the bars at nearly 2 a.m., a little girl was dancing. She was wearing a short skirt, heavy blue eye shadow, and bright red lipstick. A man grabbed her by the waist when she ran to him.

Harper explained with shock and it was as if her whole body was gesticulating, 'This is the girl we've been looking for the past six months. The first time we encountered this little girl, she was dancing for money in a very skimpy outfit in the middle of the street. They give her speed, and they let her dance for about eight hours. She's between three and four years old. We need to get her off the street, and we need to get her some help!'

She bent over and took a deep breath. It was the first time I had seen a vulnerable side to Harper. She looked so broken by seeing this tiny girl. I felt distressed too beyond anything I had ever experienced in the frontlines of human trafficking.

Social workers and police were not available to rescue this girl in the middle of the night. And NGOs could not just take kids off the streets or from bars. 'When we have a child who's admitted being abused and beaten, then right away we call the police and call the social worker. Then they come in and the police does a rescue,' she said.

Harper was working with police and social workers in a pioneer programme to save former child slaves. She told me that rescues didn't happen every week but every few months. Her first successful rescue case was a girl named Bec who was in bondage to a begging ring in Pattaya. 'She's suffered severe abuse and STDs. She's only ten,' she said with a sad smile. 'My job is to take the child into a long-term facility where they specialize in sexual abuse or trauma healing for children. She'd lived on the streets for a long time. I think she's going to have a really good life.'

Harper is truly a hero. She later told me her faith helped keep her grounded.

During another night in Bangkok, Harper approached a young mother sitting on the sidewalk with a baby in her arms and a three-year-old child clinging to her shoulder. 'Why did you come here?' she asked in Thai. The woman did not respond to the question.

I learnt that the mother was part of a 'begging ring'—pretend mothers with rented kids. 'These begging rings are one of the most horrific forms of exploitation of children on the streets. They're completely taken advantage of, both sexually and physically,' she said. 'The babies perform oral sex. That is very common.' I was in total shock after hearing of this.

I wanted to understand why there is a market for children to be exploited in this way, so I met with Chris Lenty who was heading a Christian group that befriended and counselled men who buy sex.

'There is so much hatred for men,' he said 'They're the reason this injustice is so prevalent throughout Asia and the world. And I began to think to myself . . . that's just not true. Because as I look into my own life, as I sit and talk to men on the side of the road, they are not waking up wondering how can they inflict pain on somebody else. There are issues. All of us have issues.'

Chris told me that he used to be addicted to sex. 'You begin to develop a more deviant nature, then you begin to buy sex. And I know this from my own life with pornography. It gradually led down a path like that. And it was awful. It began to eat away at the relationships I was trying to build with people. It began to eat away who I was.'

He had a sense of calling to Thailand and moved there from the US in 2001. He and his team had mapped out hundreds of massage parlours, nightclubs, and sex bars in the city for their outreach plans, and they showed me their impressive wall with stickers in different colours. In a span of five years, they had spoken with more than two thousand men. I believe they were one of the few groups that were trying to reach and tackle the issue of prostitution and sex trafficking from the buyer's side, reaching the johns who purchased sex with compassion and viewing them as victims too.

'There's one man who told me, "Yes I have a wife at home, but this is what men do. She knows I come down." In the course of our conversation, we were able to share with him, "If you love your wife so much then why do you need the lies of this area?" A couple weeks later we get an email, and this man's like, "You guys were right. My wife is my perfect gift. And there is no reason to come down here."'

When I expressed interest in interviewing someone about Thai prisons where many Cambodian trafficking victims are sent, Harper connected me with Margie Grainger, the director of the Hand to Hand Foundation. Margie was an American with curly brown hair, a tanned face without make-up, and a laid-back disposition. She reminded me of a hippie from the 1960s. Margie regularly delivered food and clothing to trafficked children who were in prison. 'For as long as people can make money out of these children and it's profitable to bring these children back to Thailand, you're never going to break the system. A lot of the children are by themselves when they're arrested, and they get put in an adult jail with no bedding. They get one meal a day,' she said.

Being on Thailand's anti-human trafficking advisory panel, Margie has brought this issue of children being forced to stay in adult prisons to top officials. 'The last meeting I attended, I said to the major general, "We have this problem in the jails in Pattaya." He said, "No, there are no children in the jail in Pattaya." He honestly and sincerely did not know that this problem existed.' We also spent time at her day care, and there were happy children laughing and playing together. Margie said softly to me that some of these children were former trafficking victims. I would not have guessed that to be the case judging by the huge smiles on their faces.

Matt said to me when I had first interviewed him, 'Thailand has a law that basically states that if you have been trafficked, they will offer certain protections to you. Identified trafficking victims are offered shelter, medical, and legal support and prepared for reintegration into life in their home country. You could even work in Thailand while your case is moving forward. So one of the key solutions is more emphasis on victim identification. To do that, you need good translation services. And that's one of the biggest constraints the Thai government has.'

As for why trafficking hasn't been abolished in the red-light districts, Matt added that there's often corruption associated with law enforcement in the sex trade, and there's a tremendous amount of money to be made.

According to the US State Department's *2021 Trafficking in Persons Report*:

> The Government of Thailand does not fully meet the minimum standards for the elimination of trafficking but is making significant efforts to do so . . , However, the government did not demonstrate overall increasing efforts compared to the previous reporting period, even considering the impact of the COVID-19 pandemic on its anti-trafficking capacity . . . The government's provision of services to victims remained inadequate, and some victims residing in government shelters lacked freedom of movement. Corruption and official complicity continued to impede anti-trafficking efforts, and the government convicted five complicit officials in 2020. Therefore Thailand was downgraded to Tier 2 Watch List.

* * *

In the heart of Bangkok, I accompanied an outreach worker named Su who was with a Bangkok-based Christian NGO. She was a short, rotund Chinese–Thai woman with a jovial personality and an easy smile. Her short hair and glasses made her look like an university student rather than a social worker.

She was highly connected with the Thai police because she was personable, trustworthy, and reliable. She got the job done and did it very well. They contacted her when they identified trafficked women, and she then placed them in a safe home while they made preparations for their return to their homeland. Su shared with me that she wanted to help these vulnerable women start businesses as a long-term way of sustaining themselves, or else they would be at risk of being trafficked again. 'I want to find an organization that can help them set up a small enterprise to help meet their financial needs and not just rescue them and send them back without a job. They'll probably come back next month looking for work and get trafficked again because they're stuck in a cycle of poverty and desperate to make money,' she said and asked if I could help her. I told her that I would speak with my contacts. But she didn't follow up even though we exchanged a few emails.

Su had brought me to a notorious three-star hotel that was known as a hangout for trafficked women. Security was tight. The traffickers were protecting their 'investments'. In the basement, there was a coffee shop where the women were waiting for customers. Su told me that the women had been trafficked from Uzbekistan and sold by a local recruiter to a mama-san. 'They have to pay to their mama-san 4,000–5,000 baht each night,' she said. I was petrified to gather footage of these women. I debated and deliberated for an hour. Finally, the cameraman had to push me and rebuked me and said, 'Just do it!' I took a huge breath even though I was frightened and felt like fainting from the adrenalin rush. I walked in and asked the mama-sans if they knew the time. What an awkward question I thought to myself as these hardened women looked at me suspiciously. At any minute, I feared the traffickers would rush out with machine guns to take me away. Thankfully that didn't happen, and after several minutes of filming these ladies and the area, I walked out of there with the cameraman. I was shaken to my core but unscathed. I swore to myself that I wouldn't do that kind of undercover work ever again.

Su then pointed out several African women who were hanging out on the street. We approached them, and I asked them for their stories but they refused. One woman's trafficker came up to intimidate me, and then two African men tried to grab me. Several women gave us the middle finger. I was taken aback and wanted to scream, 'Hey we're trying to help you!'

After spending an eye-opening evening with Su, I was about to interview her boss, Judy. She was a soft-spoken American woman and looked wispy and fragile outwardly. Yet, inwardly, she was very gutsy. Judy has helped rescue more than 150 victims of forced sexual exploitation through her organization. Often she would go into the bars with only a few women and bravely talk with the girls and the owners in the hope of rescuing the trafficked women who didn't want to work there. Coincidentally, several years earlier, I had processed her grant application when I was working as a philanthropy advisor I knew her work well on paper and was looking forward to getting to know her and her work in person.

She told me that at least ninety-five per cent of the foreign women who come to the area are initially trafficked. She said she'd met trafficked women from a dizzying list of countries such as China, North Korea, Romania, Turkey and Nepal as well as numerous countries from South America and Africa.

One African woman told Judy of how she was approached by a recruiter who promised to take care of her travel expenses. 'When she got to China, the woman said there's no job here,' said Judy. 'Prostitution is your only option. Now she owed the woman US$4,000. She naturally didn't have a return ticket. She had left home believing that she was going to send money home. She had no choice but to go to the street. Then they said, "Well then we're going to teach you what it means to be a prostitute." So they sent in two foreign men who raped her. They took turns violently raping her until she was completely broken. She couldn't work for five days. She knew that if she wanted to survive, she had to start working as a prostitute. She was stuck in it for two years before we met her and were able to help send her home.'

Judy recounted another incident in gentle tones. 'Two women had run away from a trafficking ring, and a group of mafia were sent after them. When they caught up, they gang-raped the girls and filmed their ordeal. When the girls refused to go back to prostitution, they were told, "We'll take this film of you being raped and we'll post it on the Internet and we'll send it back to your country and everybody will see you in this position."'

I spoke with a former prostitute named Aom who was helped by the organization. She was one of five siblings who were abandoned by a drunken father. 'When I was a child, I cried a lot. I would hide behind the house and cry,' she said. One day, a friend took her to work in the bars. 'I'd never been to this area before. I'd never gone out into the red-light areas. I was shocked. I went home and thought about my family. Mom would call and ask, "Why haven't you sent any money home?"'

Once, Aom barely escaped from a client. 'I had a customer who took me. He didn't pay me, and he also hurt me badly.' She ended up contracting HIV. 'One night I prayed when I was in hospital. I said, "God if you're real, then help me." I had sores all over my body but they disappeared miraculously. My mother was speechless.' She was visibly joyful.

'It's Russian Roulette,' Judy explained. The next one could be the guy that takes her to the room and has five men waiting to gang-rape her, beat her up, kick her out the door with absolutely no money and have her end up with HIV.'

I spoke with Mint next. She was especially vulnerable to sexual exploitation and trafficking. She told me that she was a single mother at sixteen and an orphan with no job skills. An auntie from her village recruited her to sell sex in bars. 'I didn't know any foreigners but had to have sex with foreigners,' she said. 'I was afraid. I had to prepare myself every time. I felt like I didn't have any value. My family didn't have any money. The bar was set up in such a way that I had no choice. There was a mama-san and a pimp, and they would push really hard to sell me. It was a terrible time. I was drinking heavily. I didn't know how to pray but I cried, "God get me out of this place and bring me into the light."'

Her story echoed the sentiments of all of the trafficked Filipina women working at bars in Hong Kong. There was a universal thread that ran through their stories of worthlessness, of vulnerability as orphans, of families with no money, and their choices being snatched away from them by virtue of their birthplace. It could happen to anyone.

Somehow, Mint met Judy, and she was given a long-term job. Her face glowed as she testified, 'My life has changed. I feel safe now. I came to have a dream to help prostitutes.' How I wished all of the victims I had met could escape their ordeal and have the option of a long-term safe job.

* * *

In the Philippines, tens of thousands of girls and boys are exploited through force or coercion in cybersex trafficking via webcams, videos, and photos for clients around the world. There were about 60,000 reports of online child sexual exploitation in the country in 2018. This crime is increasing globally due to the widespread use of mobile devices, social media, and online games and forums, with victims being filmed or live-streamed to anyone with an Internet connection.

Traffickers across the world usually prey on vulnerable and impoverished families to recruit their victims. In the Philippines, many victims are exploited by their own families, which makes it impossible for them to leave or speak out.

In my personal experience, I have not seen many organizations that are able to offer job skills with effective trauma healing, and I was pleasantly surprised to find one that was seeing good results. Many victims of exploitation and slavery have some level of trauma. Survivors need special care and healing before they can re-enter society, take on full-time jobs successfully, rebuild their lives, and start families of their own.

My husband had put me in touch with Sam Dharmapala, the founder of the social enterprise Regenesys, whose driving vision was to run a company that employs vulnerable people and survivors of exploitation for computer-based work. He launched the social enterprise in 2014.

Dharmapala was working in the Philippines in 2013 for a global investment bank when he met with several NGOs that were rescuing trafficked women and girls. They all said that the greatest challenge was helping these survivors find stable well-paying jobs so that they wouldn't be exploited again. These women were derailed by the constant and chronic stress that comes with understanding how to live life daily outside of shelters.

To begin with, he met with high-school graduates in rural areas. He felt that they would not be able to access opportunities for work requiring knowledge of computers because they wouldn't be able to afford the tuition fees for learning these skills. This is where his journey began to create a company from scratch to employ survivors.

Out of the 200 staff at Regenesys, 180 are survivors of exploitation and physical and sexual abuse, domestic violence or highly at risk as individuals who are escaping severe poverty. All work in photo, video, or 3D editing for real estate companies or as virtual assistants. Everyone goes through eight weeks of training that includes a healing and resilience-building component to help break negative thinking patterns.

I asked Dharmapala if I could interview a successful case of a former trafficked woman who was now thriving. He helped put me in touch with Irene, and we had an online interview.

Irene was looking timid when we first saw each other on video. I could sense that she was still grappling with trauma pain. My heart had compassion for her as I had met a range of victims of sexual enslavement and exploitation with PTSD. I told her who I was and why I was interested in documenting her story for the world to know and take action.

I asked her gingerly what she wanted to share with me. Irene was twelve years old when her aunt and uncle who had a baby invited her to live at their home in the northern part of Cebu in the Philippines. In exchange for household chores and babysitting, Irene's school tuition would be paid for. She looked up to her aunt who had graduated from college and was a role model to her.

Irene's parents were farmers and could barely support themselves. Irene dreamed of finishing high school but she knew it was out of reach, so she decided to make the move from southern Cebu to her aunt and uncle's home. She would be replacing her younger eleven year old sister who had been living with them for a few months but wanted to leave.

When her aunt asked her to show her body to strangers online for money, Irene froze from shock. But her aunt groomed and manipulated her by saying that she would be able to make enough to graduate from high school. She reassured Irene that the foreigners would not be able to touch her.

I instinctively knew, from my years of interviewing victims, that she would have felt profoundly betrayed by an authority figure, which would affect her ability to trust and form healthy relationships in the future. I didn't push for her to answer and waited for her to feel comfortable.

After Irene agreed to do this work, she called her mother who already knew about her decision. She would work in this role for four years from the age of twelve to sixteen.

She said her online nickname was Kim. The first time she showed her body was to two foreign men in their forties or fifties. Her aunt called it a 'show'. 'My aunt asked me to do this. I was at my grandma's house. That was the first time I saw a man touching himself. It was really scary. My aunt kept telling me to look at the camera. She asked me to take off my dress and bra. I felt bad about myself. She said it's normal but I felt shame,' she said in a quiet hushed voice.

Her aunt sometimes gave her 200 pesos ($4). Sometimes, she didn't pay at all because she was already sponsoring her school fee. One day after school, her aunt asked Irene to chat with a foreigner named Richard. He was waiting for her at their home.

'He asked me to touch myself. I pretended. She was happy that I had clients who asked for me. I remember the first day Richard slept beside me. I was sleeping on the floor and it was still dark. Richard came and he fell asleep. Nothing happened. I already felt that he may do something bad next time,' she said, tearing up. I expressed sadness for her, and we sat in silence as her tears rolled down. The air was pregnant with sorrow, and I dared not move or say anything.

She expressed anger at why her parents allowed her to do shameful things because of poverty. She was upset that her aunt and uncle kept up appearances by attending church and praying in front of others. But the reality of their lives was rotten and their computer room business—where people could rent a computer to play games—was a façade that hid an online pornography ring. Irene sometimes helped exchange bills into coins.

'There were other girls and a boy who were forced into online pornography. One girl was the five-year-old niece of the uncle. There was also a gay boy. They were managing it by themselves on the computer. Even in a café chatting on a computer with foreigners. They would tell them a foreigner wants a 'show'. The customers were all foreigners but I'm not sure where they were from. They took most of the money from us. They made a lot of money. They recruited other people to ask their clients to drop money in their accounts. They operated a loan shark system.

'When I graduated from high school, I promised myself that I would go home. One day, I was in their kitchen when my uncle came out with a towel on. He was in his thirties. He asked me to massage his penis. I fought him and cried non-stop. He threatened me saying, "Don't tell anyone or you'll be ashamed. Aunt shouldn't know,"' Irene said. She decided to go home to protect herself from sexual abuse from her uncle. She called her mom who instinctively knew she was almost raped. Her aunt lied to her mom and said Irene didn't want to go home after all and that she would continue to live with them to clean their home and care for their baby. After she was at home, her aunt and uncle visited her to persuade her to return to work.

'My mom was suspicious about why I didn't go near them. My sister and I told our mom about our uncle and the online cyber pornography shows. She called the police and went to the wife of my father's uncle and asked for advice,' she said.

A police case opened up in April 2015. Her aunt and uncle ran away when the police began to question them and investigate. The police are still looking for them with a warrant for their arrest. Irene said, 'I really want them to go to jail. It was the toughest time of my life. Now I'm recovering. My sister is healing. I've heard stories of other girls who were raped. I was not raped. That's how I console myself.'

Irene admits she is traumatized and has nightmares. In the aftermath, before she joined Regenesys, her parents often found her staring catatonically, and she often woke up crying. She said, 'I have forgotten the pain with the busyness of my work. My aunt and uncle were motivated by greed and forced children into cyber pornography. I think they are still forcing other children into cyberporn. They can't earn money without it. They're traffickers.'

While Irene's mom wants her aunt and uncle to go to jail as punishment for forcing her daughters into online pornography, Irene's grandmother is pressuring her and her sister to drop the case.

Irene dreams of being a teacher someday. She has a sponsor, a kind professor from Europe, for her college studies. Her life is turning around, and she also has a boyfriend she plans to marry and is pregnant with his child. '[My current job] really changed my life. I am shocked by how family-oriented they are. They care about us and not just their own selves,' she said. She found the emotional healing course for abused women to be very helpful and is grateful to have counsellors to speak with.

'I was afraid of failure. I felt terrible when I failed. They taught us that failure is the start of learning. They trust us even when we fail. They gave me a stable environment and family-like support. They made me feel cared for and accepted.'

In her role, she edits photos and offers virtual assistance by responding to clients' emails and reviews photo quality. Irene believes that she would be working at a fast-food restaurant if she didn't have this opportunity. She is most grateful for being brought out of her dark place through kind-hearted people. 'I think we can help other girl victims by offering jobs like the one I have. That's what we want—we want jobs to earn money and not to earn it in bad ways,' she said with a smile in her eyes. We ended the call with joy. I thanked her for her courage and reassured her that her story will help many other women.

* * *

Dharmapala had worked in change management in the corporate world for years, building effective technical teams before he felt compelled to leave his stable career behind. His wife, a medical doctor, wanted to offer health education to at-risk populations in the Philippines too. Both were radically motivated by their Christian faith.

Dharmapala wanted to be able to offer higher skilled work and economic independence to survivors as a way to help foster a new identity that was not centred on being a sexual object and to give them greater acceptance within their families and communities.

'Victims often experience shame, stigma, and rejection from their families and communities following rescue and attempted reintegration. This is especially if they had been trafficked for sexual exploitation, which, in turn, can not only cause ongoing psychosocial distress but also increase the risk of re-trafficking,' he said. 'Underlying this approach was a hypothesis that the survivors should be highly motivated because a good, stable job means escape from exploitation and a path towards restoration. And that through the best people development tools in the corporate world, it is possible to tap into this motivation to see some incredible life transformation.'

Another shining example of success is twenty-two-year-old Marie, a mother of three and a child-trafficking victim since she was fourteen. Her parents physically abused her. She had several boyfriends after escaping multiple times from shelters for sex trafficking victims. She would often call her social worker for help when things became difficult. One of her friends at the shelter began to work at Regenesys. Marie witnessed her friend's emotional and physical transformation and wanted this for herself. She signed up for the training as a photo editor. Initially, she was known to be difficult to work with, but after receiving caring feedback from her supervisors, she has gained more emotional intelligence in the way she deals with her colleagues. She sets a high standard for herself and mentors the new employees.

The company is self-sustaining. 'It is also painfully obvious that the need for large-scale businesses is so significant for survivors. There are 46 million slaves across the world and there needs to be a better answer to what happens to them after they are rescued,' said Dharmapala.

* * *

As I look back at the beginning of my long road to justice during that fateful call with Gay McDougall, I can discern a series of serendipitous connections and events that led me to find myself and then birth my life's message in the form of this book as a voice for suffering girls and women. The epic journey I went on to document the historical truth and experiences of wartime sex slaves for the Japanese military and the people involved in this human rights issue helped me process my old wounds, my painful setbacks and failures and allowed me to fully accept my Korean identity. Through this journey, I was able to connect the dots between historical sex military slavery with modern human trafficking. I want the world to know about this horrific cycle of sex slavery. Indeed, my desperate search for justice and meaning led to a healing acceptance of who I am and solidified my calling to stand for modern slavery victims and the most marginalized people on earth.

I feel humbled, as a deeply flawed person, to be a voice for many women, children and former mama-sans and pimps. Meeting them has been a huge privilege and helped to shape me and crystallize my convictions over the years. I've come to firmly determine through the years of meeting survivors, frontline workers, and former traffickers that we need more sustainable job opportunities for survivors of modern-day slavery and other vulnerable people that go beyond ubiquitous jewellery-making, which may not be enough to provide for their families. These people need safe employment options that empower them to work with dignity and allow them to use and develop their talents. Frontline workers need more trauma care and support to sustain their vital efforts that may be the only lifeline for the enslaved in some regions.

As a campaigner, I feel that we need as many people as possible to commit to take action. We need people from all sectors—donors, governments, schools and more to stand for what's right and help abolish modern slavery in our lifetime.

In my experience as a philanthropy advisor managing millions of dollars directed to anti-human trafficking and humanitarian work, I have come to conclude that we need to better coordinate funding and strategic efforts to maximize our impact and curb the sometimes toxic impact of competition among NGOs. Businesses are more efficient than NGOs and have a key role to play in the next global wave of combating the buying and selling of humans and in ridding their value chains of human trafficking and exploitation. Goods and services made by slave labour are products borne of criminal activity.

I wholeheartedly support Matt Friedman and his partners, Phil Marshall and Adam Harper—they have launched a 'Moon Goal' initiative that has a collective ambitious goal of ensuring that 'the private sector will eliminate forced labour from its supply chains by 2028 without a negative impact on profitability.' After all the time I've spent on the frontlines, it is surprising for me to conclude— and I believe this with all my heart—that the private sector has the influence, resources, and talents to lead the way globally in helping to end exploitation in our lifetime.

Lastly, it's the youth generation that has helped shape world history since time immemorial, leading every social revolution. It brings tears to my eyes when I see inspiring young people rising up in their social justice awakening in their fields of choice. If more people can help empower and raise them up, they will be an unstoppable force for social change.

\* \* \*

By equipping the Filipina survivors of abuse with the skills and opportunities required for a life of independence and dignity, Sam Dharmapala is helping turn the tide against child abuse and modern slavery.

Pastors Selamet Yap, Eni Lestari, Cynthia Abdon-Tellez and other frontline workers have stepped up to help exploited and underage domestic workers in Hong Kong, Singapore, and elsewhere.

David Kang shifted the focus of his life from making profits to helping North Korean refugees escape oppression and trafficking, to the extent that he ended up in a Chinese prison for four years.

Tim Peters has spent decades fighting for human rights in North Korea.

Takashi Uemura, Gay McDougall, and many campaigners in Korea, East Asia, and around the world have fought for justice on behalf of the elderly survivors of Japanese military sex slavery.

The sincere and heartfelt apologies given by Tomoko Hasegawa, Cindy Goh, and friends to the survivors of wartime forced prostitution have brought some conciliation and healing to a historical wound.

The ex-Japanese soldiers Waichi Okumura, Tetsuro Takahashi, and Yasuji Kaneko have all bravely faced their troubled past lives and tried to move forward with empathy for those who have been enslaved and abused.

Kaushic Biswas, Guo, and Mary Zardilla have been on similar journeys of seeking redemption and personal transformation after moving on from lives of pimping and trafficking.

Caring people such as Agnes, Su, Judy, Linda Chan, Melissa Wu, Amy and the Door of Hope volunteers have at times risked their lives to rescue women and girls from a life of exploitation and misery in the flesh trade.

Matt Friedman continues to educate, lead, and inspire the global business community with the aim of eradicating modern slavery in Asia and around the world, once and for all.

These inspirational unsung heroes have found in their selfless service a profound sense of meaningful living, an unending well of contentment that comes from sacrifice to bring love and change to one person at a time—to make this world a better place for the most marginalized.

By sharing their stories with me, the survivors of abuse and enslavement have drawn a line in the sand and taken a moral responsibility—future generations of women and girls must not suffer the same fate.

The channels of Imperial Japan's military sex slavery never died. It was one of the worst human rights abuses in history, and it's a horrific cycle that continues on in war zones, it rages in brothels across cities and in the nefarious trafficking of women and girls around the world. Only a few hundred elderly women came forward publicly to bear witness to systematic sexual enslavement by the Japanese military in the first #MeToo movement in the world. These women were way ahead of their time. They have all voiced a wish for a sincere apology from the Japanese government that would bring restoration and healing.

Countless other wartime sex slavery victims were murdered or perished due to horrific conditions or as casualties of war. Still many others have chosen to take their traumatic secrets to their graves. Today, only a handful of these elderly women are still alive, and they continue to wait for closure of their war wounds.

Those who have been trafficked into sex slavery are at risk of getting infected with HIV and venereal disease, or suffering violence from their pimps and the johns. They are not able to form families of their own, and their traumas have a compounding effect, leading them astray into more devastating situations, from one living hell to another. They often come from impoverished and challenging backgrounds. These vulnerable young women are at higher risk of deception, coercion, and exploitation by traffickers because of their desperate bid to support their families. No one should live in the kind of abject poverty that crushes the human spirit and brings indignity. Poverty causes two untimely deaths: death to dreams and death to self-respect.

It is within our power to eradicate the evil of sex trafficking and offer hope and a new life for those caught in its web. We can use our privilege and our freedom to help those who cannot pay us back. When we turn a blind eye, we are effectively endorsing the traffickers' view that their victims are garbage, that their lives are cheap.

Consider William Wilberforce and his network of supporters who campaigned to abolish slavery in the British empire. They were just a group of friends who were perceived as having an idealistic, naive, and impossible dream. Yet, through their vision, perseverance, and diligence, they were able to combine their talent and mine their connections to change the face of society and the course of history.

If a member of your family were being enslaved and abused, wouldn't you galvanize every weapon in your arsenal and tirelessly fight to save them? Those who are in the chains of sex trafficking and slavery of any form are our brothers and sisters. They are part of our human family.

The sale of human beings is a threat to our collective freedom and safety. It's a different kind of terrorism. It's subtle and heinous, and will eventually infect us all.

# Afterword

I immigrated back to Asia more than twenty-eight years after my parents departed from their homeland for Canada. I reluctantly left my comfort zone to go on an adventurous journey that led to heartache but eventually helped me find myself. To top this, I also had a miracle happy ending of marrying a man who loves me unconditionally and partners with me on my human rights work. I found my calling through bearing witness for the wartime sex slaves of the Japanese military.

Martin Luther King said it best: 'Life's most persistent and urgent question is "What are you doing for others?"'

I feel honoured to have met so many extraordinary people across East Asia and around the world. I've had the privilege of interviewing survivors of modern slavery who have experienced the unspeakable. Their courage, perseverance, and dignity have changed me. They have led me on a long road to justice—to tell the untold stories of human slavery survivors and to help bring attention, funding, and change to those who are suffering.

As I examined my brokenness, I was inspired and felt healed by the resilience and hope within these people.

They helped me far more than I could ever help them.

They helped me find faith.

They have transcended their past to embrace the present and transform the future. I am a different person from when I first started my journey investigating Japanese wartime sex slavery more than two decades ago. Each survivor has enriched my world and enlarged my thinking, my capacity for compassion, and my passion for social change.

This is a call to action to young people and professionals who have the gift of choice, to use their abilities, their talents, and their finances to influence social change for the most marginalized people on Earth. As I reflect upon the legacy I wish to leave behind for future generations, I hope we can someday tell them that we have brought healing and restoration to at-risk children, broken lives, and the poor. This is the dream that's burning in my heart, and I hope that it burns in the hearts of the next generation, too.

Each of us can take a step forward to do more to help children, women and men trapped in modern slavery.

You can help through one small act at a time and by spreading kindness. You can start by educating others and sharing information on your social media about a global issue, volunteer with a non-profit organization, or donate the equivalent of the cost of a lunch to a non-profit organization. These individual, seemingly insignificant, actions, multiplied by millions of people, can change our world.

For more information on our Be the Hero Campaign on global volunteerism, visit: www.betheherocampaign.com

# Acknowledgements

Words cannot describe how grateful I am to the love of my life, my husband Matt Friedman, for his partnership in our common mission to help make the world a better place. Matt's unconditional love for me, his sacrificial lifestyle and pure dedication to the freedom of millions of enslaved people has inspired me to pen their stories. Thanks, Matt, for your extraordinary work in inspiring so many over the years. It's because of you that I can finish this book, and I hope it honours every single person who has experienced the horrors of modern slavery.

I would also like to express my deepest gratitude to my parents and siblings for their love and encouragement. Without my mother's unwavering devotion and belief in me and her incredible encouragement to pursue my dreams over the years, this book would have remained an idea in my head. I resonate with Abraham Lincoln who said, 'All that I am, or hope to be, I owe to my angel mother.' A million thanks to my friends and mentors on different continents who have inspired me, prayed for me and walked together on this journey—my cup overflows.

A heartfelt thanks to Karen Cooper for her care and sharp eye as she read and edited an early part of my manuscript. Thanks to

Nelson Chiu for wonderful assistance with first drafts of this book. I'll never forget our epic work trips to Yunnan. Thank you to my dear friends who gave timely encouragement to finish this book— you know who you are.

A huge thanks to Amberdawn Manaois for incredible edits and to Matthew Keeler who has been a great editor and helped get this book ready for publication. A special thanks to my SCMP editor, Andrew Raine.

Last but not least, I want to express my deepest gratitude to Nora Nazerene Abu Bakar of Penguin Random House for her support and for believing in my book's message.

Finally, I would like to thank the many victims and frontline workers who have shared their stories with me over the years. In most cases, for their safety and to protect their privacy, I have not used their real names in this book.